Skid Row
and Its
Alternatives

SKID ROW AREA

CITY OF PHILADELPHIA

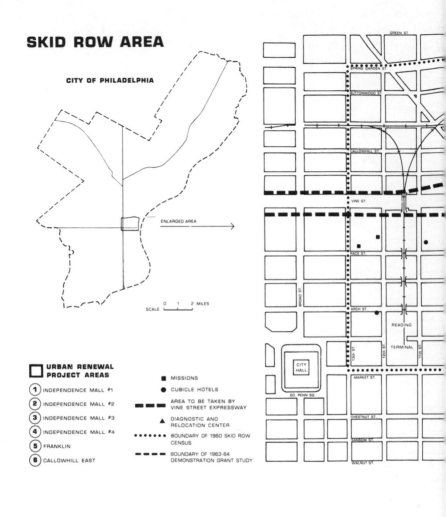

ENLARGED AREA →

0   1   2 MILES
SCALE

URBAN RENEWAL
PROJECT AREAS

1 INDEPENDENCE MALL #1

2 INDEPENDENCE MALL #2

3 INDEPENDENCE MALL #3

4 INDEPENDENCE MALL #4

5 FRANKLIN

6 CALLOWHILL EAST

■ MISSIONS

● CUBICLE HOTELS

━ ━ ━ AREA TO BE TAKEN BY
VINE STREET EXPRESSWAY

▲ DIAGNOSTIC AND
RELOCATION CENTER

•••••••• BOUNDARY OF 1960 SKID ROW
CENSUS

━━ ━━ ━━ BOUNDARY OF 1963-64
DEMONSTRATION GRANT STUDY

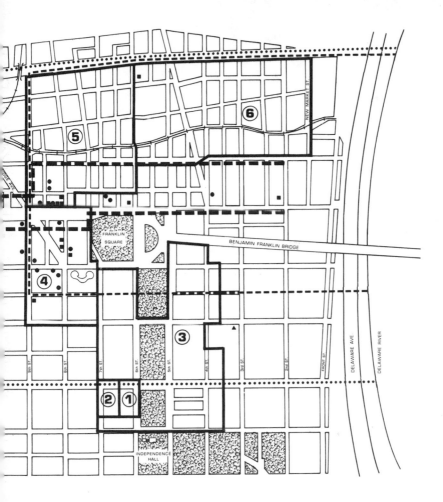

FRANKLIN
SQUARE

BENJAMIN FRANKLIN BRIDGE

NEW MARKET ST

DELAWARE AVE.

DELAWARE RIVER

9th ST
8th ST
7th ST
6th ST
5th ST
4th ST
3rd ST
2nd ST
FRONT ST

INDEPENDENCE
HALL

⑤ ⑥ ④ ③ ② ①

Skid Row and Its Alternatives

Research and Recommendations from Philadelphia

Leonard Blumberg
Thomas E. Shipley, Jr.
Irving W. Shandler

Temple University Press
Philadelphia

Temple University Press, Philadelphia 19122
© 1973 by Temple University. All rights reserved
Published 1973
Printed in the United States of America

International Standard Book Number: 0-87722-055-7

Library of Congress Catalog Card Number: 72-92877

To the men of Skid Row: clients, staff, and friends; to those who wanted to help and to those who bitched at our failings; to those who conned us into an understanding of their problems; and, especially to those who found *their* way.

Contents

Appendixes

Foreword

What began in 1960 as a massive attempt to survey the characteristics of all homeless men in one blighted area in Philadelphia has developed in the authors' hands into the first and, to date, the only statistically controlled study of the complex problems of Skid Row and alcoholism. The study concludes with a discussion of what "ought to be done about those men down there on Skid Row" and offers clear, detailed, and precise recommendations, based on data garnered from years of dedicated work by the staff of the Philadelphia Diagnostic and Rehabilitation Center. Even more important, these data are based on the best traditions of responsible, professional attitudes in the fields of health and social welfare, attitudes unfortunately lacking in many other attempts to intervene in Skid Row problems. The report can well serve as the survey for a program worthy of consideration by every urban community across the nation.

Skid Row and Its Alternatives is being published during an unprecedented ferment about alcohol abuse and alcoholism in the United States. In 1970 President Nixon signed into law P.L. 91-616, the Comprehensive Alcohol Abuse and Alcoholism Prevention, Treatment and Rehabilitation Act. Spearheaded by Senator Harold Hughes of Iowa, the passage of the bill was unanimous in both houses of Congress. Within a short time the National Conference of Commissioners on Uniform State Laws adopted a Uniform Alcoholism and Intoxication Treatment Act, which, among other provisions, makes public intoxication no longer a criminal act. The United States Department of Transportation has awarded some eighty million dollars for a period of three years, in contract with thirty-five communities, to develop Alcohol Safety Action Programs to find the earliest evidence of alcoholism in problem-drinking drivers. The National Institute on Alcohol Abuse and Alcoholism has provided occupational program advisors to forty-nine states for a "broad-brush approach" to early diagnosis of alcohol-related problems of employees in industry. Finally, one notices a gradually accelerated public education campaign through the mass media.

All these measures will no doubt tend to alter the stereotype of all alcoholics as end-stage victims—the Skid Row denizens. It is hoped that these measures will enlarge the scope of alcoholism services to cover the average citizen showing signs of incipient trouble. The long-concealed truth that 95 percent of those addicted to or dependent on alcohol are still functioning as family members and workers will finally surface, but the relatively small number of Skid Row residents will in any event remain the most visible segment of this population—and the most neglected.

The cost to the larger community of this neglect cannot be exaggerated. As the authors show, crimes on Skid Row flourish, with the habitué more often than not in the role of the victim. His physical debility and his state of intoxication make him easy prey to mugging, rolling, and other crimes, both major and minor. He is the natural target of oppression and exploitation: kidnapping for indentured farm labor, usury on the part of employment agencies, and schemes by landlords to gain control of welfare checks. Because he avoids contact with law enforcement officers whenever possible, he fails to seek protection from abuse.

Skid Row is also a reservoir of contagious disease which can quickly and insidiously penetrate the larger community. While physical contact with the Skid Row resident is usually avoided by other citizens, the reverse may not be true. The common cohabitants of Skid Row—the rats, mice and lice—may also travel. Polluted blood sold by the Skid Row resident to commercial blood banks may travel even farther. Skid Row, the authors point out, is unhealthy not only for those who live in it but for the entire citizenry.

Why then is so little attention paid to so serious a public health menace as Skid Row? We may speculate that society's attitudes toward the alcoholic in general, and the most socially deteriorated victims in particular, are potent factors in maintaining the status quo.

In spite of the increasing acceptance of the disease concept of alcoholism by professionals and paraprofessionals who work directly with alcoholics, and in spite of the clinical impression that such a concept is therapeutically effective in providing hope and motivation for an alcoholic to enter treatment, society has resisted adopting the concept or acting upon it. That public intoxication should be considered criminal behavior rather than a symptom of a complex disease is still a widespread attitude. Only a handful of states have enacted any laws similar to the Uniform Alcoholism and Intoxication Treatment Act removing drunkenness per se from the criminal justice system. On the other hand, drunkenness is also widely regarded as a sin or a sign of moral weakness, with the result that alcoholics are subjected to essentially hortatory appeals but are scarcely expected to heed them.

Personal involvement with alcoholics or close awareness of the experience of others tends to confirm another widely held attitude: that alcoholics are hopeless cases for whom recovery is impossible or at best temporary, once they have descended to Skid Row. The helping person will, time and again, reach out to counsel, support, and treat the sick and suffering alcoholic. He will be told, repeatedly perhaps, that the drinking is now under control, that no more alcohol will be consumed, that the alcoholic can "take it or leave it." Bitter disappointment usually follows, when such "promises" cannot be kept. The helper now rationalizes his rejection of the alcoholic by telling him: "You're not motivated yet." He scarcely realizes (and verbalizes even less) that he himself is not motivated to offer further treatment, since he cannot tolerate a sense of failure. He feels utterly helpless, especially when he has not investigated the allies that may be available: Alcoholics Anonymous, Al-Anon and Alateen, family members, clergy, or alcoholism counselors. The therapist also often falls too quickly into the trap of diagnosing "organic brain damage," an interpretation which may have no basis other than the therapist's need to find clinical justification for his rejection of a suffering fellow human. The authors point to so many vivid examples of recoveries when by traditional criteria the prognosis would have been unfavorable, that one must be impressed by the impossibility of declaring any alcoholic hopeless, except as a statistical abstraction.

But even when the helping persons recognize alcoholism as a disease, with the concomitant hope of arresting it, a confusion in attitudes may result in failure to *reach* the alcoholic and may actually tend to perpetuate the Skid Rows of this country. The benefactor often feels that the alcoholic is responsible for his disease and that he bears a measure of guilt for having contracted it. ("After all, no one twists the alcoholic's arm to take a drink.") The simple truth, however, is that no alcoholic sets out to become an alcoholic nor does he want to suffer from this devastating illness. He is no more "responsible" for having succumbed to alcoholism than cardiac patients are responsible for having coronary infarctions or diabetic patients for their altered carbohydrate metabolism. He has succumbed somehow to a condition whose causes are not known but whose progress seems inevitable, leading to early death if not treated.

Alcoholics may begin their drinking careers identically with all other drinkers, although in many cases insignificant differences could perhaps be found in the initial experiences—in the degree of individual tolerance and in the patterns of drinking. But sooner or later marked differences occur in quantity consumed, in frequency, in incidence of unacceptable behavior, in blackouts, in loss of control. Alcoholics begin by doing precisely what their colleagues do—"drink"—but later they can scarcely be said to be doing the same. The confusion arises, as Selden Bacon pointed out some fifteen years ago, in identifying the term "drinking" with "alcoholism." If drinking a beverage is a voluntary act, the alcoholic may justly be viewed as responsible for his disease, for having "brought it on himself." But "alcoholics do not drink," Bacon indicated. They consume alcohol but they do not drink! (See Selden Bacon, "Alcoholics Do Not Drink," *Annals of the American Academy of Political and Social Science* 315 [1958]: 55 ff.)

The alcoholic carries with him into Skid Row a heavy burden of guilt and shame and deeply feels his rejection by society. The therapist who simply confirms these views and whose crippling attitudes militate against the alcoholic's resuming an active role in controlling his destructive behavior is actually helping to preserve the Skid Row condition.

Fortunately, *Skid Row and Its Alternatives* makes it undeniably clear that therapeutic results can be achieved among this very population. Rehabilitation consists in most cases of a long series of small steps, each aimed at a realistic and recognizable goal, however minor it may seem. The Skid Row alcoholic is most interested in taking these steps after someone has demonstrated a genuine concern for his well-being. Providing for his immediate, urgent needs is more important than the question of tomorrow's sobriety, since the latter eventually evolves from the former when the helper has achieved a deep personal interest and involvement with the alcoholic, based on realistic expectations for his progress.

Successful methods in Skid Row, while similar, will vary with time and local circumstances. The Baltimore Public Inebriate Program began with the need for a shelter to implement the Maryland Comprehensive Intoxication and Alcoholism Control Act (1968). This pioneering law states in part: "There are some chronic alcoholics for whom recovery is unlikely. For these supportive services and residential facilities shall be provided so that they may survive in a decent manner" (Section 305, 1b). Close consultation with the Philadelphia experience resulted in the addition of a screening and evaluation center, a therapeutic community, and a number of boarding homes, all funded by the National Institute on Alcohol Abuse and Alcoholism. The programs in Seattle and Milwaukee, similarly funded, will undoubtedly present their own variations.

Experience across the country already tends to confirm the conclusions in the Philadelphia report, and one hopes for additional, carefully documented reports of innovative treatment approaches to the Skid Row problem. The present study will remain, however, as a model for the future and will continue to inspire hope in the hearts of those who suffer from alcoholism and of those who attempt to help them.

Maxwell N. Weisman, M.D.

Director, Division of Alcoholism Control
Mental Health Administration
Department of Health and Mental Hygiene for the State of
Maryland

Preface

Redevelopment or renewal of blighted areas and slums peripheral to the central business districts of major cities has been a growing concern in the United States. Joined with an increasing recognition of the seriousness of the problem of the urban alcoholic and the contribution of alcoholism to social disorganization in urban areas, this drive to reclaim city slums has given impetus to renewed interest in the "homeless men" of America.

Philadelphia's active interest in her Skid Row began in 1956. It took more than a decade to develop the city's relocation program and to establish the Diagnostic and Relocation Center, which formed the working core of the program.

The growth and shaping of Philadelphia's efforts to solve the problem of Skid Row involved all levels of government. We discovered that for the complex problems of Skid Row and of alcoholism there can be no small plans. The sums of money and the scope of operations needed in a project to rehabilitate Skid Row require the participation of citizens from all sociopolitical levels, from neighborhood groups to federal government agencies. It has become clear to us that the development of such programs as Philadelphia's is necessarily a political process in the broadest meaning of the term.

In Philadelphia this political process had several goals: to establish a program of action-research on civic problems; to conduct an action-research experiment on the relocation of Skid Row men to healthy environments, and thus to provide suggestions and guidelines for other cities in the United States; to establish alternative facilities for men who could not survive independent living outside institutions or Skid Row; and to develop a set of theoretical notions that would permit generalizing our findings to other localities and other programs designed to achieve similar goals.

The primary purpose of this book is to present the findings of the Philadelphia project for other civic groups to use in planning service programs for their own cities. This book is directed to that mixed public of academics, public officials, professional health and welfare workers, and other citizens who are interested in determining what can be done about Skid Row. We hope that it will give them substantial help.

We want to call attention to the combination of action and research which formed the basis of our work on the Philadelphia project. Throughout the program the need to obtain reliable data and to keep the assessment of our findings accurate was tempered with the important need to keep a genuine concern for the human beings with whom we were working.

This approach, which calls for casework to be truly centered on the client, represents our concept of professional social welfare work. We believe that such an approach is particularly applicable to programs of residential relocation for urban redevelopment, and we have written our book from this point of view.

This book is divided into four parts. In part I, we explain the development of the Philadelphia Skid Row project. The philosophy and the services of the Diagnostic and Rehabilitation Center are explained and related to the general characteristics of the Skid Row men, for whom it was planned. Because we believe that it is important to convey the human situation, we have included a number of biographical statements about Skid Row men. These were written some weeks after the authors had joined the staff of the center, and should put some flesh on the bones of the statistics that will occupy us during much of the balance of the book. All person's names used in this book are pseudonyms.

Part II discusses the intersection of alcohol and the slum. There are a number of ways of defining "alcoholism," and we have relied primarily upon loss of control as measured by self-reports of spree drinking, although we also give some attention to blood-level drinking (which is less common in the United States). We use this approach to suggest that the "assimilated Skid Row man" is likely to be a daily drinker and that he approximates the blood-level alcoholic rather than the spree drinker. We also discuss Sunday drinking in Philadelphia by Skid Row men—some go to private drinking clubs, but many resort to bootleggers.

We then examine the relationship of the Skid Row man to law enforcement agencies and conclude that, while this is an oversimplification, the police do constitute oppressors of Skid Row men under some circumstances. With respect to housing, there is little doubt that Skid Row is a slum whether housing is made available by private enterprise or by gospel missions. Many men are employed in part-time jobs. They are underemployed partly as a matter of choice and partly as a consequence of preoccupation with alcohol. This is in contrast with most of the rest of our society, in which one's job is a preoccupation and alcohol is peripheral. In a variety of contexts we discuss the relationship of the Skid Row man and his employer; although it is a mixed picture, the lasting impression is that Skid Row men are exploited not only in their housing but in their jobs as well.

Skid Row is an unhealthy place. The center's medical program provided examinations and referrals. The overall impression is that many Skid Row men are sick and in need of care; much of the disease is chronic, requiring long-term medical treatment or surgical correction. This unhealthy quality of Skid Row is further emphasized by a consideration of the very high death rate. The fact of death calls forth the same kind of problems and social organization for Skid Row men that it does for all others; however, when relatives do not arrange for burial, it is our impression that Skid Row men are exploited in death as well as in life. Skid Row is also a public health problem, as evidenced in an extremely high tuberculosis rate and in the high probability that blood obtained from Skid Row men and sold to hospitals by commercial blood banks is infected with serum hepatitis.

But our conclusion that Skid Row is an unhealthy and unhappy place does not negate the fact that some men have been assimilated into a Skid Row life style. Is Skid Row a community? This important question has implications for the program recommendations made in Chapter 13.

Part III considers our efforts to assess the effectiveness of rehabilitation procedures. These include a group therapy experiment at the Philadelphia House of Correction, housing relocation away from Skid Row, and a residential "halfway house" between Skid Row and the larger community. From these efforts we have selected for detailed consideration an intensive casework procedure which we believe shows great promise. On that basis we offer some theory for the successes of this intensive casework procedure, which is based on optimal discrepancy theory from psychology and exchange theory from sociology.

In Chapter 13 we offer a series of recommendations that are rooted in the chapters that have gone before, and combine these recommendations with a humanistic approach. We realize that our approach may be controversial, and we seek to facilitate the debate which is basic to community participation in the formation of social welfare policy by setting forth a series of propositions. We realize too that Skid Row residents are but one small segment of the urban poor and that much of what we recommend is equally applicable to that larger population.

We are concerned that social welfare policy be informed by research (we call it action-research), but we recognize that many readers will not want to be burdened with questions of research design, sampling, reliability, and the like. As much as we could, we have placed this kind of technical discussion in the Appendixes, where it will be available but not intrusive.

With other social scientists, as well as with other cities in mind, we have throughout the book sought to relate our findings to those of previous writers and investigators. We believe that knowledge is cumulative and that, within reason, the replication of research findings is both necessary and desirable. Our research methods bear some resemblance to those of others, as do our findings, and we have not hesitated to comment on the similarity as well as the dissimilarity of findings and conclusions. Insofar as Philadelphia's Skid Row population is similar to those in other cities, the recommendations in Chapter 13 have a general quality. Firmly rooted in the data, knowing the thrust of the literature about Skid Row as well as the present findings, we hope that the reader will enter into the social policy debate that we have outlined in Chapter 13 and that from that debate will come new efforts to offer alternatives to Skid Row and new programs to evaluate the success of these new programs.

Acknowledgments

The programs on which this book is based were supported from several sources:

A demonstration grant (Penna. D-7) under Section 314 of the Housing Act of 1954, administered by the U.S. Housing and Home Finance Agency (now the Department of Housing and Urban Development).

A contract between the Redevelopment Authority of the City of Philadelphia and the Greater Philadelphia Movement with the Department of Psychiatry, Temple University School of Medicine.

A grant (RD-1611 P) from the Vocational Rehabilitation Administration.

A grant (MH 15081) from the National Institute of Mental Health, Department of Health, Education, and Welfare.

Temple University granted faculty research leaves.

The contents of this volume are solely the responsibility of the authors. They are not the responsibility of the Department of Housing and Urban Development, the Redevelopment Authority of the City of Philadelphia through which the demonstration grant program was administered, or of the Department of Health, Education, and Welfare.

We wish also to make a public acknowledgment of a more personal sort to the many agencies and persons who have been helpful to us over the years. We have tried to give the names of some of these in conjunction with the various chapters, but there are many

xxiii

others who we cannot list. In their own special way, the residents of the Philadelphia Skid Row have been helpful to us beyond simply being a source of information about themselves. We wish to express our appreciation to them, and we hope that some benefit will accrue to them from what we have done and what we say in this book.

The Redevelopment Authority of the City of Philadelphia, through its former chairman Gustave Amsterdam and others on its board of directors, committed themselves to the program with a degree of involvement and support that fully demonstrated their desire to resolve the real estate problems of Skid Row and to provide needed rehabilitation services. While the policy was set at the board level, it was fully implemented at the operational level. Francis Lammer, executive director; Joseph Turchi, director of operations; and Chester Hayes, director of the Centralized Relocation Bureau—all gave the problem a great deal of personal attention and always in a solid supporting fashion. The key liaison member of the authority staff between the DRC/P and the authority has always been William Ludlow, director of programs. He proved to be of invaluable assistance in many ways. Hugh Hill was site manager of the Centralized Relocation Bureau and a valued colleague.

Data collection in the House of Correction study had the active support of Randolph Wise, commissioner of public welfare, and Edward Hendricks, superintendent of Philadelphia prisons. Similarly, health data and death statistics were secured with the support of: Dr. Norman Ingraham, commissioner of public health; the late Dr. Joseph O. Spelman, medical examiner of the city of Philadelphia; and Dr. F. Herbert Colwell, director, Division of Statistics and Research, Philadelphia Department of Public Health.

We cannot fail to mention the Greater Philadelphia Movement. It was the catalytic agent that helped make the program go. This key civic organization provided strong backing in every phase of the operations through its Committee for the Study of Skid Row, comprising the late Harry Batten, Joseph Keady, Elias Wolf, and chairman Lewis H. Van Dusen, Jr. Special recognition must also be given to William H. Wilcox, former executive director of the Greater Philadelphia Movement (and now Secretary for Community Affairs in the governor's cabinet), whose ready availability and knowledge eased many an anguished moment for us.

Temple University's involvement and concern for urban affairs was evidenced in the strong personal support offered by Dr. Millard Gladfelter, chancellor of the university. We would also like to acknowledge the interest and active support of other members of the administration of Temple University: Dr. Paul Anderson, president; and Dr. George Huganir, formerly dean of the graduate school; Dr. John Adams, assistant vice-president for financial affairs, and Dr. Herman Niebuhr, associate vice-president for community affairs.

There are those who have been close to us throughout the years as members of the DRC/P staff. Again, we cannot provide the complete list that justice would demand, but we hope that this book justifies the investment of their time and efforts. We hope that this book will measure up to the quality that our good friend, Jean Lilly, wished for it; her untimely death made it impossible for her to see it through. We cannot fail to mention gratefully the assistance of James Rooney, Paul Miller, Stephen Barsky, and Leonard Moore, who as research associates did so much to accumulate and organize the data. Dr. Walter Stanger's direction of the Halfway House was a major contribution, and William Hood's careful casework research was invaluable. Joseph O. Moor, Jr., and James A. Cassidy, as our deputy directors during the course of the NIMH project, managed our daily affairs. Joan Dennihy helped with editorial advice. How can we ever say enough about the efforts of Barbara A. Christmas and Marilyn F. Whitt, who typed the manuscript?

Finally, we wish to acknowledge that, especially in Chapter 1, we have drawn on material previously published in the *Quarterly Journal of Studies on Alcohol.*

Part I

Points of View

1   The Diagnostic and Rehabilitation Center/ Philadelphia

Skid Row has been a social phenomenon of United States cities for many years. The Row and its inhabitants have sometimes become a civic concern, but until recently little action of any real consequence has resulted.

The stereotypical idea of Skid Row is that of a sort of "hobohemia," where down-and-outers hang out, drinking, bumming, perhaps suffering, but living the kind of life they have in some way chosen, a life that is shunned by most citizens as a sort of dead end, a life that creates a cluster of problems that have to be dealt with in some way by the larger community. The actual troubles of Skid Row people have not often been understood from the viewpoint of the people themselves.

In recent years, however, urban renewal plans have precipitated a new and more urgent concern for Skid Row areas. With this concern and the resulting redevelopment programs in various cities, the need to define and understand Skid Row in terms of its real existence has become increasingly important.

We believe that in the social sciences some definitions may be more helpful in one context than in another. The criteria we have adopted here may not be the most helpful as constructs in a sociological theory of the structure of Skid Rows or of the functional relationships that existed within them in the past. But these criteria are in our opinion sociologically relevant and necessary as

3

guides for considered decisions in matters of social policy. We
believe that a flexible approach also makes it easier to understand
the relationship of Skid Row to the larger community.

Skid Row has been approached in terms of a place, a way of
life, a group of people.[1] And when we refer to Skid Row in this
book, we are usually referring to that part of the city that is cus-
tomarily labeled Skid Row by the community. But we have found
it more useful from the perspective of social policy and planning
to view Skid Row as a set of human relationships that are also
likely to occur in the inner city slums and poorer working-class
districts than to think of it as a geographical area, a place. We
have discarded the land-use approach to Skid Row, well described
elsewhere, in favor of the above point of view.[2]

For our purposes, Skid Row is considered: as a sustenance, or
socioeconomic survival, relationship in the metropolitan community; as a set of power relationships; and as a status relationship.
These three relationships are central to the concept of the community relationship.[3]

There are various ways to analyze this set of human relationships. Sustenance relationships have to do most directly with problems of human survival: food, housing and shelter, illness and
medical care, sex, work and sources of money, and (for many)
alcohol. Power relationships arise in dealing with agencies of civil
control—the police and the courts—and other persons or institutions by which Skid Row men are vulnerable to exploitation, such
as landlords, employment agencies, bartenders and other operators,
public and private welfare groups, and so on. Skid Row also represents a status relationship—that is, Skid Row people are extremely
low in terms of the degree of status and honor accorded them by
the larger community. They are perceived as the unsalvageable
remnant of the larger human community. Skid Row people are
not the only ones disesteemed in our society, but the differences
between Skid Row people and others are usually connected with
the fact that those from Skid Row are rapidly moving down in
esteem while those from other groups are more often moving
upward, even though slowly. The Skid Row condition, the consequences of the Skid Row life style, and the relationship of Skid
Row to the larger community are the problems that lie at the core
of Chapters 2 through 9.

We see few redeeming features in the Skid Row way of life.

In most cases Skid Row men have a minimal code of mutual duties and obligations, and we maintain that their needs as related to the larger community can be met by persons within that larger community better than in Skid Row.

In general, programs designed to meet these needs should demonstrate that identification with the larger community has higher rewards than identification with Skid Row. Any such program would have to provide at least adequate and nutritious food and ready accessibility of health services during periods of personal crisis. Of necessity, succoring for the basic elements of life, including decent, safe, and sanitary housing, would also need to be established as an expression of basic policy. Further, winning the effort to effect reaffiliation would involve the treatment of the Skid Row man as a citizen with his own rights of freedom to participate in decisions that directly affect his life, thus according him dignity in the face of his adversity (without respect to the question of whether or not it is his own fault), and intervention on the part of the larger community to prevent his victimization. Under these conditions the commitment to extreme consumption of alcohol as a core element of the Skid Row life style might become more subject to change and abandonment so that other bases of social relationship might then become possible for Skid Row men. We have discussed programs that take this approach in Chapter 13.

We have suggested elsewhere a theory—the optimal goal discrepancy theory—that may be of use in proposing ways to bring Skid Row men back within the larger community.[4] This theory is derived most directly from the theoretical scheme presented by D.C. McClelland and others, and conceptualizes the theoretical problem in terms of the relationship of achievement and goal opportunities with aspiration.[5]

The kinds of problems that an individual will meet in the wider community will depend, in part, upon his level of aspiration, as well as upon his achievement level and the varieties of opportunities available to him. Thus, if a man's achievement and aspiration are practically nonexistent, reality and lack of motivation will conspire to keep him on Skid Row. If, on the other hand, his achievement is low and his achievement aspirations are unrealistically high, the man will remain on Skid Row and be continuously frustrated by his plight.[6]

The Philadelphia program was geared to raise the level of achievement of Skid Row inhabitants and to provide wider opportunities for them. But the most appropriate opportunities were those which were not greatly divergent from their present levels of achievement.

We believe that a person will work harder and with greater effectiveness for immediate goals that are not widely different from his present level of achievement but which, for him, represent a challenge. In this regard, the determination of optimal goals is difficult. Nevertheless, we believe that this general scheme may be applied to a broad range of problems. Its applicability was demonstrated in the Philadelphia project.

PHILADELPHIA'S SKID ROW PROJECT

In 1952, because of its concern for the city's slum areas, the Health and Welfare Council of Philadelphia published its recommendations for a comprehensive casework program. This proposal was repeated in 1956 in a publication of the Philadelphia Prison Society.[7] By 1956 the Greater Philadelphia Movement, a civic organization representing the top leadership of the community, had also developed an interest in the problems of Skid Row in the city. "Interest was motivated by the known public costs of Skid Row, the human problems of men who exist there, a concern over the public health aspects of the problem, the effect of Skid Row on our historic area . . . planned for restoration, and the adverse impact of Skid Row on downtown commercial growth."[8]

Philadelphia's Skid Row is adjacent to the historical Independence Hall area, peripheral to the central business district, and close to the Society Hill upper-income redevelopment area. Its strategic location in regard to rail and highway transportation is important to plans to redevelop the area for high-prestige office buildings and light industry.

The concern for Skid Row and its problems was further deepened by the evidence of the magnitude of tuberculosis and alcoholism on the Row. Therefore in 1958 Dr. Earl Rubington, consultant to the Greater Philadelphia Movement, proposed the establishment of a temporary diagnostic and relocation center. He also suggested that a survey be undertaken to ascertain the characteristics of the Skid Row population.

In 1959 a three-party contract was signed by the Greater Philadelphia Movement (GPM), the Temple University Medical School Department of Psychiatry, and the Redevelopment Authority of the City of Philadelphia. The contract called for a census of the men living in the Skid Row neighborhood and an analysis of their characteristics focused on problems that might be encountered when relocation of the men became necessary. The census was completed and the results reported to GPM and the Redevelopment Authority early in 1961.[9] Approximately 80 percent of the men living in Philadelphia's Skid Row in late February 1960 had been interviewed (2,249 out of an estimated 2,857), and the findings indicated a need for the proposed diagnostic and relocation center to provide vocational counseling and medical help, especially for those suffering from alcoholism.

On the basis of the census data, a recommendation was made for a center to be opened on or near Skid Row, to be staffed by professionals who would try to get to know, and to be known by, the men so that a relationship of trust could be developed. It was recommended that the center offer vocational planning, job placement, medical and psychiatric diagnostic service, and housing relocation assistance.

A three-party contract was then undertaken by the Redevelopment Authority, the GPM, and the newly organized Temple University Center for Community Studies (which replaced the Department of Psychiatry of Temple University in the Section 314 grant phase). Negotiations were begun for a Section 314 demonstration grant from the federal Urban Renewal Administration (URA). The major formal objective of the demonstration grant project was the development of procedure and information that might be generalized to other cities, providing guidance for urban centers which intended to undertake redevelopment of their own Skid Row areas. When approval of the project appeared imminent, it was decided to employ a project director who would have the overall responsibility for developing, implementing, and evaluating the project, and the planning begun in 1956 was ready to be translated into action on August 1, 1962.

Meanwhile, the Department of Psychiatry had already been engaged in a diagnostic and group therapy project for Skid Row alcoholics at the Philadelphia House of Correction. In the period from 1960 to 1962, after the Skid Row census was finished and before the demonstration grant came into force, a systematic effort was made to assess the effectiveness of a group therapy program with Skid Row alcoholics within the House of Correction. The results of that research are reported in Chapter 10.

THE DIAGNOSTIC AND RELOCATION CENTER

Perhaps the most critical concern in planning the program of the center was the question of the extent of its diagnostic service. The funds granted to the city by URA were inadequate to carry out a comprehensive program, since the plan had shifted from an emphasis on the use of community resources outside the center to more intensive concentration within the center. The question became one of funding the increased staff. The new project director, previously director of rehabilitation and patient service for a state voluntary health agency, was able to arrange further financial assistance from the state departments of Health, Public Welfare, and Labor and Industry. The Health Department allotted funds for a part-time physician; the Department of Public Welfare added funds for a psychiatric team, plus a staff liaison with the County Board of Assistance; the Department of Labor and Industry provided a liaison staff member from the Bureau of Vocational Rehabilitation; in addition, a close working tie was established with the Bureau of Employment Security. As a consequence, the project staff was able to set up a dynamic program in which the major public agencies of the state were involved.

Representatives of the three principal agencies in the demonstration project—the Redevelopment Authority, the GPM, and the Temple University Center for Community Studies—met regularly with the center staff; meetings were also held with representatives of key city agencies to inform them of the progress of the project and to gain their support. It was decided not to have a formal advisory board but to limit meetings to information sharing and agency endorsement. These meetings continued throughout the first early activities of the center, and the plan of gradual involvement of city agency representatives was successful.

What kind of men came into the center? The data that we will discuss in this book come from a number of different studies. We want the reader to understand Skid Row as a social welfare problem and to be prepared to enter into our discussion of proposed alternatives to Skid Row, which begins with Chapter 10 and culminates in Chapter 13; to make this easier, we have relegated to the Appendixes much of the discussion of research design and research methods. Appendix A discusses the 1960 Skid Row census and also the Section 314 demonstration grant research design; Appendix C presents a comparison of the characteristics of these two populations with respect to selected variables, and seeks to answer the questions about the extent to which the data we report are characteristics of all Skid Row men. Appendix B discusses our attempts to assess the degree to which the men we interviewed were reliable in what they said—for Skid Row men do not always tell the truth.

Many of our tables are drawn from the 1960 Skid Row census or from the demonstration grant study, but other data are also used when this seems appropriate. For example, Chapter 4 discusses the relationship of the Skid Row man and the law enforcement agencies. During the course of that discussion, we cite a study of the House of Correction that was done as a part of the psychiatry department project. We also cite a special ten-day study done at the police station which handles most of the Skid Row arrests. In that study, we were interested in knowing more about the kind of men who were brought in so that we could make recommendations that would effect a meaningful change in law enforcement practices in Philadelphia as they concerned Skid Row men. Another source of data was a series of substudies done under a grant from the National Institute of Mental Health. These data include studies of the employment practices that affect Skid Row men, blood banking, the rooming houses and slum housing, and the discussion of bootlegging that is included in Chapter 3. Chapters 10, 11, and 12 discuss experiments in rehabilitation; there we describe the related procedures as a part of the presentation of the data because we think that it makes greater sense to do it that way.

In selecting a site for the Diagnostic and Relocation Center, it was decided not to locate on or adjacent to Skid Row, for a number of reasons.

The center was established as an action-research project for working primarily with men selected at random from Skid Row. Near, but not adjacent to the Row, it would eliminate the casual walk-in and allow the program to focus on the men in the sample group.

If located on the Row, the center would have been more readily stereotyped as a mission-type or other similar Skid Row institution.

For the men who became involved in the program, the location of the center away from the Row in pleasant surroundings would set the tone for rehabilitation. (We underestimated the needs of the Skid Row men; once the center was accepted by the Row, it was viewed by all the men as a means of securing help. The distance, however, about a quarter of a mile, was no handicap to those who wanted to come to the center.) Special attention was given to finding a site that was physically pleasant and had kitchen facilities. The pleasant environment and availability of good food were to serve as a subtle frame for the therapeutic milieu.

The final selection, a former hotel-residence at 304 Arch Street, next to a Friends meeting house, several blocks from the Row, was strongly influenced by practical limitations. Several of the center staff literally walked every street in and near the Row seeking appropriate housing. Decrepit buildings, the high cost of remodeling, and reluctant neighbors combined to limit the alternatives.

The director was largely free to hire his own staff without pressure, political or otherwise. Thus it was possible to employ people who had both the professional competence and the personality to fit into the center's program and philosophy. Job specifications were not bound by rigid educational or residential requirements, and the staff were selected to be client-oriented—with the Skid Row men their focus of attention.

The staff members had varied backgrounds and experience, ranging from former Skid Row men to trained professionals. The former Skid Row men knew what Skid Row really meant to those who lived there; they were familiar with the residents, their life style, and their mood. As a result, their ability to communicate with the men and to bring the center's program to the Row was invaluable. On the other side, the professionals on the staff adapted their skills to the unique problems of the men on the Row.

The administrative policy was to establish a warm, flexible, therapeutic atmosphere in the center; the resulting morale seemed sound and healthy. The staff met formally and informally in total freedom to express opinions and feelings and, above all, to learn.

Since the center was initially planned to be a diagnostic unit, not a long-term treatment facility, a first step was to seek out the appropriate community agencies and to inform them of the forthcoming project; these included the full range of service agencies such as hospitals, churches, Alcoholics Anonymous, social agencies. A staff member presented each agency with the background of the project, and each agency was asked to lend its general support and to offer suggestions for the most appropriate use of its program. Periodically, groups of the agencies or key people in Skid Row institutions would be invited to meet and share their ideas regarding the project. The response was generally favorable; the agencies offered a strong moral endorsement of the program. Key people in the power structure provided the center with an open sesame to most doors.

Experience proved, however, that in spite of the center's plans and the community agencies' stated interest, it was difficult to "tie in" a man to an agency in the community. The consequence was that eventually it became necessary to develop treatment facilities as a part of the center's program. The halfway house was an early step in that direction (see Chapters 11 and 12) and ultimately brought about a change in name—to the Diagnostic and Rehabilitation Center/Philadelphia.

The Diagnostic and Relocation Center was officially opened on May 13, 1963. A major question from the start was whether it would be possible to get men to come to the center at all, much less in accordance with a random sampling procedure.

Many men in Skid Row are residentially highly mobile; they spend each night in a different mission, cubicle hotel, all-night movie, or parked car. Some men "ship out" to resort jobs and may be gone for months in institutional live-in jobs. Addresses of residentially stable men receiving Public Assistance payments can be secured, but men whose only income is from Social Security payments and spot labor can be found only by going into the row and asking for them. Then too, strangers are always viewed with suspicion. Appendix C presents a comparison between those we reached out in the field and those who came into the center.

Our philosophy was to reach out to the men rather than wait for them to come to us. We knew that the first contact with the Row, both in a collective sense and in an individual sense, would be critically important. In the first interviews with the men selected, the contact counselor was to find the man and conduct the first ("doorstep") interview. In many cases the contact counselor was an ex-Skid Row man who still had some sense of identification with Skid Row men. He wanted to be sure that the men in the Row got a break; at the same time, he had not been away from Skid Row very long, so that he knew and was known by most of the men still living in the Row. He knew the hotel owners, room clerks, bartenders, mission clerks, and foremen of work crews.

In the beginning these contact counselers had doubts about whether the professional staff of the center were really sincere about helping Skid Row men. Nevertheless, these counselors con-

vinced the Skid Row men that the center was "for real" and that
it offered help and not just another rejection.

In the first interview, when the contact counselor was not an
ex-Skid Row man, an ex-Skid Row man would often accompany
him to help identify the prospective respondent and to reassure
him. After the interview was completed, the respondent would be
brought back to the center if he agreed to come.

We ourselves had some early doubts about whether the men
living in Skid Row would come to the center. But during the first
few months after the center opened, men appeared in such overwhelming numbers that the lunch facilities and the staff were
swamped. The men came to look over the center for themselves,
and it soon became less vital for the contact counselor to be an
ex-Skid Row man. Within months, the center had become a recognized part of the lives of the men of Skid Row.

The major social welfare goal of the Diagnostic and Rehabilitation Center/Philadelphia was to develop procedures for rehabilitative relocation. In this process one of the most important elements
was the anchor counselor, who provided a consistent tie to the
Skid Row man, whatever service he received, whether in the center or through referral. The anchor counselor coordinated services
for clients who came to the center or for those who made use of
the center's facilities as a direct or indirect result of the doorstep
interviews. After the intake interview, the anchor counselor scheduled appointments for the client to have a complete medical examination, including chest X-ray, blood tests, urinalysis, and electrocardiogram. Psychological and psychiatric interviews and testing
followed. In the beginning, dental examinations were available, but
these were discontinued because virtually all the men had dental
problems, which resulted in a massive referral problem rather than
a diagnostic one.

The diagnostic appointments usually took about a week. The
client continued to live where he had been if he had his own
checks coming in. If he had no money, a limited number of beds
were available for a reasonable length of time at St. John's Hospice and at the Salvation Army (Sally), with no requirement for
participation further in the Sally's program. A hot meal was served
at noon each day at the center for clients who had participated in
the program that day, coffee and doughnuts were available in
ample supply, and the caseworker saw the men daily.

During the demonstration grant period the anchor counselor

also discussed the question of anticipated relocation. He made an effort to persuade the client to accept the idea and to agree to an appointment with one of the relocation staff quartered in the center, if he himself was not acting as relocation worker. We discuss our efforts to assess the success of these activities in Chapter 10.

The men who came to the center gave the anchor counselor an oversimplified description of what they wanted. They seldom looked further than their immediate needs, and frequently did not perceive their more fundamental needs or have the conceptual ability or language facility to express them. Even if it seemed obvious that a man needed long-term hospitalization for acute alcoholism, he might ask for nothing more than a pair of pants, a meal, a flop for the night, or a physician to fix an ulcerated leg. The anchor counselor tried to help the man develop the view that more than a meal or a free flop for a couple of nights was possible. To do this he had to show the Skid Row man that someone would listen solely to him, would understand. Understanding was demonstrated by doing something then—not just talking. Doing something involved assistance in getting medical care, job training, a chance to get off the Row by way of an alcohol program, or a check from the County Board of Assistance, or an expedited referral-admission to a Veterans Administration hospital.

The center's casework approach was different from that of a health clinic, in which social workers are defined as auxiliary (or paramedical) personnel and the physician-psychiatrist has the central role. The policy of the center was that the social worker had permanent responsibility for his case; the hope was that this approach would further client-counselor rapport.

Skid Row men find it a hardship to be passed from one caseworker to another, often between agencies. The location of multidisciplinary diagnostic and counseling services under one roof made it easy for the clients to receive these services. Anchor counselors had easy access to all the information gathered and to all personnel on the staff for consultation. They had considerable latitude and authority, and rarely had to pass the buck up the administrative line to the director. The anchor counselor could therefore serve as a true anchor to his client, listening to his opinions, complaints, fears, and desires. This sympathetic counseling was extremely important to the Skid Row men, many of whom were suspicious and pathologically dependent and felt isolated and worthless.

The centrality of the role of anchor counselor made it possible to cut red tape to a minimum. When contact counselors made contact with a man in Skid Row who was a part of the demonstration project sample, they made no specific appointments; they either accompanied the man back to the center immediately or gave him an appointment card to use whenever he was ready. Assigned anchor counselors kept no rigid appointment schedules, but saw clients as soon as possible after they arrived. When a new client came in, a short, friendly greeting was given him even if sometimes it meant interrupting a formal interview. Often a few words of encouragement by the anchor counselor were enough to induce him to stay for an interview himself. Frequently a warm, friendly approach and encouragement by the office personnel persuaded clients to wait. This type of procedure was adopted because of the Skid Row man's concept and use of time, which did not easily adapt to fixed appointment schedules. We did not attempt to use set casework conference times as a therapeutic device but, instead, used flexibility of time and availability of staff to extend rapport.

Every effort was made to develop informal staff-client ties. First names were used; the anchor counselor was Phil, Andy, or Chet, rather than Mister. The contact counselor or the anchor counselor might decide that the situation warranted having a drink together in a neighborhood bar (a practice permitted but not encouraged) or a cup of coffee in a local restaurant, and he knew that his supervisors would not look askance at this nonprofessional conduct. The anchor counselor might even help the Skid Row man get deloused as a first step in his relationship with the center.

Skid Row men easily accepted the need for medical examinations and, in the main, welcomed medical diagnosis and referral, particularly since it was often accompanied by immediate medication to relieve hangovers, pains from stomach ulcers, and the like. Sometimes they came into the center for some other purpose and while there began to experience the d.t.'s. Then it became necessary to arrange for immediate hospitalization.

Skid Row men walked for hours in Skid Row and in the adjacent business streets. Some had jobs that required much walking (muzzling—that is, distributing handbills) or standing (dishwashing); podiatric assistance was therefore welcome. Many needed eyeglasses, and anchor counselors made referrals to the College of Optometry for free attention. If a man did not have money to get to the college, he was given carfare or was taken there by a member of the center staff. Finally, minor treatment by the center's physicians helped to cement relationships between the anchor counselor and his clients.

Staff physicians at the center were paid through grants made by the State Department of Health. The Philadelphia Health Department added a physician to the staff of the center. Dental services and podiatric services were provided by professionals who volunteered. Students from the College of Podiatry and the College of Osteopathic Medicine volunteered in order to gain clinical experience. Temple University Medical School students worked in the center for field placement experience and as part of a training program in psychiatry and comprehensive medicine. The head of the medical department was an internist with special competence in pulmonary problems and a special interest in alcoholism. The chief staff physician was an osteopath with a special interest in the biochemistry of alcoholism.

Some Skid Row men welcomed the evaluations resulting from the psychiatric interview and psychological testing conducted within the center. Others accepted the situation when they were assured that it was a study project and that their names would not be used and when they were told, "You won't be committed to any institution against your will." Some clients resisted vigorously and expressed great fear. ("What do you think I am—nuts?") Sometimes we were able to secure cooperation by demonstrating the immediate usefulness of the psychiatric interview. For example, one man's case was about to be closed at the Office of the Blind because of "lack of motivation." His caseworker at the Office of the Blind agreed that the client's cooperation with our diagnostic services would probably assure him of eyeglasses and shoes that the man needed, but the caseworker doubted that the client would agree to a psychiatric interview. The anchor counselor at the center spent much time allaying the client's fear of this interview, virtually guaranteeing that if he cooperated he would receive eyeglasses and shoes. The client finally agreed to the interview and did receive the glasses and shoes; a minor victory indeed, but the man got what he needed at the time and doors were opened.

The anchor counselors made numerous referrals to other agencies, but they had to consider that most agencies did not welcome Skid Row men—especially alcoholics. It was therefore essential for anchor counselors to follow through on their referrals. To refer and forget was to destroy the anchor role. Despite early approaches to agencies, it was still necessary for the director to interpret the center's program and goals to those agencies which received most of our referrals. Frequent telephone calls were needed to assure sympathetic and necessary treatment. When this was done in the client's presence, it tended to reinforce the man's perception of our continuing interest and willingness to go out on a limb for him. One anchor counselor found it necessary to testify for his client in court, and his client later commented, "I never had anybody go to bat for me like that before."

An anchor counselor sometimes had to prepare a client to cope with "punitive" treatment in another agency. A number of clients were referred for Public Assistance, and anchor counselors learned which interviewers at that agency were punitive. It was then the anchor counselor's task to encourage his client to get conclusive eligibility evidence, to prepare him for harsh treatment, to write a detailed referral note, and to assure the client of support if he had difficulty. Under these circumstances, the Skid Row man was often able to get assistance without the need for intervention, and he developed more confidence in handling interpersonal situations. There were added gains if the man was an alcoholic, for he learned something of the possibility of handling situations without going on a spree, and also developed a greater sense of confidence in the anchor counselor.

Another service that counted with the men was the center's lunchroom. Coffee and doughnuts (occasionally even home-baked coffee cake) were out on the table every morning; there was an ever flowing coffee pot; a hot dinner was served. The staff paid for their own dinners, but for Skid Row men this meal was free. The men got the same food as the staff.

A brief informal chat between client and anchor counselor in the lunchroom often did more to cement a meaningful relationship than a formal office interview. Not infrequently such informal conversations were held with several clients at once. We believe that the availability of the lunchroom was an important motivating factor in the cooperation of the Skid Row men.

We are aware of the strong analogy that may be drawn between the center and the missions. But we believe that at the center the food was substantially better than at most missions and that it was important to the men that they sat down at a dining room table and did not have to go through a cafeteria line. We believe, further, that the considerable attention given to the man as a person when he came to the center was ego-enhancing rather than ego-debasing. Among the factors involved, the lunchroom and the available medical services figured importantly in achieving good relationships with Skid Row men.

2   The Skid Row Condition

Behind the statistical and other research data of this book are highly dramatic human materials. In this chapter we highlight the human condition through biographies. Frank Schell describes his alcohol-centered life and his feelings as he adopted the Skid Row life style. We understand a little better, after reading about how he hid from his niece as she walked through the kitchen where he was washing dishes, why the homeless man denies the relatives who probably live somewhere else in the metropolitan area. He is living outside family life, but he is not without a family.

All the men whose biographies are reported here are "alcoholics"; their lives and their relationships with other people have been disrupted profoundly by their use of alcohol and by the fact that their lives have become centered on alcohol. Mike Kelly is an example of mutual rejection by both a Skid Row man and his respectable son in which alcohol is central. Bill Dunn is an example of a man whose father became a Skid Row alcoholic and who, in turn, adopted the Skid Row life style—two generations in which alcohol was a factor in the disrupted family pattern. One of the most important contributions of Dunn's biography is that it directs us to the significance of the social ties that keep men off the Row. When these are gone, there is a strong likelihood that a move will be made. Dunn's case suggests further

18

that for many men the move to Skid Row involves a transition
with occasional visits long before the final move is made. We
discuss the entire problem of alcohol in considerable detail in
Chapter 3.

Only an unusual Skid Row man is able to avoid the police to
the degree that Pat Fitzhugh did. On the other hand, few Skid
Row men would fight the police as consistently as Mike Kelly did;
few are strong enough to take the beatings that would follow.
Therefore, neither of these men is typical of Skid Row men in this
respect. We discuss police practices in detail in Chapter 4.

Aside from alcohol and the police, the basic elements of the
Skid Row life style are food and shelter. The biographies of both
Pat Fitzhugh and Mike Kelly bring out the relationship between
the gospel missions, the Salvation Army, and the Skid Row men.
While the missions see their activities as a religious ministry, the
men tend to look at them as resources to be exploited; however,
because the men dislike the way the services are made available,
they use the missions only as a last resort. We discuss this matter
in greater detail in Chapter 5.

The Salvation Army Men's Social Service Center is one of the
several industrial, or work-related, mission programs in the city.
Chapter 6 discusses Skid Row jobs and mission employment. The
biography of Mike Kelly makes clear that the men regard the missions as exploitative, thus justifying Kelly's own counterexploitation
of the Salvation Army.

A move into the Skid Row area does not change a man's racial
attitudes. Skid Row housing is racially segregated as much because
the white Skid Row men insist upon it as because those in charge
of housing impose segregation. The center had both black and
white anchor counselors. Assignment of cases was made without
regard to race, but such practices had no apparent effect on the
attitudes of the men. At best, the anchor counselor was probably
viewed as an exception to the accepted racial segregation. In Mike
Kelly's biography we see some of these elements. Among all the
complexities of our research, we did not feel prepared to mount a
major research project on attitude change. Chapter 5 discusses the
segregative practices that prevail in Skid Row housing. Chapter 6
describes some of the consequences of racial discrimination in
employment of Skid Row men.

The author of Mike Kelly's biography, who was an intake counselor at the time, warns us that in our formal interviews we cannot

easily learn about the warm humanity of Mike himself. That is one
of the reasons for our including this chapter. Furthermore, he
warns us that our interview material may be inaccurate. We were
not unaware of that possibility. One of our research failures
involved an attempt to get information about Skid Row men from
their next of kin; the effort failed because we needed the consent
of the men themselves, and many of them refused to give it,
although they usually gave us the name of the next of kin—in case
of emergency. Appendix B discusses other, more successful, efforts
to come to grips with the problem of reliability.

We have not censored the following materials, and we have not
smoothed out the rough details. A number of places, persons, and
activities need explanation. Such explanations, which we have kept
at a minimum, are in brackets. All names of clients are of course
pseudonyms.

MIKE KELLY: A BIOGRAPHICAL STATEMENT

"I find myself in the unique position of comparing an interview
with a close personal relationship. I'm sure my 'living' experience
with Mike Kelly reflects a different character than the intake interview Michael Aloysius Kelly.

"I had been on and off the Row for a few years before I ran
into Mike. I recall our first meeting quite clearly. It was at the
Sally in Roxborough around 1954–55. We were both sober and
worked as helpers on a Sally truck for the fantastic sum of one
(1) dollar per week.

"Mike and I hit it off immediately because we had many things
in common: we were alkys, Irish, ex-Marines, and Philadelphians.
These were important, but not necessarily in that order.

"By the end of a month of hustling and 'unloading' [stealing
items from the Sally to peddle] we had accrued enough loot and
clothes [to peddle on the Row] to head for the Skid and the
first of many binges that came to pass in a ten-year relationship.

"I learned, very quickly, many things about Mike—some good
and some not so good. The fact that I have a long period of sobriety behind me now, indicates to me that I can see these highlights
in Mike's personality much more clearly now than I ever could
have perceived them then. The memory bank being what it is, the
imprintations come back loud and clear on recall.

"Mike like most alcoholics was a supreme paradox. He was
angry most of the time because inside him was an ever-shifting

caldron of hate and violence. Yet there were times when a real warm and human Mike shone through. Mike had lost his sense of smell [but] he never lost his emotional ability to cry on sober occasions when we would rehash our 'might-have-beens' [which] brought on fits of anger and expressions of hate for his wife [an alcoholic], the blacks, the cops, and the rotten bastards who ran the Reading Railroad. Also his son, Mike, Jr.

"Anyone in their right mind would steer clear of Mike on a drinking bout where a confrontation with the cops might arise. That is, drinking outside a flop house or squeezing a can in an empty house or lot where your chances of being grabbed were good. Never in my right mind in those days, I seemed to wind up with Mike in a cop-fighting situation where the cops did all the fighting. Mike was, to put it mildly, a cop-hater of the first water. You never got locked up peacefully with Mike. He would call any cop, big or small, the most vile and obscene names in the book and make a few violent thrusts at their jaw or try to grab their gun and even bite them. This would result in Mike being beaten with a club on every part of his body, especially on the nose and head. Consequently, who ever happened to be with Mike would get the hell beat out of him, too. Strangely though, I have, to the best of my memory, never seen Mike lose consciousness. My technique was to feign unconsciousness almost immediately—Mike would battle till the cell door clanged. He'd then roll over and we'd sleep in Mike's blood.

"In retrospect, I wonder if Mike hated cops because they represented authority or because the uniform represented his son, who wore a similar uniform, Lieutenant of Fire, who he hated because he rejected him completely.

"Mike and I shared every misery on the Row. As I see it now, we seemed to go out of our way to get into the most miserable situations. Many times we'd have enough for a flop but spend it on a jug or a few cans of squeeze, on a cold wintry night, and wind up holeing-up in an old station wagon across from the Twelfth Street Mission. I would go along with this because Mike was the dominant of the duo in the earlier stages of our relationship. As the beatings progressed, and the booze intake became constant, Mike's brain started scrambling, then he became a follower for survival.

"The son, Mike, Jr., I understand once told Mike, that he, Mike, wasn't around when he, Junior, needed him so never to bother him. Junior felt this way even after Mike had some periods of sobriety here at the Center.

"It may seem to the reader I was with Mike night and day constantly observing his behavior on the Row. This is not the case. Many times, Mike and I would go on separate drunks on the Row, sometimes staying in the same flop but never meeting for days or even weeks at a time. It was our habit of looking each other up because we were familiar with each other's haunts. What I'm writing about is some of the highlights of our association as I recall them soberly.

"Another hate object of Mike's was the black men. 'Spooks' as Mike referred to them. He would purposely seek them out for combat early in his Row days. He became more tolerant when he became associated with the DRC/P and fellows like Bart, Andy, and Bill [all black members of the DRC/P staff at that time]. He developed a good feeling about Jim [also a black member of the DRC/P staff] that I think was genuine. Nevertheless way down Mike hated blacks with a passion.

"Mike was also in conflict with his God. He couldn't understand why God would play a dirty trick on a good (?) Catholic. I supported him in this type of thinking because God was the only one I had left to blame things on. In moments of clarity though, Mike would concede that part of our predicament was of our own making.

"Mike and I drank everything under the sun together, we worked together, we shared many of the real miseries of the Row—jail, beatings, rolled [jack-rolled, robbed] and violently sick and miserable. But, with it all, I doubt if I knew the real Michael Kelly. I knew the alcoholic Mike Kelly and thank God there is a difference.

"Finally, on June 17, 1966, Mike found what he so desperately sought, consciously or unconsciously, death. . . . "

PATRICK FITZHUGH: A BIOGRAPHICAL STATEMENT

"Pat was a unique character in terms of Skid Row habitués. I say this because the guy who becomes Skid Row oriented over a period of years takes on a Skid Row 'personality' to such an extent that most Skid Row guys become typed: they look, think, and behave overtly pretty much the same with slight variations. Pat had preferences, which is rare or nonexistent in most Row Joes.

"I met Pat on the steps of the Galilee Mission one dismal A.M.

in 1950. I struck up a conversation by asking what time the cellar opened: for warmth, shaving, wash sox, and so forth. This began a relationship that was to last with few interruptions for about fifteen years until, like our mutual drinking buddy, Mike Kelly, Pat died on the floor of a bar, from a cardiac arrest brought on during an alcoholic convulsion. Ironically, both guys with whom I was most closely associated on the Row died in 1966, the year I was beginning to come back to life.

"In the undignified environment of the Row, Pat maintained a certain dignity that was a mystery to me and his many buddies on the Row. This dignity was not necessarily reflected in his mode of dress, because at times he suffered from run-down heels and failing of the room rent, just like the rest of us. Though dignity and Skid Row do not seem compatible, this is the label I would have to pin on Pat: a dignified Rower.

"Pat came from Brockton, Mass., and Rocky Marciano was, of course, his idol. He was a walking encyclopedia when it came to sports—any sport.

"Pat talked very little of his parents and two sisters. I gathered he had a fairly normal middle-class bringing up. Irish Catholic, not too rigid. For years Pat would sneak down to midnight mass at St. John's [formerly the Roman Catholic Cathedral Church, located in Center City Philadelphia], but he finally cut that out. He refused to take ear bangings [sermons] in the missions for coffee and he'd do without. Pat was what we called a holer-upper. He would hibernate in his cubicle for weeks at a time. He was able to do this because of the unique operation of the flophouse he stayed at: the Ace Hotel, on Wood Street just east of Eighth. . . . Pat would stay in his room, as I said, for weeks holding court for his more intimate buddies . . . Mike, George, Joe, and myself. He enjoyed discussing sports, politics and the Battle of the Bulge which most of us had been involved in. As I look back, some of, or possibly only, the most sensible times I spent on the Row, were at Pat's 'suite,' sharing jugs and squeeze [a nonbeverage alcohol] and being happy in the knowledge that the country was safely in the hands of an Irish Catholic—J.F.K.

"As I mentioned, Pat was different, he never made 11th and Winter [the nearest police lockup] let alone up the Creek [in the Philadelphia House of Correction]. He drank in only three bars on the Row: Butch's at 8th and Wood, the Log Cabin on the other corner of 8th and Wood, and Mommies at Franklin and

Wood. [Thus, room and liquor were within two blocks of each other.] To this extent he was predictable—you could always find him if he was out of his flop. Pat would never ship out on a live-in job. He did once, got drunk and became terrified of being out of the Row area. Pat would never, but never, get involved with a bottle-gang—which just about every drinking Rower does at times. Pat's only work on the Row was muzzling. He would work six weeks steady, with no drinking. Pat could 'get out' every day, he was well liked at Park's and Cassidy's [day-labor contractors]. Then he would 'hole up' after getting started in one of his favorite bars for a week, two weeks, or until he became so sick he had to stop. While he was holed up and making sense, we, and his other associates, Rowers and businessmen in the area, saw to it he had eats when he could eat, and drinks when he needed them. Pat loved wine and ale, but he would easily settle for 'heat' [squeeze, nonbeverage alcohol] if need be. Pat never sold blood—Pat was never seen on the street unshaven. To this day, when I drop into some of the stores where Pat was known—second-hand shops, bars, hock shops—and rehash the scuttle-butt, we always bring up Pat and his unusual, un-Row-like behavior.

"I never heard Pat refer to a black man as a 'nigger' or a Jew as a 'smuck' or, as a matter of fact, say anything derogatory about anyone. He never tried to blame the war or any incident on any person for his own predicament. This was unusual in a situation where everyone else was hanging blame crepes everywhere. Actually, Pat never discussed the how of his being on the Row. He would always encourage others to 'make a move' from the Row, but never thought about it in terms of himself. As I look back, it's ironic, because Pat was the least of a 'typical Rower' than the lot of us.

"Pat finally got so sick in 1964 they carried him out on a stretcher to Hahnemann Hospital where they found he had TB. They shipped him to South Mountain for treatment.

"I saw Pat for the last time in January 1965. He had just eloped from Alto [the tuberculosis hospital]. It was snowing like hell and I was headed for Brother John's [St. John's Hospice for Men, a Roman Catholic facility.] I was in the process of being sent to Norristown [State Hospital]. Pat looked good and I told him what I was doing and we agreed it would be a good 'stop' for the winter. (Little did I realize that was to be the beginning of my recovery.) He gave me $10 and wished me well. I never saw Pat again.

"Pat, I later found out, went on a binge to end all binges, away from the Row, because he was 'hot' from the Health Department. He finally cashed in his chips in Pentony's Bar, 13th and Arch. The end of a nice guy and in my mind an enigma of the Row. Age 48."

CHARLES WASHINGTON: AN AUTOBIOGRAPHICAL STATEMENT

"My first introduction to muzzling came at the lowest period of my life. It was in the winter of 1953 in Baltimore, Maryland . . . a bitter cold winter, which found me homeless and destitute in a strange city where I knew no one. I had no place to stay and no job in sight . . . and no money. It was there, also, that I was introduced to my first mission and my first flophouse.

"I had severed relations with my home life . . . my family and my friends, and my pride was too great to permit me to call home and admit defeat, to admit that I was wrong. There was only one place to go and that was to the Helping Up Mission, then located on East Baltimore Street, known as The Strip. I was in from the cold and the rain, anyway they did give us something to eat after we had 'received the blessing,' or taken the 'ear beating.'

"At the Helping Up Mission you were allowed to stay five nights free. The man who admitted us let me stay an extra night and told me that I might get a day's work at Fedder's Distributing Company on Sharp Street near the railway station. I worked there two days and was paid just over $3 per day for an eight-hour day. That gave me enough money to pay two nights 'flop' at a dormitory-type flophouse and get something to eat and drink. I recall spending seventy-five cents for food and the rest for cigarettes and wine.

"At that time I had not heard of employment agencies who had live-in jobs, so I continued working at muzzling for awhile until I got a job washing dishes at Miller Brothers Restaurant for $6 per day. I was promoted to pantryman and stayed there at $45 per week until the first of the year, when I came to Philadelphia to visit my aunt who lived . . . in Melrose Park. I looked around for a job at the hotels here and got a part-time job as pantryman at the Bellevue Stratford Hotel making $13 per day.

"I promptly moved into a high-class flophouse located at 148 North Eighth Street and started learning the ropes of Skid Row existence. I learned of the best places to go to get dishwashing jobs, the best dishwashing jobs, the places to go to get work muzzling, the best employment agencies for live-in jobs, and the best places to go to get day-labor jobs. I also learned how to get into a rut and stay there for over ten years without communicating with my family. I buried myself on Skid Row and became content to live there and stay drunk there and lose my identity there.

"Every once in a while I got tired of it and took a live-in job somewhere out of the city. The summer months took me to the shore, where I worked in such places as the Riverview Hotel, Toms River, for $85 per week and my keep, the Surf City Hotel on Long Beach Island, $65 per week plus my keep, and the Sea Gull, $150 per week plus my keep. I would always return to the Row and spend my hard-earned money until I was 'sick and broke.' Then I would muzzle for awhile and ship out to some country club.

"To get on with the muzzling bit. It was a sad day in hell when I got on that route. I can recall some miserable days in every area of Philadelphia and surrounding countryside, including New Jersey and Delaware. When I first started working for Cassidy-Richiar they were paying eight dollars a day. At the end of the day you received six dollars and the rest was given to you the following week in the form of what was (and still is) called a 'kick-back.' Taxes, etc., are taken out of the remaining two bucks and you get the rest. It's hardly worth going back for, and many people didn't bother to. I often wondered where that money went to, that so many people never returned for.

"The going rate now is the minimum wage rate of $1.60 per hour plus time and a half for overtime. If a fellow is lucky enough to make five days he can earn a fair enough wage for that type of work. It's hard to make a buck. Anyone who calls a muzzler a bum has got to be crazy. All he asks for is a day's work. He is not on D.P.A. and he even takes pride in his job. At the end of any work day you might visit any bar on the Row where the muzzlers go to drink and all you can hear is muzzling talk, who put out the most paper in the toughest neighborhood.

"Sometimes it seems the worse the weather, the better they like it. They will actually brag about how wet they got and how hard the job was to do. I can recall many terrible days at that job. There is nothing like West Philadelphia on a day when the thermometer reads 92 degrees and you are walking up the street with a bag on your shoulder, going up and down the steps to put the paper on the damned door knob. You are wet all over from sweat, and you stink. All the good port wine you drank the night before comes out of your pores and you actually smell like wine, and you can hardly wait to get some more wine.

"The muzzler likes to drink, usually wine, and he will muzzle every day of the week to get it. His system craves it, I remember the day when I would hit the bar, filthy dirty from newsprint ink, and would become irritated as hell if I weren't waited on right away. That first Taylor's Port on the rocks tasted so good I usually killed a whole bottle before I even thought about eating, if I bothered to eat. After I ate, I would usually return to the bar and kill another bottle before I could face the loneliness of the flophouse or rooming house, or wherever I decided to stay.

"Then I can recall those wonderful days in Levittown when the temperature dropped to the near zero mark, a fine mist falling, and the seemingly endless miles there were to walk before the truck finally came around to pick you up. Your hair would be frozen. If you had a beard, it would be frozen. Icicles would actually be hanging from your eyebrows. You would have a headache and your bones would be cold, and at lunch time the goddamned foreman would stop at Dunkin Doughnuts and not a bar in sight where a man could get a drink. The lousy son-of-a-bitch would even read you off if you missed a house that had a big German police dog waiting to take a hunk out of your leg.

"Approximately 15 years ago was my first experience with muzzling in Philadelphia. I will try to tell what I know of it briefly.

"Muzzling dates back to the horse and buggy days when Philadelphia was still comparatively small. I can't go back that far. Where the term 'muzzler' came from is a mystery to me. I have asked about that several times and have yet to come up with an answer.

"The companies I am familiar with are Reuben H. Donnelley, 13th and Callowhill, A.A., 11th and Spring Garden, Ad1, 8th and Wood, Parks Distribution Co., 5th and Spring Garden and Cassidy-Richlar, 4th and Callowhill. It is with that last company mentioned that I have had the most experience, and which I will describe the practices of as I understand them.

"In past days the problem of manpower was nonexistent. There were enough flophouses and missions in the area housing enough men to more than supply the needs of all the companies mentioned. Usually the companies would determine how many men were needed for each day of the following week and post it where the men came to 'shape up.' The shop steward would post the information in the union hall located somewhere on Eleventh Street. The flophouses and missions were informed, and the bartenders of all the Skid Row bars were informed. It was not an uncommon practice for the bartenders to tell the muzzlers and the caddies where there was a day's work to be had.

"The Theatrical Bar, 8th and Race, used to be well informed along those lines. We had information from the distribution companies, hotels and restaurants, country clubs, employment agencies and the like. If anyone needed a day-labor job we could usually tell them a place to go. It was sort of an information center.

"The men would report to the various companies and turn in their employee identification cards and wait to be called. It was usually a motley looking gathering. Men, still dirty from the previous day, men who had obviously spent the night on the street, people who had stayed in the missions and flophouses. Once in a while you might notice someone clean and wonder what the hell he was doing there. Of course, all the foremen and drivers were allowed in the office where they would make a big production of going over the cards to get their 'key men.' They would also make a big production of telling certain men that they were not working because they were too dirty or too drunk, always loud enough so the big boss could hear it. In all probability the foreman himself was pretty damned dirty and feeling no pain.

"There were some foremen who would let a man work if he gave them a dollar out of his pay. There are some foremen who would take a couple of men with them from the flophouse, sign him up for the day, and drop him off before leaving for his territory. On the way home at night the man or men were picked up and taken to the office to get paid. He would keep three dollars and give the foreman five dollars, and was known as a 'ghost rider.'

"The usual crew was made up of a driver, a foreman, and eight to ten men. In cases where there were over ten men the foreman had an assistant who was called a *fishcake*. It was the fishcake's duty to load the bags and help the foreman spot the men and, at times when the foreman got too drunk, to run the crew and make sure the foreman was sober enough to present himself at the office at the end of the day. Before getting to the assigned territory it was a custom to make a coffee stop. A chicken-shit foreman would advance his men a quarter for coffee and would make sure to stop where there were no bars open. A good foreman would stop where there was a restaurant and a bar open. He would actually advance his men a dollar for two glasses of wine and a pack of cigarettes. Sometimes, at Howard and York [Jack Cousin's Bar], there would be three or four crews in at one time and Jack would ask one of his steady customers to help behind the bar until we had all been served. In places like that the foreman never paid for his drinks, a form of 'thank you' for bringing the crew in. We liked to make stops like that. At lunch he would advance them another dollar and again stop where you could eat and drink. At the end of the day, if we finished early, another stop was made where another dollar was advanced for more liquid refreshment. A man would be lucky at times to have five dollars coming at the end of the day.

"A *good territory* was a section of the city where there were plenty of row houses where you never had to leave the sidewalk to hang the paper on the door, and where there were plenty of bars a man could quench his thirst in. South Philadelphia, Kensington and the like were known as good territory. *Bad territory* was territory like southwest Philadelphia where you have to climb steps to hang the paper on the door knob. Other bad territories were places like Normandy Park or Levittown [near city limits or beyond]. They were called 'dog heaven.' The muzzler is afraid of dogs, and probably afraid of his own shadow. The houses are far apart and the going is slow, and there is no place to relieve yourself. It isn't uncommon in areas like that for a man to shit or piss his pants.

"In Fairless Hills [in the suburbs] one of my men was picked up by the police for urinating in a car port. I had to round up my entire crew and report to the police station. I finally talked my way into paying a $19 fine to keep the man out of jail. After paying the fine I promptly picked up all my men and headed back to Philadelphia, straight to Richmond and Elkhart Streets where there is a junk shop. I sold the rest of the paper and holed up in a bar until time to report back to the office. Very little work was done in Levittown and Fairless Hills that day, but the President of Cassidy-Richlar met us at the office and said that it was a good job. He must have gone to the area where we did a little work and skipped the rest or there would have been hell to pay.

"Junking paper was another source of income for the foreman.

He might tell his men to do a 'good decorating' job, which meant to put paper where it would show up good, but not to put too much paper there. The more paper left over, the more money he will get for junking it. I have known foremen to take a crew out on a raining day and junk the whole load, mark their work sheet completed and spend the whole day in a bar.

"The ordinary work day is eight hours, although a man seldom works that long. The present rate is the minimum rate of $1.60 per hour plus time and a half for overtime. Overtime is accrued on a daily basis, not weekly hours worked.

"I forgot to mention the fact that a man who pissed or shitted himself was automatically ostracized, shunned by the other members of the crew, and made to sit on the tail gate of the truck on the way home. I don't want to sit by you. You shit yourself. It's because of you we won't get to make a stop on the way in. After all, it wouldn't be fair to the bar owner to bring a man in who smelled like shit, and you can't let the man sit alone in the truck. If you were to take him into the bar he would go over like a turd in a punch bowl. . . . "

FRANK SCHELL: AN AUTOBIOGRAPHICAL STATEMENT

"I don't think there is such a thing as a typical case of a typical client, because each man has hurt and been hurt in a thousand ways from Sunday, and while they all have a common denominator in the fact that they're all alcoholics, each man thinks and feels and dreams—and bleeds—in a somewhat different way. For purposes of this statement, let's concern ourselves with a guy I know well and, if I can, I'll try to get right inside him and tell you his story as I know it. It won't be a pretty story, and you might not like it, because it contains a lot of pain and fear and dirt, and it also concerns people he met along the way. So I suppose it will be mostly about people and pain, and a guy that's dead in every sense of the word except he's still breathing—when we first meet him.

"His name is Frankie. He's walking up Vine Street toward 13th Street with his head down, and he isn't really walking—he's shuffling and his head is down because he's looking for a dry cigarette butt. It rained last night and the goddamn butts are wet and even if you put them in a little paper bag, it takes too long to dry them out so you can get a smoke. And those sons-of-bitches that smoke filters should drop dead right now, because you spot a big one and when you bend over to pick it up it's a Salem or a Kent. The bastard—why can't he smoke a decent cigarette like other people so a guy could get a couple of drags out of it? And what he wouldn't give for a drink. A drink of wine or squeeze or witch hazel or *anything!* If it only had alcohol in it!

"He conned the clerk at the Palace Hotel to put him in last night, because the clerk remembered he bought him a couple drinks the last time he was flush. When he opened the door to the room he saw a bottle on the floor that was half full—Jesus Christ! Did some dumb bastard leave a jug in the room? Great day in the morning! But wait a minute—it looks like white port or Sauterne but is it? Could be piss. He can't tell from the smell because he's got a bad cold from sleeping in that empty car the night before. Well, there's only one way to find out—taste the son-of-a-bitch. Christ—it's piss alright. Might of known. Nobody's gonna be that dumb no matter how slopped up he was. Hold it—who's that next door? Big Jim Smith. Haven't seen him since we worked in Lakewood [New Jersey] together. He's as broke and sick as Frankie is but at least it's somebody to talk to. At least that's something, because when you lay there without a drink, the minutes seem like hours, and you look up at the chicken wire ceiling, and you can't even fantasize properly. At least if you have a jug, you can pull on that and lay back and make the secret life of Walter Mitty seem like a piker. Conan Doyle, in a Sherlock Holmes adventure called 'The Man with the Twisted Lip,' describes the interior of an opium den located in the bowels of London, and he very well could have been describing the Palace Hotel. The same broken men, the vacant stares mirroring the nameless fears. And those nameless fears are pure unadulterated hell. You cringe in a corner like a whipped dog—because you *are* a whipped dog. And if anybody you don't know comes near you, every hair on your head stands up, every nerve in your body screams a warning and every muscle tightens instinctively. Because you're scared. You don't know why you are scared or how you got that way, because it wasn't always that way. There was a time when you had an identity—you were a thinking, feeling contributing human being—capable of loving and being loved. Love? How the very word nauseates you, and if you even hear anyone use it you immediately move away because this has got to be some kind of a nut. The only kind of love you know comes in a dark brown bottle, and when you hold it up to the light it's a beautiful deep red, more beautiful than any ruby ever was, more faithful than any woman, because when

you drink it you kill the pain—if only for a little while. So you're
in love with a bottle of port wine and she's as demanding and
capricious as any woman ever was. And you go to any lengths to
get her. You lie, cheat, steal, con, promise only Christ don't turn
me down! Please give me one more on the tab and I swear I'll
get the money tomorrow. I'll go see my brother or I'll sell my
jacket or even my shoes but christ don't turn me down! He looks
at you with contempt, and he makes you dance on a string like a
puppet and you get down and grovel and you're no longer a
human being but a geek like Tyrone Power was in a movie long
ago. But you don't care because God is dead and the Devil is
alive and he's got to be paid because you belong to him just as
much as you ever did to your mother. When he sees you're shaking so much you're ready to crack and he's had his kicks he gives
you the bottle and you thrust it under your jacket and held it
tighter than you ever did a woman. Then you run back to the
flop through the alley and if any son-of-a-bitch tries to take it
away from you he'll have to kill you first! You run through the
lobby and up the stairs and the bent key doesn't work in the half-
hinged door so you kick it in and slam it to and lean against it,
trying to breathe.

"Frankie became a no-person. A zombie. One year Frankie
worked for an employment agency in Miami and the boss—a
sadistic bastard—would take a job order from an employer, and
it would read as follows: 'Needed at once—10 zombie's for ban-
quet department—Roney Plaza—must have strong back—no
mind—3 days work, long hours, 60¢ an hour. Comb the row.' So
Frankie would shake his head and wonder—how does a man
become a zombie, a no-person? It's a very gradual process. It's
impossible to spell out in detail just how it happens, because the
millions of Frankies don't know it's happening. They know that
something is wrong, but what? I think the key word is bewilder-
ment. Sure, he knows he is drinking too much, and he just got
fired, and his wife or girlfriend says 'You better straighten out or
we're through,' but he's walking around in a daze, continually
saying 'What's wrong, what's wrong?' And then he reaches a point
of no return. A point where he says, 'I no longer care what happens to me—my wife or girlfriend, my job and society, the church
and God and country and mothers and fathers and sisters and
brothers can all go f--- themselves—I am now a nothing.' I will
ship out on lousy jobs, wear the clothes on my back, change my

socks when I can no longer stand the squashing sound when I walk, get deloused at a mission when the 'geese bits' [lice bites] get so bad people notice I'm always scratching myself, and I am now a part of a shadow society. I'm back in the hotel kitchen washing mountains of dishes when Susie gets married, and when she passes through on her way to change her clothes, you pray she won't see you, because you knew her and her mother and father before you became a no-person—she's your niece. . . . "

BILL DUNN: AN AUTOBIOGRAPHICAL STATEMENT

"I was born here in the city [Philadelphia]. My family had come here a few years earlier. They had wandered a lot before that— New York—Ohio—Jersey—finally Philadelphia. I guess my father thought this was a good place to find steady work. He never really had a trade. I think he sometimes did construction work. Anyway he left home several years after the 'crash.' I was just about eight or nine years old then.

"I have one brother—about a year older than me. I don't really remember too much about those years before my father left. I remember we moved a lot—from one room to another. I remember my father was thin and tired and sad. He'd go out early in the morning to look for work, and come home each day a little more tired. And after a while a little more drunk.

"I remember my mother always being cheerful though and always saying 'It's o.k., we'll *make do*' and she did. God! I remember yards of cheap printed cotton goods that covered orange-crate dish cupboards and formed make-believe walls between their 'room' and ours—my brother's and mine.

"After my father left home she wasn't so cheerful anymore. She still made do—but she was strong in a different way then, a grim, tight-lipped way. She did cleaning for other people sometimes, and sewed piecework at home. She finally rented a small row house and we kind of settled down as a family again.

"We seldom talked about my father. I remember my aunt would come over once in a while with all kinds of rumors—about where he'd been seen who he was with—that he was drinking more and more. Mostly I remember the time when she said she heard he'd hit the 'skids.' I remember my mother's eyes then. Worse than if she'd been standing over his grave.

"Anyway, my brother and I grew up, not much different than any other kids on any other crowded city block, with hand-me-down clothes, jelly sandwiches, skinned knees, mumblety-peg and bad report cards. My brother was the scrapper. He fought in streets, schoolyards, the war—and I guess fights his way pretty well through life—even now. I was always the quieter one, the loner.

"What I remember most is that when I got older, maybe 14 or 15, I used to go down to the Row a lot. I'd find an excuse to walk through there on my way into town or something. Partly curiosity, but mostly the rumor that my father was there. I guess it was my age as much as anything. I was looking, like all kids that age I guess, for parts of myself, for searching out roots—for that part of my lost father in me. I didn't tell anyone about it. It took me a long time—walking the Row, asking around.

"Finally I found him. He was standing outside a bar, leaning a little uncertainly against the glass, squinting into the sun. He didn't look much like the old photographs my mother had kept, his hair was matted, he was filthy and unshaven. When I told him who I was he just stared at me. His mouth dropped open a little, and then his hands moved up shaking and slowly covering his face. I just said 'Why?' But he didn't say anything. He just pushed me away and staggered into the bar. I'll never forget that. He didn't say anything.

"I didn't go back. Not for a long while. Several years later when I was in the Navy, I'd go back, hit the bars and ask around. A buddy of his finally told me he'd died. He died in some stinking alley, piled with garbage and broken bottles. His buddy had found him. I got the story in bits and pieces from others. He'd been through all the 'revolving doors.' P.G.H. [Philadelphia General Hospital] drunk tanks, House of Correction—you name it, he'd been there.

"I never told anybody. I never knew how you could tell this. I kept it to myself, thinking I'll go back—inside of me—someday and look at it, see what it meant. I was in the service then, and there was enough rotten in war, and enough booze on leave, to do that—to forget about it for a little while.

"My brother married a girl from California while he was in the service, and headed out there when the war was over. He was making out good the last I heard—haven't been in touch with him for years.

"I came back home in '46, lived with my mother till she died a few years later. I used to drink a lot even then. It killed her. I guess it really killed her.

"Anyway, I always worked pretty steady. I had a job as a machine operator then. Finally I got married, but my wife and me fought most of the time. She was a good woman, couldn't stand my drinking. When she got pregnant she left me. That was around '57. I don't blame her. I heard it was a boy. I've never even seen him. It's funny, but that part of my life—the 'realest' part—all seems so very unreal to me now. I guess too much has happened since.

"I hung on for a few years. I drank on the Row sometimes when I was broke but I never stayed till I lost my job. Then I started drinking more and taking any work I could get—cook, dishwasher, whatever. In '62 I hit the Row for good and before I left I'd hit every stop my father had made. I've sold my blood for booze and my soul for mission soup. I guess I'm stuck now with the same 'why' I once confronted my father with. . . .

"I've thought a lot about the Row and what it means. First of all it's damned important that the Row is being torn down. Maybe not too many guys there are 'second generation' like myself, and not too many kids saw it the way I did for the first time. Yet as long as it's there—as long as it physically exists—it's a possibility for some men. You know, that's what you see in a stranger's eyes sometimes when you panhandle—that fear. And they either cuss you to get out of their way or mumble and push a quarter in your hand, bribing you to get out of their sight. It's the failure they see that reminds them of something inside themselves. And their own guilt for being part of the system that created the Row.

"There is something about that place that adds permanence to your sense of failure, and yet allows you the mixed blessing of a place to belong. It has to come down because there have to be other alternatives to that feeling in human beings.

"You know from that day on, as a kid—when I first saw the Row—'failure' wasn't just a word for me anymore. It was real. It had a shape in the crumbling bricks that form the bars, flops and eateries of the Row. When I hit the 'bottom'—inside myself, my own despair—I knew where to go. 'The bottom' was a place. It was something you could touch and taste and smell.

"I remember when I first hit the Row for good, and I was still alive enough to feel it. I remember patrol cars—and dark bottle-strewn alleys and nights. And my own flesh crawling with lice, and with half-forgotten shame. I remember the smell of warm port wine, and the sounds of groans, and men puking in doorways.

"I remember waking up alone and scared in the middle of the night on a urine-soaked, cigarette-scorched mattress. And that lousy cubicle—that 5′ by 7′ hole—seemed suddenly too big, with all the loneliness inside me.

"I remember watching the old men, and waiting for my brain to be numbed like theirs. I remember the waiting—and only the small struggles against it—for that chronic disease of the Row, hopelessness, to take firm hold of the body, dull the senses, still the torment. Booze could only do it for such a short time—wash down the anger and the pain that choked up in you. I waited for the stinking clothes, the bottle, the invisible walls of the Row to become a simple logical extension of the self. I've seen it happen to men. It began to happen to me.

"The hopelessness—the sense of failure. That begins before you get to the Row, but it's like a slight infection then—if you could get over it while you're still out there. If there was anything—anyone—out there to stop you. . . ."

Part II

The Intersection
of Alcohol
and the Slum

3

Drinking Patterns
and Alcoholism

Almost all discussions of Skid Row make it clear that alcohol is used heavily by many Skid Row men, and that their style of using alcohol influences almost all social and institutional relationships that take place on Skid Row. As Chapter 2 brings out, for many Skid Row men alcohol is the tie that binds them together while it helps to dissolve their relationships with others in the larger community. We believe that a broad spectrum of programs for Skid Row men should include at least care for those who have alcohol-related problems.

We see no point in a lengthy discussion of the effects of alcohol, with which most Americans are familiar. Further, getting drunk and alcoholism are not the same. Getting drunk is the precursor to alcoholism, but the latter condition involves considerably more.

In field and clinical studies alcoholism is defined in different ways. One way is to emphasize the effects of alcohol consumption, in which one's consumption is related to personal disorganization, ill health, marital and family disruption, jail, crime, and unemployment. These effects usually bring the alcoholic to the attention of the physician, social agency, police, or court. Consequently, this approach is adopted by people interested in

In the preparation of this chapter, we wish to acknowledge the assistance of Donald B. Wallace and William Hood.

individual and public welfare. (Studies by Pittman and Gordon and Brantner are of this type.[1]) In this approach, it is necessary to obtain accurate information about personal problems as well as their social concomitants; and in addition, the relationship between alcohol consumption and this social disorganization needs to be demonstrated. Dunham, Lovald, Wallace, Wiseman, and Spradley discuss this complex set of relationships.[2]

A second approach is to determine the amount of alcohol consumed by the individual in any given period of time; the degree of alcoholism is often qualified by the percent of income spent or by the norms of the particular community. However, it is difficult to get accurate information about both the amount of alcohol consumed and community norms. Bogue relied primarily upon a self-report of amount of alcohol consumed, and he related this measure to personal history, current individual activity, and social functioning.[3] Although we gathered some information on expenditures, we have never really felt comfortable with this procedure when used with Skid Row men. Especially when a man is on a prolonged drinking bout or spree, he is not likely to have an accurate knowledge of the amount of alcohol he has recently consumed. Further, since poor Skid Row men often club together to buy wine (the "bottle gang"), statements of quantity are, at best, approximations. However, this does not deny the usefulness of the procedure with more moderate drinkers.

In a third approach, an alcoholic is defined as one who is unable to maintain control over his drinking behavior. We may think of the degree of control as the probability of taking a drink at any given moment or at any given day or, more generally, as the probability of taking a drink under any set of circumstances. For instance, consider the man for whom the probability of taking a drink on any day is very low, but if he takes a drink, then the probability of taking a second drink is very high; indeed, it soars to a probability of 1.0. This is a classic spree or binge drinker, or Jellinek's Gamma type.[4] On the other hand, we have a man for whom the probability at any moment of taking a drink is somewhat higher than for the spree drinker and for whom the probability of taking a drink on any given day is almost 1.0. This is the so-called blood-level drinker who does not necessarily—or may only rarely—drink to insensibility. This is Jellinek's Delta type.

If we look at the differences in the probability of drinking as a function of circumstances, we may be able to understand the problem of control a little better. Presumably the neurotic—Jellinek's Alpha type—loses control of his drinking under certain particularly anxiety-provoking circumstances. It may also be that the probability of taking the first drink rises rapidly for the spree drinker under circumstances such as anniversaries or adverse trauma (such as losing a job). The blood-level drinker may simply drink more, more regularly, as a function of circumstances. Thus, the question of who does or does not have control over drinking may not be as appropriate as the question of when or under what circumstances he has control.

There are probably fashions and cultural factors which characterize any diagnosis of loss of control of the use of alcohol. In the United States, loss of control is now usually ascribed to a spree drinker and less frequently to a blood-level drinker. Because it is difficult to get reliable information, and because loss of control may be situationally specific, we chose to rely heavily upon spree drinking as our indicator of alcoholism. We used the following categories to describe serious drinking styles: spree, daily, off and on throughout the week, weekends only, a few times a month, and no drinking. All these categories were of course based on self-reports. However, it is not enough to ask about drinking style directly. One should also seek to determine the answers to such questions as: How long must there be a loss of control before it is called alcoholism? And, must this be a chronic condition? On Skid Row, this condition has of course often continued long enough to satisfy most definitions of chronicity. Consequently, we have usually relied upon this criterion before we labeled a client as alcoholic. Chronicity for a year or longer is relatively easy to detect in a Skid Row client after working with him for a few days, and we have used this as one of our diagnostic criteria. Bahr's study in New York relied heavily upon the style of drinking approach, although some data on quantities consumed were also collected.[5]

All definitions present difficulties and limitations when applied in the field. Therefore most researchers have used combinations of approaches and whatever information was available to specify the degree of alcoholism. Regardless of how alcoholism is defined, it is important that drinking behavior and the effects of drinking be kept separate conceptually.

Another approach to the concept of alcoholism relies on a clinical definition. Clinical definitions tend to describe the syndrome in terms of the degree of apparent control that a person has over his drinking. We made clinical determinations on the basis of the degree of (or, more accurately, lack of) control exhibited by a client. We relied upon estimates of lack of control made by physicians, psychiatrists, psychologists, and social workers. A final diagnosis was made by reviewing each case in terms of the original diagnosis and of our casework experience. As a result, some men were diagnosed as alcoholics who had not been so originally.

DRINKING PATTERNS

Spree Drinking

At least 30 percent of the Philadelphia Skid Row population were diagnosed as spree drinkers (Table 3-1)—that is, men who chronically lose control.

TABLE 3-1   DRINKING PATTERNS OF THE 1960 AND 1964 SAMPLES, BY PERCENTAGE

| SAMPLES | | DRINKING PATTERNS | | | | | | TOTAL | |
	Spree Drinker	Daily	Off and on Through Week	Week-ends Only	Few Times per Month	No Drink-ing	Other and DK, NA, RA*	Per-centage	N
1960 sample	29	16	9	8	14	17	7	100	1474
1964 sample (Total)	30	14	9	9	15	16	7	100	552
Doorstep	22	17	11	11	11	19	9	100	288
Returnee	38	11	8	7	18	11	7	100	264
1964 walk-in	56	5	6	6	12	11	4	100	269

* DK = Don't Know; NA = No Answer; RA = Refuse to Answer.

Of the men given the diagnostic work-up at the center, roughly half (51 percent) were diagnosed as alcoholic. Table 3-2 presents the relationship between the clinical diagnosis of alcoholism and the report of drinking patterns. Of those reporting different drinking patterns, almost three-fourths of those who reported that they were spree drinkers were subsequently diagnosed as alcoholics. In contrast, about one-fourth of those who reported that they drank infrequently or moderately were diagnosed as alcoholics. The percentages of diagnosed alcoholics among the daily drinkers and the off and on throughout the week drinkers were intermediate. The data suggest that, despite limitations, interviews which focus upon a man's style of drinking (easier to obtain than the amount of alcohol consumed) have good diagnostic validity insofar as the criterion of alcoholism is loss of control and fair validity with respect to other drinking styles.

TABLE 3-2   DIAGNOSIS OF ALCOHOLISM AND DRINKING PATTERNS, BY PERCENTAGE

DRINKING PATTERNS	DIAGNOSIS OF ALCOHOLISM		TOTAL	
	Alcoholic	Non-alcoholic	Percentage	N[a]
Spree drinker	74	26	100	97
Daily	66	34	100	29
Off and on throughout week	55	45	100	20
Weekends only	24	76	100	17
Few times per month	24	76	100	38
Less than once per month	22	78	100	9
Nondrinker	24	76	100	29

[a] Other and DK, NA, RA omitted.

In Appendix C we present the characteristics of those who voluntarily came into the center's program. We distinguish those interviewed where they lived but who did not come to the center (doorsteps), those who came to the center after having been interviewed where they live (returnees), and those who simply came in without a previous interview (walk-ins). There were more spree drinkers among the returnees than among the doorsteps; most of the walk-ins were spree drinkers. These differences prevailed with respect to all drinking styles even when the data were controlled for age. However, the proportion of spree drinkers decreased with age for all three groupings; the decline in the percentage of spree drinkers was most notable for those over 65 years of age.

Spree drinkers had slightly higher educational levels than those . of the nonspree drinkers; the nondrinkers, lower than the nonspree drinkers. Again, age made a difference, if only because the youngest group was likely to have more education as a consequence of recent trends in our society. However, there did not seem to be any obvious interaction between present age and present drinking pattern with respect to education. A comparison of the clinical alcoholics and the nonalcoholics also indicates the educational superiority of the alcoholics over the nonalcoholics; the median grade for the alcoholics was the eighth grade, in comparison with the seventh grade for the nonalcoholics. In addition, a greater percentage of spree drinkers had been married at some time (64 percent) than had the nonspree drinkers (53 percent), and the nondrinkers (45 percent). There seemed to be no striking interaction between marital status, age, and drinking pattern. As was expected the relationship between loss of spouse was apparently linear with age, and, here again, there is no apparent interaction as a function of the drinking pattern. Finally, spree drinkers and daily drinkers had greater residential instability and tended to pay for shelter on a daily basis.

There were relatively few blacks actually in the Philadelphia Skid Row during the 1960 study and the demonstration grant period. Of those blacks included in the data, we were uncertain about which should be included as regular inhabitants of Skid Row. One reason for our uncertainty was that a larger black slum abuts the northern boundary of what we have called Skid Row. Consequently we have excluded from our analyses a section of the redevelopment area which was largely black.

Our data show that the drinking patterns of whites and blacks in Skid Row are different. Blacks comprise a minority of all categories except for the weekend drinkers only. This is true primarily of the younger members of our sample, but it is also relatively true for the whole sample. Neither did the blacks have such serious problems with alcohol as did the whites living in the area. Thus, a larger percentage of whites (74 percent) were diagnosed as alcoholics than blacks (44 percent). The black sample on Skid Row was younger than the white.

We found that almost half of the spree drinkers and daily drinkers had been in jail two or more times in the past five years, in comparison with about 10 percent of those who drink less frequently. For clinical alcoholics, the comparable figure was 43 percent, in comparison with 21 percent of the nonalcoholics. However, almost 50 percent of the nonalcoholics had been in jail at least once in the past five years. This is an amazing figure for any single section of the population of Philadelphia, and serves to emphasize the importance of reconsidering our legal and judicial procedures as they relate to this segment of our society. Our data give some support to Spradley's conclusions that one function of the law enforcement agencies is to "convert" some of our citizens from marginal, nonconforming persons into Skid Row men.[6]

We used many different approaches in assessing the severity of problem drinking on Skid Row. For instance, we asked all who came to the center if they had ever been heavy or periodic drinkers. Of those who said they had been, at some time in the past, a large majority (86 percent) had been spree drinkers, in contrast to about two-thirds of those who said they drank off and on during the week, and about four-tenths of the daily drinkers. The relatively high proportion of those men who drank off and on during the week and had been heavy drinkers in the past suggests that this category may include more men who were defensive about reporting the amount they drank or the frequency of their drinking.

We also asked the men specifically about losing control of their drinking. The spree drinkers, much more so than the others, were most likely to admit losing control (70 percent). The fact that those who reported drinking off and on throughout the week reported loss of control less often (20 percent) than did the daily drinkers (28 percent) tends to confirm the hypothesis that they are more defensive about their drinking. In the comparable analysis for alcoholism diagnosis, about half the alcoholics (55 percent) admit that their drinking has been out of control, in comparison with only 2 percent of the nonalcoholics.

In a slightly different approach, we also asked if they had ever experienced a blackout or "pulled a blank," a condition often used as the diagnostic sign for confirmed alcoholism and clearly indicative of loss of control. Seventy-six percent of the spree drinkers reported blackouts, which is substantially higher than the off and on throughout the week drinkers (45 percent) and the daily drinkers (30 percent). These data also tend to support the hypothesis that those who reported drinking off and on during the week were defensive in their attitudes about drinking and alcoholism. The data on the clinical alcoholics are consistent with the self-report of drinking pattern; thus 67 percent of the alcoholics reported that they had had blackouts, in contrast to 4 percent of the nonalcoholics.

Not only drinking styles and the effects of drinking but also the place where drinking takes place appear to differentiate the clinical alcoholics from the nonalcoholics. Both types tended to do their drinking in bars. However, a far larger percent of the alcoholics (50 percent) reported drinking outside bars during the week before their interview than did the nonalcoholics (17 percent). The place where drinking took place is also of interest in that it is prognostic of arrest for drunkenness. This will be discussed in greater detail in Chapter 4.

Finally, the probability that a spree drinker will take a drink to cure the effects of a hangover is 66 percent for our sample (Table 3-3). The probability decreases regularly for other drinking categories. This suggests that the addictive pattern of using alcohol as a remedy for the effects of alcohol may have etiological significance for the development of at least the spree drinking pattern. The fact that a small percentage of those categorized as nondrinkers reported this addictive behavior may be an indication of the reliability of the men's reports. The data are consistent with other findings on the nondrinkers, and may simply be a consequence of the fact that the man was asked whether he had had a drink in the past year. He may well have stopped drinking in the past year, but may have had an addictive pattern before that.

TABLE 3-3   REPORTED HANGOVER REMEDY AND DRINKING PATTERNS, BY PERCENTAGE

DRINKING PATTERNS	HANGOVER REMEDY			TOTAL	
	Take a Drink	Other	No Drink or No Hangover	Percentage	N[a]
Spree drinker	66	32	2	100	158
Daily and off and on throughout week	35	42	23	100	132
Other drinkers	18	46	36	100	131
Nondrinkers	9	32	59	100	75

[a] DK, NA, RA omitted.

In brief summary, the data lend support to the usefulness of spree drinking as a way to approach the concept of alcoholism in the Skid Row context and, in a general way, also tend to support Bogue's postion that alcoholism has probably been overemphasized in discussions of Skid Row men and their problems.[7] The significance of alcohol varies among individual Skid Row men. Health and welfare services offered on the basis of the alcoholism stereotype are less likely to reach men who drink but are not alcoholics. Since Skid Row men live below any reasonable level for our affluent society, greater effectiveness is needed in reaching those who are not alcoholics. The more desperate a man, related to his loss of control, the more willing he is to seek out any help he can find. The problem that always remains is the disparity between the concepts of help that are held by the man and by the helping agency.

Blood-Level Drinking

We asked men who returned to the center which of the following terms best described themselves: drunk, lush, wino, teetotaler, worker, or retired worker. The first three are pejorative, and the last three are not; all describe types of men found on Skid Row. Sixty-one percent of the daily drinkers, 43 percent of the spree drinkers, and 27 percent of those who drink off and on during the week referred to themselves in pejorative terms. If all the men or even extremely high proportions had elected the pejorative terms, we might have been inclined to accept the theory that this was another example of the nose dive in which the Skid Row man appears to accept the debasement as part of his strategy for survival. Wallace and Wiseman point out that the man learns to conform to the expectations of missions and social agencies—he "cons" the agency in order to get service.[8] The differential distribution of the responses, however, leads us to doubt the nose-dive theory. Instead, we may have an example of the stabilization of alcohol as a personal and social value after socialization into Skid Row, such as Wallace presents.[9] The men were under no particular pressure to select the pejorative terms, and we can easily believe that this was their honest response rather than a "put on." If so, then we suggest that Wallace's "assimilated Skid Row man" is likely to be a daily drinker and that he approximates a blood-level rather than a spree drinker. If we consider these latter two as unstable rather than as fixed behavioral patterns, then we need to know what relationship there is between the two and between these two and other patterns of drinking. There may be situational and unique elements that are critical to the process. For example, a man can stay "dry" for three or four years and then "bomb out" during a particularly active Christmas-New Year holiday. But the matter remains problematical at present because we are not equipped to make a systematic study that would demonstrate empirical relationships between daily and blood-level drinking.

Off-Hours Drinking

For blood-level and spree drinkers, the need for alcohol does not stop at legal closing hours. How do men get their alcohol during the off hours—late at night and on Sundays, when neither bars nor state liquor stores are open? Many heavy drinkers on Skid Row are unable or unwilling to lay in a supply of booze to carry them over. There are three principal sources of alcohol on Sundays, according to our informants. First is a bootlegger, whom we shall call Joe (a pseudonym). Joe operates within the Skid Row area itself. Second is the Rose Club (pseudonym), a legal drinking club outside the redevelopment area. Third is a store in the neighborhood, reportedly owned by Joe, which sells large quantities of witch hazel. Some men on Skid Row believe that there is a financial tie between the owners of the Rose Club and Joe the bootlegger and that the owners of the Rose Club controlled the rackets in the area from Spring Garden Street to Arch Street and from Broad Street to Franklin Street during Prohibition. These men say that another member of the same family controlled the balance of the Spring Garden–Arch area to the Schuylkill. (We have not tried to verify these allegations.) At that time the Row had three flourishing burlesques, bootleggers, prostitution, and "flea circuses" (which had several small sideshows outside and a girlie show inside for an extra twenty-five cents). These informants say that in those days the Rose Club was a speakeasy and apparently the theatrical crowd with its hangers-on were its principal customers. With the end of Prohibition things got difficult for these places, and Skid Row gradually expanded into the area. The Rose Club eventually became a Skid Row Sunday drinking club and a hotel owned by the same family became a higher-class Skid Row rooming house.

A number of alternative strategies are available to the Skid Row man, depending on how much money he has and what his inclinations are. If he has no money and there is no one around who "owes him a favor," he may sit in his hotel lobby hoping that someone will pay him for a "run" to the bootlegger's, for which he will usually insist on fifty cents and a glass of wine as his fee. If it is night, he will insist on more because of the danger of mugging. If a man has less than a dollar, he may buy a pint of witch hazel for forty cents and take it to his cubicle. Alternatively, he may promote a bottle group with his fifty cents to buy a pint of wine from the bootlegger. If he has between one dollar and two dollars, he will probably buy his own pint of wine from Joe. This will cost him a dollar, which is a 100 percent markup from the New Jersey retail liquor store price. Pennsylvania State Liquor Commission stores do not sell pints of wine. Many men use the bootlegger exclusively, especially if they are nonworkers who live on a fixed income. The reason is not clear. If a man has between two and three dollars, he may go to the Rose Club in order to have some companionship, even though it is more expensive than buying a pint of wine from Joe. A man's appearance is no obstacle to his membership in the Rose Club (one dollar a year); drinks at the club cost five cents more on Sundays than on weekdays. If a man has more than three dollars, he probably will go to a hotel in the Spruce Street area or to a veteran's club not far away, where he will drink shots and beer.

Some men use other local hotel bars or go to licensed clubs when they have enough money and are careful about their appearance. There they will drink cheap whiskey or beer instead of wine. A number of men go to drinking clubs further out from the center of the city in the working-class neighborhoods where they formerly lived and are still well known. Many of these are nationality clubs whose membership-clientele is white. (There are 79 drinking clubs in South Philadelphia, 67 in the Kensington-Fishtown area, 39 in the Port Richmond–Bridesburg–Tacony–Holmesburg sector, 27 in the Nicetown area, 17 in Germantown, 15 in the Kingsessing area of southwest Philadelphia, and 8 in the old borough of Manayunk. However, all North Philadelphia from Girard Avenue to Allegheny has only 31, many of which are old white nationality clubs in an area which is now predominantly black.)[10] Several clubs in the Kensington-Fishtown area are reported to be willing to serve Skid Row-like men on Sundays if they are not conspicuous in their behavior or dress. Most of these clubs increase their prices only 5 cents a drink on Sundays; hotel bars usually increase 10 to 15 cents. Our Skid Row informants say that most clubs do not sell cheap wine on Sundays or may discourage its sale by serving a small glass and giving wine drinkers poor service. Thus, the Skid Row man may drink at a club or a hotel bar when he has money, or he may go to the local bootlegger when he has run out of money or is drinking cheap wine. It is in this sense that the connection exists between the drinking club and Skid Row.

Since Joe the bootlegger is the major source of supply of cheap wine on Sunday, more should be said about his operation. Most of the sales are package goods at one dollar a pint. However, depending on who you are, whether you are a regular customer, and how much he likes you, Joe may charge more. If you drink in his place, you pay a minimum of twenty-five cents extra for the first bottle. A client told us that he was charged fifty cents extra, and it is said that Joe may short change a customer (e.g., give change for five dollars when the customer had given him ten). When this happens they are told, "You'd better not squawk!" Joe's prices can go higher under special circumstances too. For instance, during the week that the mayor of Philadelphia closed all bars by proclamation following the assassination of the Reverend Martin Luther King, prices were doubled. It is reported that at two dollars a pint sales were still heavy.

Our informants tell us that police cars are frequently parked outside Joe's and they infer that there are payoffs. Certain norms are supposed to be practiced when the police are in the vicinity, say our informants. The purchaser is supposed to keep his bottle out of sight under his clothes when he leaves, and he is supposed to be able to navigate fairly well. If these rules are broken, the men believe that the police confiscate the bottle, and then go in and demand an extra payoff from Joe. Skid Row men believe that many of these confiscated bottles are resold by the police. (We do not infer that the administration of the Police Department condones such venality. Indeed, we believe that they have taken positive efforts to crack down from time to time. Nonetheless, it is extremely difficult to prevent these practices. Furthermore, we are not sure just where the line should be drawn between fact and distortion in the present case.)

A well-informed client reported to us that Joe's bootlegging franchise extends from Sixth to Ninth Streets and from Race to Noble Streets. We say "franchise" because apparently the restriction of sales is enforced for Joe's benefit within that area. For example, it is reported that when some Row men have set up small bootlegging operations of their own in their rooms or cubicles, a "goon squad" goes into action and the competition is eliminated. In addition, it is reported that the police recently busted a small-time bootlegger in a hotel near Joe's place. The one reported exception to this monopoly is a bootlegger who sells wine to farm laborers who leave from the area on trucks or old school buses early in the morning. These sales actually take place outside his territory, and Joe would have no direct basis for action.

Finally, a man who lives in one of the Skid Row cubicle hotels and buys wine exclusively from Joe on Sundays, reports that there is a connection not only between a hotel and a restaurant, but that a bar and a bootlegger are also tied in. Herman Wright (pseudonym), who owns a bar and a hotel, also owns a cheap rooming house in the area. He deducts from his tenants' checks the following: rent, meal tickets at a local restaurant, six wines a day in his bar, two dollars a day repayment for the one dollar a day advance to tenants for bootleg wine on weekends and after hours. Practically speaking, this wine money can only be spent at Joe's.

This discussion of off-hours drinking has led us to realize how deeply implicated non-Skid Row people are in the continuation of the alcohol problems of Skid Row men. The bootlegger's function, however, does not seem to be much different from the social club or hotel which has a Sunday liquor license. In general, most Skid Row men cannot afford the social club or the hotel bar. This being so, a call for law enforcement against bootleggers has some of the same implications about class justice that Spradley observed in Seattle where the difference between a Skid Row man and other citizens was that Skid Row men don't have bail money when they are arrested for drunken behavior while other people do.[11]

DOWNWARD CLASS MOBILITY

In Chapter 2 and in Appendix C, we have tried to "place" the Skid Row men whom we reached either in the neighborhood or in the center. We did this demographically and in terms of personal characteristics. In this chapter, we have attempted to place them with respect to alcoholism and problem drinking. There is still another dimension—social class—which can be related to alcoholism and problem drinking. Here we want not only to dispel the myths of the descent of the drunkard but also to lay the groundwork for the position that rehabilitation of Skid Row men should not involve the implicit plan of returning them to the fringes of the middle class (a point which Wiseman develops[12]) but, rather, should help them participate within the working classes. We see class placement as an abbreviated way of casting the Skid Row population into the perspective of the larger American society with respect to racial and ethnic background, style of life, competitive achievement, relative control over one's own life, and relative power with respect to other people. We have relied upon occupational information for class placement. What a man does for a living may have greater status value in the middle classes than in the working classes, but, insofar as the worlds of the Skid Row man and of the larger community intersect, jobs are sources of money for drink, shelter, food, and clothing. Skid Row men also rely heavily upon Social Security retirement benefits and public welfare.

Discussion of class mobility has long been a part of the larger methodological discussion of social class in American communities. It seems to have first been given major attention by Sorokin.[13] Most of this discussion has been in terms of upward mobility— that is, movement from a lower to a higher social class. However, there has been some recognition that the American system is also characterized by downward mobility. The extent of this downward mobility is not well known; for the moment we should probably accept McGuire's estimate of about 5 percent.[14] A similar finding was made by Van Tulder[15] for the Netherlands for about a 35-year period, which lends support to the interesting speculation that such rates are common for mature industrial systems, a position also suggested by Schnore[16] and others.

Merton and Kitt, in an attempt to extend the theoretical value of *The American Soldier* studies, write of anticipatory socialization of the upwardly mobile enlisted soldier into the officer reference group and of his alienation and marginality from his present enlisted man membership group.[17] They point out that most of the problems of the upwardly mobile person may be objectively solved if he is accepted into his reference group; if he is rejected by that reference group, he is likely to be a rootless social isolate (an almost classic condition for the development of anomie). Rootlessness and social isolation are not synonymous with Skid Row. Wallace argues that as a man becomes a part of the Skid Row way of life he associates with others for whom alcohol is the focal element of the relationship. Spradley, on the other hand, argues that it is during the jail experience that the process of stripping away the man's identity takes place with its replacement by a Skid Row identity.[18] Nonetheless, both describe the Skid Row man as associating with others in the same circumstances, and challenge the idea that Skid Row men in general are social isolates. Some men on Skid Row say they have no close friends, either on the Row or outside, but the numbers in our sample were too small to permit extensive cross-tabulations. However, we found no significant difference between these isolates and the balance of the population with respect to class mobility.

Greenblum and Pearlin[19] tested hypotheses on racial and religious prejudice. They report that persons who are downwardly mobile from the middle class to the working class are generally more prejudiced than those in the stable middle class from which they came or those in the stable working class into which they moved. Greenblum and Pearlin observe that the process of move-ment from higher to lower occupational status may lead to frustra-tions that, in turn, are channeled into hostility towards minority groups, especially if these minority groups are status competitors. Greenblum and Pearlin also seek to present their data in terms of class identification-reference group theory, and conclude that "downward mobile persons retain the exclusive attitudes of the status they are leaving, but assume and even tend to exceed in fre-quency the cognitive manifestations of prejudice of their new mem-bership group."[20] We have no data that would enable us to test this conclusion, but we believe that racial segregation at present is closely related to the attitudes of the white Skid Row residents. The restaurants and bars will serve blacks, although they may not be welcomed. The owners may have their own prejudices, but we believe that they would forgo these prejudices in order to make more money if it were not for the likelihood of violence by the whites. Skid Row men are "whitetowners" in their origins and atti-tudes,[21] and are downwardly mobile from the aggressively hostile working classes.

Social isolation may be measured by degree of participation in formally organized voluntary associations (such as churches) or occupationally based associations (such as labor unions). Lipset and Gordon made a secondary analysis of a San Francisco–Oak-land labor market study.[22] While their data seem to be more rele-vant for upwardly mobile persons, they conclude that class-mobile persons are less likely to be active members of labor unions than are those who have been stable in the working class. Roth and Peck found that the downwardly mobile had significantly lower marital adjustment scores than did the total population of respon-dents.[23] They interpret their findings in terms of the social disap-proval directed toward persons who are downwardly mobile, and suggest that the downwardly mobile person is "apt to be a rebel against convention, and to be a person who rejects responsibili-ties." This relationship of personal instability, rebellion, and down-ward mobility is also stressed by Ruesch, who interprets psycho-somatic symptoms in terms of class behavior as expressions of the attitudes of the child toward the parent and in terms of the pro-cess of acculturation to the new class of membership. If the child rejects the parent, he may work against the mobility patterns of his parents; for example, if the parental family was oriented upward, the child's rebellion might be evidenced in downward mobility. Ruesch comments that downwardly mobile persons have a poor prognosis in therapy.[24] His conclusion is supported by the conclusions of Hollingshead and Redlich, who admit that the downwardly mobile person, even though relatively scarce in our society, presents special difficulties to the therapist.[25] They point out that the downwardly mobile are often the first referred to the psychiatrist because they are perceived in the larger community as troublemakers, and may be diagnosed as having character disorders with destructive or self-destructive personalities. "Even when insight is reached in downward mobile persons by dynamic psychotherapy, their self-destructive urges in the form of negative therapeutic reaction prevent any real success in treatment."[26]

Blau points out that class mobility is fraught with dilemmas which are of the essence of the dialectic of interpersonal behavior.[27] The downwardly mobile person is faced with the dilemma of seeking to maintain social obligations which are beyond his means or accepting his inability to offer the desired status symbols and thereby losing his status in both his own eyes and the eyes of others. The downwardly mobile must choose between two kinds of social deprivation.

Both alternatives available to the *downwardly* mobile inhibit social integration. If he attempts to maintain his affiliation with his class of origin, social interaction with friends whose superior economic position continually revives his sense of frustration and failure undermines his security, his relations with these friends, and thus his integrated position as one of them. And if, to escape from such experiences, he seeks the companionship of members of the working class, differences between his values and theirs make it most difficult for him to accept them unequivocally and to become completely accepted by them. Few people reject an individual simply because he has been unsuccessful in his career, but the predicament of the downwardly mobile is that the social conditions of his existence make it nevertheless likely that he will find himself without close friends.[28]

In this type of situation, the isolation is due to rejection of the new membership group and rejection by the old membership group, the reverse of the Merton and Kitt situation.

Blau was of course not thinking of a Skid Row man, who is the extreme case. A common initial reaction is to say that as he becomes a Skid Row man he abandons the middle- and working-class values or that most of the abandonment is already in process, at least for the heavy drinker before he arrives on Skid Row.

More to the point is the fact that the conditions of Skid Row life do not permit normal middle- and working-class values much opportunity for application or fulfillment. These values therefore corrode, since attitudes, norms, and values must be situationally reinforced if they are to persist. When a man behaves in terms of a conflicting set of attitudes, norms, and values in order to establish and maintain his social relationships on Skid Row, he temporarily puts some of his former values aside. It becomes difficult to predict which set of values will influence his behavior at the appropriate opportunity.

Most Skid Row men have not been sharply downwardly class-mobile from their parental families. They originated in the working classes (Table 3-4). Nonetheless, they seem to have been skidders from the working classes for most of their adult lives. Our conclusions in this matter are essentially similar to those reported by Bogue and Bahr.[29]

In collecting and processing our data, we used a seven-position procedure for what we call the "occupational prestige class," in which position 1 was the highest and 7 the lowest. (A listing of kinds of occupations as they were classified into each status level is presented in Appendix D.) We have labeled these class positions as: upper class, middle class, lower middle class, marginal middle working class, working class, lower class, and lower lower class and lumpenproletariat. (While we have also categorized our data according to the system of socioeconomic status used by Bogue, as Appendix D shows, here we use the simpler system because we want to avoid an impression of spurious accuracy.)

The fathers of those with different drinking patterns were remarkably similar in occupational prestige rank at the time the client was growing up. The median fell within the marginal middle working class for all groups except for the weekend-only drinkers, which was slightly lower; this is undoubtedly because blacks tend to be overrepresented among the weekend-only drinkers. With respect to the client's best job—presumably one way to measure a peak of status achievement—the spree drinkers said they had a higher prestige rank than the others; 33 percent of the spree drinkers held marginal middle-class jobs or higher. However, about 62 percent of the fathers of spree drinkers held marginal middle-class jobs or higher, and about 50 percent of the fathers of all other groups held comparably ranked jobs. So it may be con-

TABLE 3-4   COMPARISON OF PRESTIGE CLASS OF JOBS, BY PERCENTAGE

PRESTIGE CLASS	PARENTAL FAMILY 1960	PARENTAL FAMILY 1964[a]	TEEN ASPIRATION 1964[b]	FIRST FULL JOB 1964[b]	LONGEST JOB 1960	BEST JOB 1964[a]	JOB AFTER LONGEST 1964[b]	SURVEY WEEK 1960	LAST JOB 1964[a]
Upper to lower middle	16	20	18	1	6	5	1	2	1
Marginal middle, upper working	39	32	25	7	25	20	10	7	6
Working	18	18	20	35	36	36	21	19	15
Lower	21	17	14	40	27	29	33	37	37
Lumpenproletariat	1	4	1	12	5	5	22	32	39
None	—	—	12	—	—	—	5	—	—
DK, NA, RA	5	9	10	5	1	5	8	3	2
Total percentage	100	100	100	100	100	100	100	100	100
N	2249	550	269	238	2249	547	238	1062	550

[a] Sample.   [b] Intake interview.

cluded that all categories of men showed some downward mobility with respect to their fathers.

In addition, all groups were downwardly mobile within their own lifetimes. Thus, for no more than 10 percent in any drinking category were their last jobs in the marginal middle working class or higher. Indeed, for about 80 percent of all groups, except the nondrinkers, the jobs were lower class or lower lower class. Both the intergenerational and the intragenerational mobilities were greatest for the spree drinkers and least extreme for the non-drinkers. This was especially true for the older nondrinkers, for whom the latest job was presumably his job at the time of his retirement (which may have come well before the age of 65); a little less than half of them (46 percent) held lower-class and lower-lower-class jobs.

The men's self-identification with a class both before and after coming to Skid Row tends to confirm these conclusions. Forty-four percent of the alcoholics said that before they came to Skid Row they were in Philadelphia's middle class, but at the time of the interview only 22 percent so classified themselves. By comparison, 34 percent of the nonalcoholics considered themselves as middle class before coming to Skid Row, and 31 percent continued this identification into the present. It may be of interest that the nonalcoholics tended to report a stronger identification with the working class. In any event, the alcoholics perceived themselves as higher than the nonalcoholics before arrival and lower after arrival on Skid Row. Because of the nature of the work carried on in the center and the relationships that were established, it was not possible to explore the reason why so many men continued to make an identification with the middle class even when living on Skid Row. We will further explore the claim to middle-class identity and Skid Row identification in Chapter 9.

One of the major problems for the Skid Row man seems to be the possible discrepancy between where he is and where he might be. One of the major determinants of this discrepancy may be the problem of drinking, and the physicians' estimate of relative employability may be considered an estimate of the magnitude of this discrepancy for both alcoholics and nonalcoholics. Of all those who were judged to have greater potential for employment, 81 percent were clinical alcoholics and 19 percent nonalcoholics. Of those who were judged to be fully employable or to have no greater potential for employment, there was no preponderance of alcoholics. On the surface, one of the major concerns of those who work with Skid Row men must be the economic rehabilitation of the alcoholic—narrowing the gap between aspiration and achievement. Since the peak of achievement in the alcoholics actually occurred some years before they came to the Row, narrowing the gap is not an easy process, and helping agencies should give up the easy assumption that rehabilitation means the ability to get and hold a good job.

Some of these discrepancies are revealed in another way. During the course of our attempts to learn about the men's motivation for change, we also obtained an estimate of their occupational aspirations by asking them about the kind of job they would like their sons to have. In contrast to the unimodal percent distribution of prestige ranks for best and latest jobs for our clients, there is a bimodal distribution of prestige ranks for the jobs they would like their sons to have. Table 3-5 presents the magnitude of this bimodality. Recent research on aspiration level by McClelland, Atkinson and Feather, and others indicate that bimodality of this

TABLE 3-5   DRINKING PATTERNS AND PRESTIGE RANK OF ASPIRATION FOR SON'S OCCUPATION, BY PERCENTAGE

| DRINKING PATTERN | PRESTIGE RANK, SON'S OCCUPATION | | | | | | TOTAL | |
	1 High	2	3	4	5	6–7 Low	Percentage	N[a]
Spree drinker	10	41	10	22	14	3	100	122
Daily and off and on throughout week	14	21	12	30	20	3	100	103
Weekends only	27	33	3	17	17	3	100	36
Few or less than once per month	25	40	6	18	10	1	100	67
Nondrinker	20	28	16	21	8	7	100	61

[a] DK, NA, RA omitted.

sort may result from a fear of failure.[30] That is, these authors suggest that the fear of failure may lead people to aspire toward unreasonably high or unreasonably low goals in contrast to those with a reasonable hope of success, who tend to aspire toward those goals which present a reasonable or moderate challenge. It is of further interest that the bimodality seems to be slightly more extreme for the spree drinkers than for the nondrinkers, suggesting that the fear of failure may be more extreme for the spree drinkers than for the nondrinkers. This must, however, be taken as a very cautious suggestion, because we do not know about other factors (such as the actual jobs of their sons) which may be a reality factor in the statement of aspirations for some of the men. It would not be surprising, however, to find that those with a drinking problem had unrealistic aspirations and a strong fear of failure in the occupational area, factors which may be major determinants of their drinking problems. Our essentially retrospective data do not allow for confirmation of the hypothesis, although this fear of failure and its relationship to drinking may be major reasons for job losses by two-thirds of the spree drinkers because of drinking sometime in the past; only one-third of the daily and off and on during the week drinkers reported job losses due to drinking.

4   Are the Police and Courts Oppressors?

More than 30 years ago, Donald Clemmer wrote about the transformation that takes place when persons are convicted and sent to prison. As they move from the court to the prison and begin to experience the peculiar frustrations of prison life, they learn about prison organization as well as the attitudes and values of both the administration and other inmates. As they assimilate these experiences into their lives, they are also stigmatized as prisoners—a process that Clemmer calls "prisonization."[1] James Spradley goes further, and argues that law enforcement agencies in Seattle (and throughout the Northwest) actually create a class of petty criminals. He describes the process by which, for want of bail, men wind up in jail. This experience "not only strips away former identities, but also helps these men erect new ones on the site where they became alienated from themselves."[2] From

In the preparation of this chapter, we wish to express our appreciation to the following: the Police Department of the city of Philadelphia; the District Attorney's Office of the city of Philadelphia; Edward Hendricks, Superintendent of Prisons; Menachem Amir, Marjorie F. Blumberg; Drs. Donald Ottenberg, Jerome Kohn, Alvin Rosen, Jules Cohen; Chesterfield Cotton, William Hood, Betty Adams, Joseph O. Moor, Jr., Stephen Barsky, Leonard Moore, Judy Nelson, Martha Blumberg, Deanne McClain, Jonathan Miller, and the magistrates of the city of Philadelphia. Finally, we regret that limitations of space required us to eliminate the discussion of the legal status of Skid Row people that was written by Judah Labovitz.

60

this point of view, the jail experience is possibly even more important in the lives of Skid Row men than alcohol. Like most other people, Skid Row men do most of their drinking socially, but they sometimes do drink alone. However, a man simply cannot go to prison alone. Prisons represent the power of the larger community. Even solitary confinement is a social experience—admittedly a difficult one—that involves the forcible deprivation of human company. In this sense, the larger community may be considered a cause of Skid Row men.

About half of Philadelphia's Skid Row men who completed the 1960 long form (N = 377) said that they had been in prison at least once during their lives; about half of this number said that they had been in prison three or more times. About one-fifth of the short form respondents (N = 2249) said that they had been in prison during the past year. (Since information of this kind came from the men themselves, the figures must be regarded as conservative.)

One might argue that this prison experience provides for social relationships after leaving prison as Spradley seems to suggest.[3] However, cross-tabulations of answers about friendships within the Skid Row neighborhood show that almost half of those who said they did not have any friends in Skid Row had been convicted of Skid Row offenses, in comparison with about three-tenths who said that they did have friends within Skid Row. If we take these data conservatively, they suggest that a common prison experience is not important to forming friendships on Skid Row.

Furthermore, we believe that the process of transformation may not be as simple as Spradley suggests, since the elements which go into making Skid Row men are more complex. Thus, about one-fifth of the 1960 Long Form respondents reported that they had been convicted for offenses other than drunkenness, disorderly conduct, and vagrancy. In addition, during the course of our efforts to learn more about death on Skid Row (which is discussed elsewhere in this book), we found a number of files containing prison histories of Skid Row men. These were obtained by the Office of the Medical Examiner (OME) as a part of their efforts to identify the men, the circumstances of their death, and the next of kin who would agree to take the body. Because the material was collected after the men had died, it tells a cumulative story despite the fact that in some respects the records are incomplete. While a comprehensive statement of alternative criminal careers of Skid Row men needs further research, our OME data suggest the following types. (We do not of course contend that all types are equally common on Skid Row.)

The stereotypical Skid Row man is, for example, one who started with a period of drifting around western Pennsylvania or eastern Ohio, or from North Carolina to the District of Columbia, or possibly simply in his own home town. There were a series of early arrests for vagrancy. While there may be burglary, larceny, or even occasional robbery charges on his record, almost all recorded arrests were for such offenses as habitual drunkenness, public indecency, panhandling, vagrancy, and disorderly conduct.

The nonsupporter alcoholic may have some criminal elements in his history, but the critical issue seems to be his heavy drinking and his relationship to his wife. Typically, a local judge enforced the law and sent him to prison for nonsupport, and an apparent cat-and-mouse game was followed by long and intermittent years of prison life. During the process, he learned to be a Skid Row bum.

The hardened criminal may have started with a theft of coal from the railroad as a youth (among the poor, this was common in the past) and then become involved in a car theft across interstate lines. In adult life, he may have moved on to burglary, holdup, armed robbery, assault and battery accompanied by robbery, and robbery of a United States Post Office. This phase of his life, including time spent in prison, may have lasted 15 or 20 years and it may have been followed by a series of trips to the House of Correction for vagrancy and habitual drunkenness. Just as alcoholism may disrupt any person's normal life style, it may interfere with a criminal life style.

The loser may have started with breaking, entering, and larceny in the night, only to have his criminal career aborted. Prison was simply not a school for the perfection of criminal skills. In one case, the sexual trauma of prison was apparently so great that the man became that great exception of the gay world—the homosexual rapist. After serving his sentence on the rape charge, the man had become a Skid Row alcoholic, with a series of subsequent arrests, including charges for drunkenness and intoxication.

The transformed drug addict was a rarity in our present set of materials. One former addict pusher had evolved into an alcoholic who later died from drinking nonbeverage alcohol. The shift from drugs to alcohol is now becoming evident among clients at the center. We have heard of drug addicts who have switched to alcohol during the course of "successful" drug therapy.

Spradley emphasizes that prison not only strips away the identity of the man in a psychological sense but also tears him loose from his societal moorings.[4] This seems helpful in understanding the cases of professional criminals who later drifted toward Skid Row. Coming out of prison, they picked up drinking patterns that they may have had before they went in, or they intensified these drinking patterns, and elements of the Skid Row alcoholic life style began to consolidate.

The process of becoming a Skid Row man seems to us more complex than was suggested by Spradley. Nonetheless, the studies of police behavior by researchers in other cities reveal much the same situation Spradley found in Seattle. These include Bain in Chicago, Chevigny in New York, Wallace and Lovald in Minneapolis, and Wiseman in San Francisco.[5] The data we have summarized from the Philadelphia OME suggest similar situations in the District of Columbia and in Wilmington, Delaware, and observers report that Philadelphia police occasionally continued to "sweep the streets" as late as 1969. Certainly in this sense, then, the police-court complex can be considered an oppressor of Skid Row men.

For their justification, the police argue that, especially in the dead of winter, the arrests actually benefit the men arrested. A stay in the House of Correction certainly provides protection and helps build a man's health so that he can survive the rigors of life on Skid Row. Bain reported that, in 1950, Skid Row men voluntarily got into the ambulance-police wagon so that they could have at least one night out of the weather.[6] Foote reported self-commitments in Philadelphia in the 1951–54 period.[7] Important philosophical and political issues need discussion about a society in which a man must give up his elementary freedom in order to get food, shelter, minimal medical care, and physical safety.[8] In cases of voluntary commitment, the police and courts function to provide these needs.

Furthermore, not all policemen are oppressors. We are not concerned here with the point made by Bittner that the police are engaged in a "peace-keeping function"—to keep deviant behavior within some kind of limits.[9] His analysis suggests that the "objective interests" of the police as a class and those of Skid Row men as a class are in conflict. Nor are we concerned with Wiseman's argument that the police look at the matter one way and that Skid Row men look at it another—a matter of differential social perception.[10] Rather, Bain says that policemen on the Skid Row beat "do allow the 'O.K. guys' limited leeway of conduct."[11] Lovald observes that policemen tend to bear down on transients and to be protective and permissive with stable residents as long as they do not challenge the officer's authority.[12]

In a poor neighborhood in Philadelphia—outside Skid Row— some policemen are said to protect the neighborhood "bums" but will jail an outsider who has drifted in from the Skid Row area. On the Philadelphia Skid Row itself, one policeman is reported to have gone to the local station and arranged for the release of a man who had been picked up on a sweep, arguing that he was an old-timer in the area with a known way of making a subsistence living and not really a vagrant. This humanization of relationships between police and Skid Row men seems to develop between stable residents of the area and foot patrolmen.[13] The Philadelphia Skid Row policeman mentioned above is an exception in an area where most police activity is now based on squad cars and where relatively few officers are foot patrolmen. Thus, under some conditions, the police are protectors of Skid Row men rather than oppressors; in political rhetoric, they might be called benevolent despots.

On August 31, 1967, Judge Weinrott, of the Court of Common Pleas, signed a writ of habeas corpus in two cases filed by the Defender Association of Philadelphia, in cooperation with the Philadelphia District Attorney's office. In his decision, Judge Weinrott pointed out that the issue before the court, which had never before been decided in Pennsylvania, was whether habitual alcoholism was a crime or a disease, there being little doubt that the men in whose name the petition was filed were alcoholics within the usual meaning of the word. Judge Weinrott took the position that habitual intoxication was not a crime but would fall more nearly under the heading of a disease and that the condition was therefore not punishable according to law. The habeas corpus petitions having been granted, the men were excused from further serving their sentences in the House of Correction.

Shortly after Judge Weinrott's decision, in which the center had a part through an extensive psycho-social evaluation of the men being tried, we were asked to assess some of the possible consequences of the decision and to make recommendations.[14] With the full cooperation of the Philadelphia Police Department, we undertook a ten-day study of men arrested for drunkenness in the Sixth Police District (where the Skid Row area is located).

During the course of the study, all men who were arrested for drunkenness at a certain time of the day were seen by a physician and a social worker. All cases were referred either to a hospital as a medical emergency or to an overnight sleeping facility, left to sleep it off in the station house, or discharged immediately after a medical examination.

A total of 197 men became a part of the sample during the course of the ten-day study. A number of questionnaires and interview procedures were undertaken, including a medical examination. The size of the sample varies because neither all questionnaires nor all procedures were administered to all men. In general, the sample was an older group of men, as one might expect, with a median age of 51 years. About two-thirds of the sample were white; most of the remainder were black. (A small proportion were "other," or race was not recorded.) This proportion of whites is lower than for Philadelphia's Skid Row as a whole; it must be remembered that the Sixth District also includes slum residents, many of whom are black. We doubt whether these data indicate a greater propensity for the police to pick up black men.

It is of some interest that only about one-third of the total sample said that they lived in Skid Row (even if homeless men who said they had no address are included, the proportion is raised only to about one-half). However, when we asked social work counselors to rate men on their appearances, about two-thirds of

TABLE 4-1　　　RESIDENCY, APPEARANCE, AND RACE BY PERCENTAGE

| | RESIDENCY | | | | | |
| | HOMELESS | | LIVES ON SKID ROW | | LIVES OFF SKID ROW | |
	W	B	W	B	W	B
Appearance						
Looks like SR man	95	80	91	90	63	27
Doesn't look like						
SR man	5	20	9	10	37	73
Total N	21	6	46	10	38	33
Total percentage	100	100	100	100	100	100

Six DK's omitted.

the men appeared to be from Skid Row. If someone was homeless or living on Skid Row, there was a relatively high probability that he would be perceived by others as looking like a Skid Row man, regardless of his color status (Table 4-1). Alternatively, this is not the case for those who reported a non-Skid Row address. Since about two-thirds of the whites, in comparison with about one-third of the blacks, were homeless or lived in Skid Row, it is evident that the whites were more unfortunate and more homogeneous, in this respect, than the blacks.

The black men were not only different from the white men with respect to Skid Row residence and appearance, but they differed from the whites in their drinking patterns and related indices of problem drinking. Table 4-2 shows that a little more

TABLE 4-2   COMPARISON OF WHITE AND BLACK SAMPLE ON INDICES OF PROBLEM DRINKING BY PERCENTAGE

INDEX OF PROBLEM DRINKING	SAMPLE			
	WHITE		BLACK	
	Percentage	N	Percentage	N
**Spree drinking	72	112	45	55
*Drink to cure hangover	76	112	54	55
Tried to give up drinking	50	112	51	55
DT's	33	112	36	55
**Admission of alcoholism	60	118	33	57
**Diagnosis of chronic alcoholism, "almost certain or certain"	60	115	32	57

* P < .05.   ** P < .001.

than one-half of both whites and blacks reported daily drinking, and almost three-fourths of the whites were spree drinkers in comparison with less than one-half of the blacks. This difference is significant (chi square = 11.70, 1 df, P < .001).[15] Table 4-2 shows also that a majority of the sample were addicted alcoholics, as indicated by their drinking alcohol to cure hangovers, but generally there were greater proportions of whites than blacks who were alcoholics.

Further, most of the men in this study population probably did not have stable heterosexual relationships (one one-fifth were currently married). Indeed, we are tempted to describe them as socially isolated in view of the fact that about three-fourths of them said they lived alone. Of course, "isolated" is too extreme a word since most of them undoubtedly had other social relationships, especially those which centered on drinking. But at the moment we have no better word to describe the absence of important relationships which can be extremely helpful during recurring personal crises. We are reminded of the finding of Myerson and Mayer at the Long Island Hospital that none of their alcoholic clients who lived alone made a recovery after leaving treatment.[16] The marital relationship as such may not be as important as the ability to turn to someone day in and day out. Thus, in the course of our research we undertook the follow-up of selected men who came into the DRC/P program. Among the relatively successful follow up workers, those who were also "recovered alcoholics" seemed to have had successfully developed other post-therapy interests and social relationships, such as remarriage or activity in Alcoholics Anonymous.[17] When a job was apparently a substitute for drinking, there was a strong tendency to relapse into spree drinking behavior.

The same Skid Row men are of course often picked up more than once. Given a situation in which they cannot be jailed for drunkenness, we might expect recidivism to happen relatively often. It is hard to say how much recidivism would have taken place in a year, but our data may give some clues. In the discussion which follows, we report only important differences between the recidivists (R) and the nonrecidivists (NR).

In our ten days at the Sixth District Police Station, 23 men were rearrested at least once; for our present purposes, we call them recidivists. A significant proportion of the R group (91 percent) reported living alone, in comparison with the NR group (71 percent). Although there is no difference is residence on or off Skid Row, the R group were rated more often as appearing Skid Row-like (83 percent) than the NR group (62 percent). This finding gives further support to our discussion of the relationship between living alone and alcohol problems among such men.

Furthermore, the R men were different from the NR men with respect to some aspects of their drinking pattern. The R group tended to drink more often, to drink wine as opposed to beer (especially just before their arrest), and, finally, to have done their drinking more often in the streets in the hours before their arrest. In other words, the R group had more severe problems with alcohol, at least during this ten-day period (Table 4-3). Even

TABLE 4-3   RECIDIVISM AND INDICES OF PROBLEM
                  DRINKING BY PERCENTAGE

QUESTION	PERCENTAGE REPORTING SYMPTOM	
	R Group	NR Group
Benders	73	56
Drink to cure hangovers	95	65
Loss of control	68	56
Worried about drinking	70	53
Ever tried to give up drinking	73	53
*Blackouts	38	18
DT's	45	32
N	22	148

* Chi square = 4.28, 1 df, p < .05.

though the differences between the R and the NR men are statistically significant only for those who reported they had had blackouts in the past, there are systematic differences between the two groups. Although the proportions reporting ever having dt's did not differ significantly between the two groups, it is worth noting that of all those reporting dt's within the past year (N = 24), almost one-third were rearrested within ten days, in contrast to about one-eighth of those who had had dt's at some earlier time. There are also systematic differences between the R and the NR groups in terms of hospitalization for alcoholism in the past. Slightly less than one-half of the R group had been hospitalized for drunkenness or its effects, in contrast to one one-third of the NR group.

The R group and the NR group also differed clinically. For example, all the physicians who participated in the study were asked to make a diagnosis with respect to alcoholism in terms of: not present, suspected, probable, and almost certain. A significantly larger proportion of the R men (83 percent) were judged as probable or almost certain alcoholics, in contrast to the NR group (60 percent), chi square = 4.34, 1 df, P < .05. The medical examination included a number of other ratings such as "ability to answer questions" and "impairment of memory," which were designed to assess, at least to a small degree, some possible lasting effects of alcohol drinking. Neither group showed great damage in this respect, and there were no systematic differences between them. Nor were there important differences between the groups on such medical indices as: presence of chronic disease; number taking medication; neurological abnormalities; abnormalities of skin; abnormalities of eyes and ears; abnormalities of abdomen, including enlarged livers; abnormalities of the extremities; the physician's judgment that a man urgently needed to be hospitalized because of his drunken condition. The final disposition or referral between the two groups did not differ significantly: 36 percent of the R group were referred to a hospital, in comparison with 30 percent of the NR group; 9 percent of the R group were discharged after their medical examination, in comparison with 20 percent of the NR group.

During the course of the ten-day study, we asked the men how many times they had been arrested in the past year. Rearrest during the ten-day period represents a hard fact; but the study was relatively short, and we could not expect such an index to be very reliable. On the other hand, reports of rearrest from the men themselves are subject to all the problems of reliability of such reports. We have compared the questionnaire responses of the R group with those of the NR group, and have also compared the questionnaire responses of those reporting more than five arrests this year with those reporting fewer than five arrests (Table 4-4). In general, these comparisons are similar.

Although recidivism within the ten-day study does not correlate significantly with the number of arrests reported this year, the relationship is nevertheless positive. Thus about three-tenths of the R group reported less than five arrests this year, in comparison with one-eighth of the NR group. With respect to other questions, a comparison of the contrasting criterion groups (R versus NR; five arrests or more versus under five arrests) is similar. The direction of the difference between R and NR and between those reporting five or more arrests and those reporting less than five is almost always the same for the general characteristics, the drinking behavior, the symptoms, and the diagnostic questions. For almost all questions, the R group and the group with 5 or more arrests indicated greater preoccupation with alcohol and high incidence of symptoms resulting from heavy drinking. Indeed, the significances of the difference between the high- and low-arrest-report groups are more frequent than the significances between the R groups. We see that the difference is significant for reported spree drinking and reported drinking of nonbeverage alcohol, for example, as well as for daily drinking and for drinking wine before the present arrest.

TABLE 4-4   A Comparison of the Predictive Indices for Two Different Criteria: Recidivism vs. Nonrecidivism and Self-Reports of High vs. Low Arrest for Prior Year

Predictive Questionnaire Item	Significance of Predicted Direction			
	SAME DIRECTION		OPPOSITE DIRECTION	
	Not Sig.	Sig. Recidivism	Sig. Arrest	Not Sig.
1. Life style				
a. Not employed during prior week			<.05	
b. Lives alone	X			
c. Looks like a Skid Row man			<.05	
2. Drinking pattern				
a. Bender in past year			<.05	
b. Drinks daily		<.05	<.05	
c. Amount of wine drunk (larger amount)			<.05	
d. Drank wine before arrest		<.05	<.05	
e. No beer during prior week		<.05		
f. Nonbeverage alcohol drunk during year			<.05	
g. Drank on street before pickup			<.05	
3. Symptoms of drinking				
a. Drinks to cure hangover			<.05	
b. Reports loss of control			<.05	
c. Worried about drinking			<.05	
d. Has tried to give up drinking	X			
e. Reports blackouts		<.05	<.05	
f. Reports DT's	X			
g. Reports hospitalization for drunkeness				X
h. Admits alcoholism	X			
4. Clinical observations				
a. Alcoholism diagnosis		<.05		
b. Breathalyzer test (high)	X			
c. Liver enlarged	X			
d. Recommendation of hospitalization for alcoholism (urgent)	X			
5. Clinical action taken				
a. Referred to hospital	X			
b. Referred for discharge	X			

We conclude from these data that the results derived from two different sources (established recidivism and reported recidivism) are closely comparable, and lead to the same conclusion: that the arrest rate is consistently related to drinking pattern and the symptoms of heavy drinking for this group of center-city problem drinkers.

In terms of the Weinrott decision, then, nearly three-fourths of the white men and nearly one-half of the black men who were picked up for drunkenness on the street were probably alcoholics. Since about three-fourths of the R group and about one-half of the NR group were alcoholics, the Weinrott decision could have a major effect on law enforcement practices. Put another way—and at the risk of overgeneralizing from these data—it seems likely that the policemen's perception of Skid Row men (like the general public's) is strongly colored by their experiences with the men who "hurt the most." These experiences provide the basis for their stereotyping of all persons who live on Skid Row as "no-good drunken bums." Again, since the police most frequently come into contact with those who hurt the most, they are, willy-nilly, a case-finding agency—if the police no longer engage in case-finding as a result of the Weinrott decision, then we believe that the responsibility must be undertaken by some other agency. We discuss this further in Chapter 13.

Did the Weinrott decision significantly influence law enforcement practices? After some delay, a set of "guidelines for release of intoxicated persons" was issued from the district attorney's office in May 1968. It had three major provisions: an intoxicated person may be released in the custody of a responsible adult; after the intoxicated person has been taken to the police station and has sobered up, he may be released; when the intoxicated person appears to be suffering from the disease of alcoholism, the police officers may turn the intoxicated person over to a hospital unit or medical facility for treatment. Throughout our study period, it was understood that a man might be held for other offenses that he had committed while intoxicated.

There seem to have been two responses to this new legal situation. On the one hand, the police were helpful to the center in getting alcoholics to the hospital on an emergency basis. On the other hand, arrests for vagrancy more than doubled for the city as a whole, from 462 in 1967 to 1004 in 1968 (figures from the Philadelphia Police Department). In the Sixth District, they almost quadrupled, to 520 (over half the city's total). Almost all the arrests were in the heart of the Skid Row area. Most of this increase in vagrancy arrests was accounted for in only the last four months of 1968, after the new procedures had been put into effect.

It is hard to tell if this situation is the result of de facto policies laid down by police officials. We have heard that the sweeps of Skid Row have continued because the area is located at one of the entrances to the city and is near Independence Hall, causing civic leaders concern about the city's image. The police are caught between the law and the expectations of the larger community that they control the flagrant behavior of these deviant people whose very public presence is insulting to the sensitivities of others.

This citizen pressure is real and potent, as illustrated by events in New York. The state had a vagrancy law which provided for six months' imprisonment of persons who were "without means to maintain themselves or who live without employment"—essentially one of the provisions of the Pennsylvania law also. In July 1967 the New York Supreme Court ruled that this 170-year-old law was unconstitutional because it constituted an overreaching of police power when a person does nothing to impinge on the rights or interests of others. For a period of several months, the New York City police made arrests on such charges as disorderly conduct and violating park regulations. Then, on September 1, 1967, public drunkenness was made an offense in New York City. As a consequence, arrests for public drunkenness increased from an average of 408 per month for the first quarter of 1968 to an average of 1,053 per month for the third quarter of 1968. Police attributed the new law and its heavy enforcement to pressure from residents and merchants to do something about the winos. It is ironic that the course of judicial review led to opposite consequences: the emphasis on vagrancy arrests in Philadelphia; the emphasis on drunkenness arrests in New York City.[18]

Skid Row men tell us also that some officers engage in shakedowns just after the men receive their Social Security and Public Assistance checks. Officers have been reported to stop men on the pretext of demanding identification and to steal from their wallets during the process. Other men have had their money taken while being put into the police wagon. Still others are reported to have been forced to turn over their money to officers at the station house and to have been given no receipts. Skid Row men are afraid to talk about such incidents because they say that they have been threatened with reprisals. Our material was forthcoming only when the men received special assurances of anonymity. We have had—and continue to have—relatively close working relationships with the Philadelphia Police Department, and we have taken complaints concerning police behavior to top level administrators when it was appropriate. We have found them cooperative on specific grievances and actively concerned about eliminating flagrant abuses that have been called to their attention. This has been in addition to a charge from a *Philadelphia Inquirer* reporter, who was sent out to explore the situation, that officers had stolen $13 from him.[19] We do not believe this is typical of all Philadelphia's policemen but of a few who hide behind the honest majority.

These abuses seem hard to suppress. Few people are likely to believe a Skid Row man, especially when he himself may actually be confused about events. This petty thievery and minor tyranny are consequences of placing officers in situations of great temptation combined with a practically fool-proof opportunity. Here, indeed, those few police who do engage in these practices are oppressors of Skid Row men.

In a larger sense, these practices are simply another evidence of the relative powerlessness of Skid Row residents in their relationship to the larger community. This powerlessness is further evidenced in the way Skid Row men continue to be treated in the lower courts of Philadelphia. Spradley points out that in Seattle there is a sentencing policy which increases in severity each time a man comes before the judge and is tempered with the expectation that if a man can stay out of jail for six months he can begin the cycle again with a five-day suspended sentence.[20] Contrary to the practices that prevail in Seattle, there seems to be no systematic element in the way Skid Row men are treated in Philadelphia. We sent an observer into the Sixth District Municipal Court in the early summer of 1969. The procedures differed only slightly from those reported by Foote in the early 1950s.[21] He observed six different judges on the bench, and talked with most of them. These judges said that they believed that it was their responsibility to be protectors to the vagrants who were brought before them. They said that their function was to give counseling, to secure medical aid, and to provide protection, depending on the individual case. However, there was only one place to which they sent these vagrants—the House of Correction. While men are no longer sentenced as habitual drunkards since the Weinrott decision, those brought before the judges as vagrants were sentenced accordingly. Some judges asked the men if they wanted to go to the House of Correction; others did not. Sentencing procedures seemed to vary for individual judges, depending on how much time was taken by other cases heard earlier in the day. If they were rushed, some judges merely dismissed the men with an injunction to "go home"; others, just as casually, sentenced men to 30 days in the House of Correction. Our observer discussed some of the cases with the police officers and observed procedures from booking to sentencing. He found that men were booked for vagrancy rather than intoxication if they were dirty, appeared to be lousy, had no shoes or wallet. He saw one man booked as a vagrant who had used an identification card which police said belonged to another man. The next morning the intoxication cases were released, but the vagrant cases were taken before the judge. The observer concluded that if a man's physical appearance was still reasonably presentable after being in the lockup cell overnight he would probably be released. However, if he was dirty, he would probably be sent to the House of Correction. Much depended on how the others in his particular "bunch" appeared that day. If he was the worst-looking man that day he would most likely be sent to the House of Correction, even though his bunch was more respectable than yesterday's. Finally, our observer saw some instances in which the judge abdicated his function almost completely and asked the police officers attending the court what sentences they wanted for the men in custody. He even observed a case of an apparently senile man whom the judge dismissed but the police insisted had been sentenced and who was taken off to the House of Correction. Throughout the proceedings there was no public defender service offered to the men, although the service was available some days and offered to others not charged with vagrancy. Even though some of the judges addressed Skid Row men as "gentlemen," the police-court complex tended to denigrate them and to deprive them of whatever sense of dignity they may have had before they came into contact with it. While the Weinrott decision made it possible to begin changes, the system itself had not been effectively mobilized in a new direction.

The Tate decision of the United States Supreme Court in March 1971 held it unconstitutional to imprison a person who fails to pay a fine if he is indigent. On the basis of that decision, the president judge of the municipal court in March 1971 offered 54 vagrants release from the House of Correction; 34 accepted, while 20 elected to stay out the balance of their sentences. The full implication of this new situation for police and court practice remains to be seen. Will there simply be a continuation of the old practices under a new label? Can the judges change the pattern of which they themselves are a part?

5   Exploitation in the Skid Row Slum

In Skid Row, alcohol and poverty intersect with slum housing. The meaning and implications of "slum" have apparently changed over the past three-quarters of a century. Abrams cites an 1897 Funk and Wagnalls Dictionary in which the term referred to back alleys which were characterized by persons with considerable social and personal disorder.[1] The solution to slums from this point of view, according to Abrams, was to "ban whiskey, teach virtue, and punish sinners," since the area was a slum in terms of the characteristics and behavior of its residents.

In contrast to this usage, the 1937 Housing Act defined a slum as "any area where dwellings predominate which by reason of dilapidation, overcrowding, faulty arrangement or design, ventilation, light or sanitation facilities or any combination of those features are detrimental to safety, health, or morals." A slum, in this approach, referred to the physical situation rather than to the residents. Implicit was the assumption that the deteriorated physical environment, particularly buildings, was accompanied by personal and social maladjustment. Is it too extreme to say that the assumption was that

In the preparation of this chapter, we wish to express our appreciation to: the Department of Licenses and Inspections of the city of Philadelphia; William Hood, and Stephen Barsky, Donald Wallace, Leonard Moore, and the Reverend Thomas Fedewa, SSA.

the deteriorated environment, particularly buildings, caused the objectionable human behavior? In any case, Gans, in his careful analysis of the way of life of the Italian residents of the Boston West End, pointed out that they led an emotionally positive and a socially organized community life despite the fact that the area was certified under the law for redevelopment.[2] Later reports indicate that relocation from the West End was correlated to a decrease in mental health and to an increase in hospitalization. Apparently the quality of the housing in the area was not as bad as the formal measures seemed to indicate. All in all, we might say that, from a humanistic point of view, the clearance of the Boston West End was a social mistake. However, from the point of view of the doctrine of higher and better land use, it may have been justified since upper-income high-rise residential units have probably contributed considerably more to the tax base than did the old tenements and apartments. The conclusion must be emphasized that relocation should be accompanied by attention to community values and mental health.

We do not believe that there are mitigating arguments in the case of the Skid Row neighborhood. Even if we accept the view that this area is a community for some of the men, we believe that the quality of housing is so poor and the organization of the housing market so exploitative, that it justifies description as a residential slum.

CUBICLE HOTELS

Most Philadelphia Skid Row men live in cubicle hotels or missions—types of housing unique to the area. Table 5-1 reports the kind of housing used by Skid Row men in 1960; also included are gospel missions that were elsewhere in Philadelphia. (The limits imposed on these data by our research procedures and our research problems are discussed in Appendix A.) It shows that about two-fifths of the men were living in cubicle hotels and that about one-quarter were in mission dormitories at that time. Rooming houses ran a poor third. There tended to be systematic age differences in the kind of housing used by Skid Row men. The younger tended to be in the gospel missions and cubicle hotels, while the older were more likely to live in rooming houses. This tends to be more true for whites than for nonwhites (almost all of whom were black). Table 5-2 shows that almost half of the nonwhites were

TABLE 5-1   HOUSING ACCOMMODATIONS OF PHILADEL-
PHIA SKID ROW POPULATION, 1960, BY
PERCENTAGE

Housing Accommodations		Percentage
Gospel mission dormitory		26.4
Cubicle hotel		41.8
Room in hotel		4.2
Rooming house		
Room alone	14.1	
Room shared	1.0	
		15.1
Apartment		
Alone	1.6	
Shared	0.7	
		2.3
Institutions		
Hospitals	1.7	
House of Correction	2.0	
Police Lockup[1]	1.6	
		5.3
Had no bed		
Walked streets	2.1	
Slept outside	0.4	
Slept in building	2.3	
		4.8
DK, RA, NA		0.1
Total percentage		100.0
N		2249

[1] 6th District Station, 11th and Winter Streets.

TABLE 5-2   TYPE OF HOUSING ACCOMMODATIONS OF
WHITE AND BLACK RESPONDENTS

Housing Accommodations	White	Black	DK, RA, NA	Percentage	N
Mission	81.6	17.5	0.9	100.0	594
Cubicle hotel	97.6	0.3	2.1	100.0	941
Hotel with rooms	92.6	4.2	3.2	100.0	95
Rooming house					
Room alone	68.3	29.8	1.8	100.0	319
Room shared	31.8	63.6	4.6	100.0	22
Apartment					
Alone	37.8	62.1	0.1	100.0	37
Shared	23.5	76.5	0.0	100.0	17
Institutions	74.8	24.3	0.9	100.0	111
No Bed	55.4	42.3	2.3	100.0	110
DK, RA, NA	—	—	—	—	3
Total					2249

living in gospel missions and that most of the balance were living in rooming houses or apartments in 1960, in contrast to over one-half of the whites living in cubicle hotels. Thus Skid Row is not only a residential slum but a racially segregated slum as well. This conclusion came as something of a surprise to us when we first began our work on Skid Row; in retrospect, it seems only another example of the pervasiveness of racial segregation in American society.

Cubicles are made by erecting thin partitions in a large room or loft. In Philadelphia, abandoned bathhouses, one-story warehouses, spaces over stores or bars, and three-story former residences have all been converted into cubicle hotels. In one three-story building, the height from floor to ceiling on the first floor was 12 feet; on the other two stories, it was about 9½ feet. The cubicle walls on all floors were about 6½ feet high; the cubicles were about 6½ feet long and about 4 feet wide (about 26 square feet of floor space). A chicken wire "ceiling" is usually nailed across the top of the partitions. This insures ventilation and presumably reduces thievery. Because the cubicles are so small, a hundred or more can be fitted into a relatively small building. There are of course variations in the dimensions of cubicles; the Department of Licenses and Inspections reported on six different Skid Row hotels and found that their cubicles varied from 26 to 36 square feet.[3] This is in violation of the city housing code, which requires a minimum of 50 square feet for each person where two or more sleep in the same room. Clearly the Skid Row hotels provide low-quality housing.

Cubicle hotel prices vary, and have increased over the years. In 1960, the average cost per night was 60 cents; by 1969, the average was up to 75 cents; in 1971, the usual in the few cubicle hotels still standing was about one dollar. (Rates by the week were slightly lower.) A man who lives in a cubicle hotel can expect to pay between $5.25 and $8.75 a week (depending on whether he pays by the night or by the week) or between $22 and $30 a month. For a man who receives a Public Assistance check of $69 twice a month (who will then pay by the month), this means that his shelter cost is a little more than one-fifth of his income. This is of course more favorable than most low-income people pay, but the quality of this man's housing is also lower. Furthermore, it must be kept in mind that many of these men do not receive Public Assistance or retirement benefits and have no stable income. For them, shelter is a nightly problem.

Associated with this poverty is high residential mobility. There are still some men who drift from city to city, and some who move in and out of the city on seasonal jobs at summer resorts and camps. But it is now more common for most men to remain in or near the area all year around and to shift from one kind of housing to another, such as from one cubicle hotel to another, or from a cubicle hotel to a mission, or from mission to walking the streets and then to another mission. Thus, in 1960 we found that about one-third of the men had last moved to the address where they were interviewed less than a month before, and that another third had last moved to that address less than a year earlier. This is an exaggerated example of the classic residential instability of the unattached male. This residential instability is age-related; it is more common for men who are under 45 years of age than for older men, and least common for men who are 65 years of age and over. It is also related to length of residence on Skid Row—that is, in general, the more recently a man has moved into the Skid Row neighborhood, the more residentially unstable he is. This residential mobility has been exacerbated by the arrest and jailing practices of the police and courts.

There is of course a minimal privacy allowed by the cubicle organization of sleeping space, and the privacy referred to in Table 5-3 must be seen in the context of the mission dormitories, where it is nonexistent. The privacy in a cubicle hotel is at least

TABLE 5-3   WHAT DO YOU LIKE ABOUT YOUR PRESENT
LODGING PLACE?[a]

	Cubicle Hotel	%[b]	Mission	%	Rooming Hse.	%
Nothing	25	17	21	18	4	8
Cheap	34	23	22	19	16	33
Friendly	22	15	22	19	10	20
Convenient to work	7	5	8	7	6	12
Likes management	18	12	21	18	6	12
Clean and neat	49	33	32	28	11	22
Quiet, privacy	22	15	8	7	7	14
Other	17	11	32	28	5	10
N[c]	148		116		49	

[a] Data from 1960 Long Form. Total respondents = 377.
[b] Total response is more than 100 percent because two responses were recorded. Percentage is of respondents who gave this reply.
[c] DK, RA, NA respondents omitted.

partly a kind of social fiction because even a cough can be heard by everyone on the same floor. Tuberculosis is common on Skid Row, and the cubicle plan (as well as the mission dormitory) is an almost ideal condition for its dissemination. A professional staff member who spent the night before interviewing began in 1960 in a cubicle hotel reported the following. The toilet-washroom was at one end of the building. It was both odorous and filthy, was inadequate for the number of persons who might be expected to use it, and provided little privacy. Furthermore, while the sheets were clean, the floor of the cubicle was littered with cigarette butts left by the previous night's occupant. The most pervasive smell during the night was that of the vomit of the man in the next cubicle.

Conditions do vary from one cubicle hotel to another. In 1960, about one-third of the men who lived in cubicle hotels said that they liked the cleanliness and neatness; about one-third complained that their hotels were rundown, or smelly. Less than one-fifth of the respondents said that they liked nothing about their cubicle hotels; about one-third said that there was nothing they disliked.

When an outsider sees a drunken Skid Row man wandering down a street, lounging against a building, sitting in a park, or lying on the sidewalk, the outsider may receive a stereotyped— and entirely mistaken—idea of the personal values of the average Skid Row man. The area is dirty and unkempt, and some of the men are themselves physically filthy, particularly during and immediately after a prolonged drinking spree, but it is noteworthy that cleanliness is an important value for these men. In addition to cleanliness, the men value privacy and the maintenance of an inoffensive environment. In other words, the men want the same basic qualities in housing that richer and more powerful people want for themselves. Cubicle hotels are not completely objectionable to the residents, but the men are most interested in such matters as cleanliness, economy, and the elimination of the noise that often goes along with heavy drinking and drunkenness as well as that caused by heavy traffic on the street.

Differences in perception do not wholly account for the data in Tables 5-3 and 5-4. In our hotel interviews, there was no place where we could go to insure privacy for the respondent; the best we could do was to get off to one side. Under these circumstances we could hardly expect to get much hostile information about the management, and we must regard our data as minimal in this

TABLE 5-4   WHAT DON'T YOU LIKE ABOUT YOUR PRES-
ENT LODGING PLACE?[a]

	Cubicle Hotel	%[b]	Mission	%	Rooming Hse.	%
Everything OK	47	33	41	34	17	33
Too expensive	0	0	2	2	2	4
Other residents	16	13	19	16	4	8
Drinking, noise	36	26	12	10	10	20
Management	3	2	13	11	1	2
Dirty, run-down	31	22	17	14	14	27
Smell	2	14	0	0	1	2
Theft	0	0	3	3	1	2
Other	37	26	42	35	16	31
N[c]	141		119		51	

[a] Data from 1960 Long Form. Total respondents = 377.
[b] Total response is more than 100 percent because two responses were recorded. Percentage is of respondents who gave this reply.
[c] DK, RA, NA respondents omitted.

regard. Furthermore, we believe that the direct criticisms of management were especially muted. The case of Charlie Orange (a pseudonym) is an example.

At the time of our first interview with Mr. Orange, he was 61 years old and was receiving a Public Assistance check of $42.10 every two weeks (the maximum allowable at that time). Although he had been living in the Skid Row neighborhood for 11 years, he said that he was a temporary resident and that when he finally went on Social Security retirement he was going to move out. He was a spree drinker but had never pulled a blank. At the time of his interview, he reported the following two-week budget: $8.40 for rent in a cubicle hotel, $15 for food (including two meal tickets at the Skid Row restaurant owned by the same man who owned the hotel), $6 for alcohol, $2 for transportation, $8 for clothes, 60 cents for tobacco, and 48 cents for laundry. While this was the expenditure for "official" purposes, at a later (and obviously confidential) interview he told us that when his Public Assistance check arrived the desk clerk took it and held it until the next time when Mr. Orange would show up. The clerk would then pass the check over the counter face down and tell Charlie to sign it. Then the clerk would take out the rent for the next two-week period, sell him two meal tickets, take out loans, and hand him the remainder—usually about $20. Mr. Orange said that several times he had taken the check out of the hotel with him, but that he had been accosted nearby, relieved of the check, and given a beating by a couple of toughs. Several other times he was threatened with a beating by the clerk if he insisted on taking the check. The upshot of the whole situation was that now he does what the clerk tells him to do.

This sort of thing seems to be common in the cubicle hotels. Even though the Police Department and the Post Office Department want to assist, it is difficult to prevent the exploitation of men like Mr. Orange because of the way Skid Row housing is now organized.

ROOMING HOUSES AND BAR-HOTELS

Over the past decade, a number of cubicle hotels and rooming houses have closed. For this reason, the distribution of men in various kinds of housing is different from that given in Table 5-1. Since no new cubicle hotels will be permitted after the existing Skid Row area is cleared, we can expect rooming houses to be more important in the future.

There are still a few rooming houses in the present Skid Row area. Some are located on the edges of the downtown business section not far from the Row, while others are in declining secondary commercial areas in other sections of the city. Some rooming houses accommodate 15 to 20 persons (usually men), but some house 50 to 60 in two or three adjacent three-story row houses. In most rooming houses, the men usually eat at cheap restaurants nearby. Rooming houses are not licensed to serve alcohol, but it is common for managers to have wine available by the bottle and sometimes by the glass.

In practice, it is not easy to distinguish a rooming house from a bar-hotel. There are a number of variations in the size and location of bar-hotels as well as in the ways they operate. Some are large corner row houses in which the first floor is a bar while the upper floors are essentially a rooming house. Other buildings appear to have gone downhill over a period of years as the commercial traveler clientele has moved to better-equipped and more fashionable hotels further to the west.

Some of the bar-hotels have Sunday liquor licenses. These usually encourage a different kind of customer on weekends and during the balance of the week. Thus, one large cheap hotel encourages its residents to use the bar during the week; on weekends, it becomes a gay bar, wine is no longer sold by the glass, and the regular residents are discouraged from coming into the barroom.

Prices for rooms seem to vary from about $5 to $15 a week in rooming houses and up to about $20 a week in the largest bar-hotels. With few exceptions, the rooming houses and the bar-hotels are racially segregated.

The residential quality of the rooms varies a good deal. Rooms on the third floor tend to be dirty and dingy, and are just large enough to satisfy the code requirement of 70 square feet for single occupants; sometimes—but not always—rooms on the first and second floors are larger and more pleasant. While the law requires that bed linens and towels be changed at least once a week and that temperatures be maintained at a minimum of 68 degrees from October 1 to April 30, these requirements are not always met. For instance, one rooming house is reported to be filthy; the bed linens are rarely changed; no towels are provided; heat is turned down to 40 degrees at night, and one thin blanket is provided; toilets are often without paper; rats and roaches have not been exterminated; and empty liquor bottles often remain on the stairs and in the halls.

The following is a report from one of our participant-observer reports on a cheap hotel outside the Skid Row neighborhood, and reveals another aspect of housing quality:

After I checked in to the hotel on Friday, I sprayed the door frames, sills, and baseboards with a pyrethrum aerosol spray. I also sprayed around my bed and the bed frame. One other time on Friday evening I sprayed. Several hours after each of these sprayings, when I returned to my room I found one or two roaches on their backs kicking out their last. By the time I went to bed Friday night I counted about fifteen roaches on the floor; since I didn't make an initial count I'm not sure how big a kill I made on Friday. I also sprayed once on Saturday. By Saturday night there were about twenty dead roaches around the room. Early Sunday morning, secure in the potency of my pyrethrum I woke up and started to read. I looked up. I had missed a bed bug that was now parading across the sheet. Disgusted, I dressed and left!

EXPLOITATION

We have noted the opportunities for the exploitation of the men who live in cubicle hotels. A similar condition exists in the rooming houses and bar-hotels. Many rooming house and bar-hotel operators seem to prefer "check men." These are men who receive Public Assistance or retirement benefit checks; they tend to be older and often suffer from some kind of disability; they are not highly mobile. The most benevolent case of exploitation that we know about concerns a rooming house operator who is highly regarded by the men. As a service to his roomers, this operator sells the "biggest 35 cent wine in town" and sells a fifth of wine at only a $1.30 (but only to his roomers). Nor does he jack up the prices on Sundays. He also sells cigarettes and sandwiches. These are clearly valued services in a neighborhood where men have been mugged on the street at night. On the other hand, this same operator is reputed to get a 20 percent cut on the retail prices of drugs sold to the men in his house, having recently changed from one pharmacist to another because he could get a bigger cut. Furthermore, he is a Democratic party committeeman; of his 69 tenants, 65 were registered Democrats. At the last election, it is reported that he offered $3 and a quart of beer for each vote.

The most extreme case of exploitation that we know about involves a man who owns a bar as well as a dirty, dingy rooming house with over 20 rooms. Roomers' checks are sent to the bar, where all business is transacted, rather than to the men's rooms. The owner-operator deducts the following from each tenant's check: two weeks' rent in advance, meal tickets for two weeks at a Skid Row restaurant, the price of six glasses of wine a day at his bar, and $2 to cover the cost of a pint of bootleg wine from Joe the bootlegger on Sunday. Since Joe sells a fifty-cent bottle for a dollar, the tenant pays back this loan to his landlord at 100 percent interest within two weeks. At least one other landlord gives tenants loans at the rate of $1.25 for each dollar loaned, payable when the next check comes in. He too keeps a firm control over his tenants' checks. If a man drinks too hard for a period of time and is temporarily unacceptable for the rooming house, the landlord will put him into a cubicle hotel for a couple of weeks until he settles down again.

Not only are the landlords economically exploitative, but they tend to be politically exploitative as well. For many years the ward boundaries of the city of Philadelphia remained the same. Votes were tightly controlled by the ward leaders and committeemen, as shown by the fact that in the last successful Republican election the Skid Row wards were strongly Republican, while after the Democratic reform ticket came to power in the 1950s the committeemen switched parties and turned in large majorities for the Democrats.[4]

An examination of voter registration lists suggests that things are not much different today. In some hotels and rooming houses, more than a little political pressure is put on the men. Thus, in a series of rooming houses owned by one landlord whose family is active in politics, 26 of the 28 men registered are Democrats. In a bar-hotel just off the Row, there are 13 Democrats out of 14 men registered; in still another rooming house, there are 31 Democrats out of 33 registered. In one mission, almost all of the 37 registered men appear on the official lists as Democrats. Republicans as well as Democrats are involved. Thus, one landlord, himself a registered Republican, has seven out of eight men living above his restaurant registered as Republicans. A Republican landlady, just a few blocks away from the Skid Row area, has six Republican tenants in her house.

We believe that pressure operates in many of these cases because there are several missions in which no one is registered; we know of a rooming house in which there are no registered voters except the Republican landlady; and there are cubicle hotels in which there is nearly even distribution between the two major parties. Further, we believe that there is pressure because some men report that it is common for a political leader to ask a voter, "You can't read, can you?" The men feel that they must say, "No." This reply legally permits the political leader to assist the voter in casting his ballot, and the political leader can insure that the vote will be cast his way.

Another procedure that the men report is for the political leader to hold the men's registration cards and to make sure that they all vote. There are at least a few cases on Skid Row election lists of the same man being registered twice—in some cases, once for each party. Finally, one client reports that he was approached by a committeeman, ordered into his car, and taken to register to vote with the comment, "We're all Republicans around here." The client was afraid not to go and was driven to a traveling registrar. He then had to argue for a ride back to his rooming house. We do not doubt that much the same sort of thing may happen in other poor sections of the city. Our point is that these people are relatively powerless not only with respect to the police and their landlords but also politically; indeed, their powerlessness is compounded by the fact that their landlords are often also their political "leaders."

MISSIONS: MUTUAL EXPLOITATION

The third major kind of housing available on Skid Row is provided by the gospel missions. In the mid-1960s, there were about 17 missions and quasi-missions in Philadelphia; 9 of these were located in Skid Row, 4 were near it, and 4 were well outside the area. Most of those which focus on Skid Row men are organized around religious services which are said to be voluntary (legally, the gospel missions are churches), but in most cases the men feel pressure to attend and they resent it. They express their hostility in such slang expressions as "taking a nose dive" (taking part in a Skid Row gospel mission prayer service before the "feeding").[5] Almost all the men say that they believe in a God (we did not explore the meaning of the term for them), but the gospel mission was not the place where they came to worship that God.

Some of the missions expect men who join the program to do work related to their clothing and furniture salvaging operations. This scheme of things is justified by the missions because they give work to the men and provide necessary income to the missions beyond what comes in through fund solicitations. A variation is the gospel mission that has a woodlot as the basis of its program. This is a remnant of an earlier work test imposed on men seeking charity during the past century. As the test was originally conceived, an able-bodied man was given a meal and a night's lodging; the next morning he was expected to cut a cord of wood and if he refused he was threatened with a sentence to the House of Correction.[6] We doubt that the particular mission with the woodlot ever worked with this plan. In any case, there is now a shortage of wood to be split, and the work program consists largely of stacking cordwood and delivering orders to householders. This mission is strict in its expectations, and operates far below its housing capacity.

Most mission beds are in dormitories. Some beds are free, but better ones cost from 35 cents to one dollar a night at the present time. A free bed at one mission during the mid-1960s was a piece of canvas stretched between two pipes; a pay bed was a mattress with springs. (A canvas cot indoors is better in the dead of winter than a grating or a loading platform or walking the streets, but it is certainly not decent housing according to present-day standards.)

Racial segregation has been the common practice in mission sleeping quarters. One mission used to have black men sleep on one floor and white men sleep on another; since it now houses almost no white men, this practice no longer prevails. Another large mission has different dormitories for whites and blacks. At one time only white men would get a low-cost bed in this mission, but we understand that the practice has changed—blacks are asked to pay also. (In 1960, a man who planned carefully could manage to live on the free food and shelter circuit from mission to mission for almost the entire month. Since that time the requirements have been loosened in response to the decline in Skid Row population, so that men need not plan so carefully.)

In general, the younger the man, the greater the likelihood that he will resort to the missions for housing, whether free or pay; these are the men who have recently come into the Row, and their drinking is likely to be most intense. Furthermore, they are still in the process of learning to survive under Skid Row conditions. But, without respect to age, the most desperate men on Skid Row are the ones most likely to use the missions because it is their last resort. In 1960, we found that about one-third of the men had gone to the missions for food and that about three-tenths had depended on the missions for a place to sleep sometime during 1959. However, only about one-tenth of the men ate at the missions for more than three months, and about one-twentieth of them had slept in the missions for more than three months in 1959. Thus, for most of the residents of the Skid Row area, the missions are not immediately important. They are more like money in the bank—a resource to be used in an emergency. Given the heavy drinking, the jackrolling, the high probability of some contact with the police and courts which may lead to loss of money or a paid-in-advance bed, many men are forced to call on this resource sometime during the year.

In spite of the relatively heavy usage of the missions (for it must be inferred that a substantial, although unknown, fraction of the men in Skid Row have used the missions at sometime over the years), Skid Row men are at best ambivalent and often hostile to the gospel missions.

Ambivalence was revealed in the 1960 study when we asked the men who they thought should run any relocation housing that might be made available to Skid Row men. Over one-half said the city of Philadelphia; almost one-third said private business; less than one-tenth said the missions (the balance were "don't know" or uncodable responses). We followed this up with some questions directed to men who came back to the center. Roughly one-half of the men agreed that the missions do help the men (Table 5-5),

TABLE 5-5   Do the Missions Help the Men?[a]

	Cubicle Hotel	%	Mission	%	Rooming Hse.	%
	PLACE OF RESIDENCE OF RESPONDENT					
Yes	35	45	64	49	59	55
No	22	29	36	28	23	21
Mixed response	15	19	24	19	15	14
Other	5	7	5	4	11	10
N[b]	77	100	129	100	108	100

[a] Data from Demonstration Grant Returnees Study.
[b] DK, RA, NA omitted.

and roughly one-fifth give a mixed yes-and-no response. In 1960, we asked the men what would be the right way to help them. About two-fifths said to make jobs available; one-fifth said to provide a community or municipal shelter; and slightly less than one-tenth suggested that more or better missions be provided (Table 5-6).

TABLE 5-6   What Would Be the Right Way to Help the Men?

Type of Reasons	Frequency (Percentage)
Help with alcohol problem	8
Make jobs available	41
Abolish missions or other Skid Row agencies	4
Provide more or better missions	8
Provide a community or municipal shelter	22
Rehabilitation; group therapy	12
Human dignity; treat men fairly	3
Law enforcement, more or stricter police	2
Total percentage	100
N[a]	126

[a] DK, RA, NA and vague responses omitted, N = 426.

In addition, many of our Skid Row clients tell us that they resent the low quality of mission food. Some missions which feed at noon or night do not offer a breakfast. Even for those who do feed in the morning, it is apparently common to make men leave the building at five or six o'clock, and to stand outside until the seven o'clock feeding. On a cold winter morning, the men look at this as a hardship.

Mission officials are undoubtedly aware of the hostility and ambivalence of most of the men. Our conclusions are consistent with the discussion of the missions that Wiseman presents in *Stations of the Lost.*[7] Mission personnel have a radically different philosophy of life and view of the world than have the Skid Row men. Most misson personnel are oriented to saving souls, using techniques developed in the great revivals of the nineteenth and early twentieth centuries. They are trying to save souls for Christ as a part of the process of saving their own souls; they are willing to be conned by the men and scorned ("for Christ's sake") by the men; they believe that their job is to find the lost sheep and bring them back to the fold.[8]

However, we do not believe that the mission directors appreciate the extent of the hostility of some of the more cynical Skid Row men, who regard themselves as pawns. These men resent what they regard as a game of exploitation of the public in which they are "used" by the mission directors. Thus, one man reported that salvaged furniture of some value was taken by a mission director and sold in his own used furniture store rather than in one owned and operated by the mission; the Skid Row man was his low-paid assistant, having been asigned there from the mission. Others have reported selling furniture and articles given to a mission in order to get whiskey and a stake so that they could quit their mission jobs and return to living on Skid Row; they felt justified in doing this because they felt that the mission was exploiting them by not paying them a reasonable day's wage. Finally, we have had a report of an arrangement in which men sent out to beg by a mission split the take. After carfare, lunch money (some of the men drank their lunch), and cigarettes were taken out of what they had collected, the men were given 40 percent. Whether these reports are to be trusted, they are indicative of the mood of the men. Evidently the men see themselves as providing the excuse for the mission director's and staff's careers and as a basis of the mission's appeals for funds. The men, in turn, accept what the mission gives at the lowest possible cost to themselves in order to meet their immediate and desperate needs for food and shelter. In Skid Row terms, the men see the directors as conning the public, and they feel justified in conning the mission directors in turn.

In the past decade, the missions on Skid Row have declined, partly because the area population itself is declining and partly because many more men are getting Public Assistance money. It may be also that the essentially urban background of these men means they are less amenable to mission appeals. The proportion of older men on Social Security retirement benefits has risen. One major mission dropped 50 free beds, and now there is a scarcity on the Row. Another related change has been a shift in mission practice, so that several of them are now taking check men. The rates vary from about $65 a month to about $97 a month for room and board; sometimes several hours of light work a day is also expected. Missions which take check men are reported to exercise a tight control on the residual part of the check that does not apply to room and board. At least one mission requires a man to ask for each sum of money he wants to withdraw from his account and to justify it; and since, in some cases, no receipts are given, the men are suspicious.

The missions face a major problem that is similar to the problem faced by colonial mission enterprises in underdeveloped countries. They both used basic necessities (such as food) as a way to bring potential converts within hearing range. Subsequently their problem became how to convert rice Christians into actively committed believers. We believe that the Skid Row gospel missions have failed because they demand radical changes from the men for relatively paltry rewards after the initial period of desperation is past. Furthermore, the missions provide little room for the men to participate in the planning and execution of the rehabilitation process. The status-prestige system within mission programs is extremely inflexible; and few Skid Row men ever hope to move into the ranks of policy formation, prestige, and relatively high income, even if they are really converted, because the gap between these men and the mission officials is great. Finally, the missions rarely provide channels out into the larger community, assuming as they do that a man will either remain institutionalized within the mission program in a status just short of peonage or will return to his family. We believe that alternative approaches to rehabilitation are needed.

6　Employment: The Visible Means of Subsistence

We are interested in the visible means of subsistence of Philadelphia Skid Row men partly because the legislature makes it an important basis for the definition of vagrancy and because men continue to be jailed in Philadelphia for that offense. A person with no visible means of subsistence is a vagrant in Pennsylvania and subject to arrest and jail.[1] There are ways to circumvent the law that are apparently not available to Skid Row men, for street begging continued in Philadelphia for many years after the anti-vagrancy law was passed in 1876. The city fathers simply issued a license as a peddler— a half dozen pencils on display was enough.

THE PREMATURELY RETIRED

We are interested in the visible means of subsistence also because behind the legislature is the general society and because what a man does for a living is of importance to the community as a whole. Furthermore, whether a man works or not and what kind of work he does are basic to the definition

In the preparation of this chapter, we wish to express our appreciation to Bonnie Greenfield, Stephen Barsky, Joseph O. Moor, Jr., William Hood, Robert McCarthy; special thanks are due to Ellen Koch for her work on peripheral workers. We also thank the American Friends Service Committee for making available a staff report on the agricultural day-haul laborers; and to the employees in the Pennsylvania State Employment Service Offices in Philadelphia, Stroudsburg, and Honesdale.

of who he is. It is therefore of considerable significance to find that between one-half and three-fifths of the men living in Philadelphia's Skid Row are apparently unemployed in any given week throughout the year, and that one-third reported that they had not worked during the year before their interview (Tables 6-1 and 6-2). Indeed, almost one-half of these said they did not have a

TABLE 6-1   NUMBER OF HOURS WORKED IN PAST WEEK, BY PERCENTAGE

Hours Worked in Week	1964 Sample	1960 Study
1–8	12	10
9–32	41	33
33–40	18	23
41 or more	21	30
DK, NA, RA	8	4
Total percentage	100	100
N[a]	238	1067

[a] 314 respondents (57 percent) not employed omitted from 1964 Sample; 1182 respondents (53 percent) not employed omitted from 1960 Study.

TABLE 6-2   LENGTH OF TIME SINCE LAST DAY OF WORK, RESPONDENTS WITH NO JOB IN PAST MONTH

Number of Years	Percentage
Less than 1	30
1–2	22
3–4	17
5 or more	31
Total	100
N = 264[a]	

[a] Respondents with job in past month, 273. Total respondents, 537; DK, NA, RA omitted.

job for the past three years—for all practical purposes, they were no longer in the labor force. In the month before their doorstep interview during the demonstration period, four-fifths of those who were 65 years of age or older were unemployed (Table 6-3).[2]

The younger men, who are presumably employable, often came into the center after a binge when their money had run out and they had lost whatever steady job they may have had. Table 6-3 shows that there is a systematic increase in percentage of unemployment with increase in age. The younger men tend to be

TABLE 6-3   AGE AND JOB IN PAST MONTH, BY PER-
                 CENTAGE

| | JOB IN PAST MONTH | | TOTAL | |
	Yes	No	Percentage	N
Less than 45	71	29	100	109
45–54	61	39	100	165
55–64	45	55	100	152
65 or older	19	81	100	97
N[a]	264	259		523

[a] DK, NA, RA omitted.

heavier drinkers; many of these have recently arrived on the Row and have only recently left their jobs, and, except for their alcohol problem, are still in reasonably good health and employable. Tables 6-4 and 6-5 suggest that for the first five years on the Row there

TABLE 6-4   SELF-REPORT OF HANDICAPS AND WORK IN
                 PAST YEAR, BY PERCENTAGE

| WEEKS WORKED | NUMBER OF HANDICAPS | | TOTAL | |
	None	One or More	Percentage	N[a]
No work in past year	49	51	100	255
Less than 48	66	34	100	165
48 or more	89	11	100	76

[a] DK, NA, RA omitted.

is a steady increase in the number of handicaps which the men believe interfere with their chances of getting and holding a job; thereafter there seems to be a health plateau.

TABLE 6-5   SELF-REPORT OF HANDICAPS BY FIRST MOVE
                 TO SKID ROW NEIGHBORHOOD, BY
                 PERCENTAGE

| NUMBER OF YEARS | NUMBER OF HANDICAPS | | | TOTAL | |
	None	One	Two or More	Percentage	N[a]
Less than 1	80	17	3	100	58
1–4	70	22	8	100	112
5–9	60	30	10	100	108
10–15	59	29	12	100	85
15 or more	49	42	9	100	129

[a] DK, NA, RA omitted.

These tables suggest that many men on Skid Row are no longer direct participants in the labor force. When we asked men about their best job during their lifetime, three-fourths answered in terms of desirable wages and working conditions; and one-eighth answered that they liked the work itself as a task. (There was no significant difference with respect to race in this matter.) That is, they were willing to use "best" in substantially the same sense that most working people might be expected to use the term. Further, their best job and their longest job were either the same or similar jobs, which suggests that job stability was also an important consideration. The men were asked the following question: "Some people say that people get ahead by their own hard work; others say that lucky breaks or help from other people are more important. What do you think about this?" (We have called this the Protestant ethic question because of its relationship to the thinking of the great German sociologist Max Weber.) Of the 552 men who were asked the question, over one-half gave replies in terms of hard work; about one-quarter said that getting ahead was due to lucky breaks or the help of other people; one-seventh said it was due to all three factors (the balance were "don't know," refusal, or uncodable responses). Even if alcohol had become a major preoccupation or a central value, work was not rejected either as a necessity or as a desired activity.

In general then, Skid Row men subscribe to a positive work ethic and are little different in this respect from the working-class population of which they were a part before moving to the Skid Row locality. That work did not touch the lives of many of the men to the same degree as it did those of other workers was a consequence of their alcohol behavior, poor health, and difficulties in overcoming those problems.[3] Furthermore, in a society in which there is a lessening demand for unskilled labor, these men are likely to become unemployable after they have been living the Skid Row style of life for a period of years. In other words, some Skid Row residents are prematurely retired—there is no longer a place for them that will pay rewards high enough to lift them out of poverty.

PERIPHERAL WORKERS

Tables 6-1 through 6-3 show that not all Skid Row men are prematurely retired; one-fifth of the men who were 65 years of age or older said that they had had a job in the past month; seven-tenths of those under 45 years of age had a job at the time. Of those who had jobs, between two-fifths and one-half worked 32 hours a week or less. (Our time categories recognize that some "full-time" jobs no longer require 40 hours a week, but that the four-day work week is still a rarity in our society.) A substantial number of Skid Row men hold part-time jobs, and should be considered peripheral workers since they tend to work less than full time for a full year. In this they are similar to youths, older workers, nonwhites, immigrants, and quasi-immigrants, such as blacks, Chicanos, and Puerto Ricans.[4]

Part-time employment and unemployment are intimately associated with the prevalence of factors related to poverty, such as poor health, a broken family, poor educational opportunities, old age, low wages, irregular employment in the past, and location in an economically declining or depressed area.[5] A study of poverty by Seymour Wolfbein showed that only 8 percent of all family heads with full-time, year-round employment lived in poverty, while the corresponding proportion for part-time, year-round workers was 44 percent.[6] Hodge and Wetzel pointed out that residents of poverty areas are twice as likely to be on short work weeks as the general population living outside such areas.[7] The service industries typically hire large numbers of part-time employees. Service occupations, which tend to be found in large numbers in the metropolitan areas of the country, do not demand a high level of skill, indeed, many of them are among the most menial occupations in contemporary society. Thousands of kitchen workers, countermen, janitors, elevator operators, cleaners, waiters, ushers, and similar workers find more or less casual employment in large cities.[8] People in service occupations cannot look forward to an orderly career development from low skill to high skill, from low wages to high wages, and from casual employment to job stability. Furthermore, when the peripheral worker is not in a service occupation, he is likely to be employed by a small firm which offers little training for advancement in job skills and which operates outside labor-union wage protection, so that the workingman is always likely to be at a dead end on the job.[9] Table 6-6 suggests this pattern of employment for Skid Row men concentrated in service and other unskilled occupations. These data are consistent with Morse's observation: "Many service occupations, because of such factors as irregular work schedules and later hours, have long attracted unattached individuals. The unattached male worker is

TABLE 6-6   Types of Occupations of Skid Row Men, 1960 and 1964, by Percentage

Type of Occupation	Longest, 1960	Best, 1964	Past week, 1960	Last job, 1964
Professional	1	3	1	1
Prop., Mgr., Off.	2	2	1	1
Clerical and sales	7	5	3	4
Craftsmen and foremen	25	20	7	6
Operatives	19	26	8	6
Service	21	23	24	36
Laborers	21	19	54	34
Non-urban	4	2	2	12
Total percentage	100	100	100	100
N[a]	2204	525	1027[b]	541

[a] DK, RA, NA omitted.
[b] Those not employed in survey week omitted.

far more apt to have a peripheral work experience than the male worker who has a family."[10]

A few Skid Row men still follow a common pattern that prevailed until perhaps ten years ago and apply for work directly to such employers ("off the street") as wholesale meat dealers and packers, (many of which are still located just north and east of the Skid Row area) or wholesale fruit and vegetable merchants (now located in South Philadelphia). In contrast to the past, most of the men who now do this sort of work are black; these black workers seem to be Skid Row-like in their instability and in their drinking behavior as the employers describe them.

Most men go to the commercial (privately operated for profit) agencies. In Chapter 2, we described how muzzling firms operate. Ostensibly muzzlers are protected by a labor union. Union headquarters are not far from Skid Row in a rundown building, but we have never found anyone there. We have been told by the firms themselves that the union local has contracts covering working conditions, wages, and vacation pay. We wonder how beneficial the union is for most Skid Row men.

In addition to muzzling outfits, there are commercial agencies that send men out on so-called permanent jobs. In this circumstance, the agency requires the man to sign a payroll deduction agreement that may assign up to 40 percent of the first month's wages to the agency and which is "taken off the top" (first) by the employer. Since many men do not remain on the job beyond the first or second pay period—and the agencies know that—it sometimes happens that after the employer takes the full job-placement fee from the check the man finds that he has been working for nothing—he leaves with almost no cash in hand. The high turn-over makes for high profits for the agency, and these are made at the expense of the known instability of the man. Although this practice is legal, we regard it as exploitative, for it takes advantage of the man's weakness. A more extreme example occurs when the agency and the employer appear to be in collusion to encourage the man to quit the job, once the agency fee has been paid, by suddenly imposing what the man regards as longer, oppressive, working hours; the employer gets a kickback, while the agency profits from the high turnover and the consequently larger job placement fees. Skid Row rumors suggest that this kind of exploitation is common, and there seems to be little that can be done to protect men from it.

Skid Row men also work for temporary job agencies. In Chicago's Uptown, there are many "hillbillies" who seek work through these agencies.[11] These agencies tend to specialize. For example, one agency will have light work (such as kitchen help and porter jobs), and older men will go there; another agency will have heavy work (such as construction or loading and unloading trucks) and the younger, more able-bodied man will go there. Heavy work pays 10 or 12 cents more an hour than does light work.

The temporary help agencies send the man to a job, charge the client-employer for the man's time, and pay the man themselves. Thus, technically the man is an employee of the agency, who then assigns him to the agency's client. The agency pays taxes and workman's compensation for each employee. In such circumstances, we would expect the man to be paid from the time he leaves the agency office until he reports back at the end of the day; in fact, the agency usually tells the man where the job is located, expects him to pay his own carfare, and pays him only for the time spent actually working for the client-employer. (The issue of portal-to-portal pay is an old one in labor-union disputes, but these marginally employed people do not have any effective labor union protection.) The agency charges the employer more than it pays the man—often as much as 80 percent higher.

SKID ROW JOBS

The following kinds of job situations all affect the public interest not only because of the exploitative elements that are revealed but because the public clearly benefits from cheaper food, institutional care, recreational facilities and because the public supports the gospel missions through their charitable giving and the purchase of salvaged items. The difference between the working poor and the Skid Row man is small.

Agricultural Day Labor

We have said little in this book about black men who live on or near Skid Row. In many ways, blacks are not readily distinguishable from other poverty-stricken blacks who live in the surrounding slum area. We have already discussed the residential segregation on Skid Row; while such data are difficult to obtain, we believe that there is also discrimination in hiring men for Skid Row jobs. Thus, there are only a few black men working on muzzling crews. Furthermore, our observer (who was white) found that black men were also looking for work when he registered in the commercial employment agencies, but that he was called first and sent out on a job while the blacks continued to wait. Indeed, as Skid Row has declined, most temporary job applicants are now black. In contrast, we believe that at the present time agricultural day labor is almost exclusively black. Most of these blacks are transported on old buses to parts of nearby Bucks County, Pennsylvania, and to farms across the Delaware River in New Jersey. We have seen crews of black men, women, and adolescents (who appeared to be as young as 14) stopping for wine on their way home from the fields. Many of these are former migrants from the South who have settled in the ghettos of metropolitan Philadelphia. The day-haul situation is exploitative in several respects, as the following staff report of the American Friends Service Committee suggests.[12]

The life of a day-haul worker is a hard one. For our Field Workers it was often necessary to get up at 3 A.M. to catch the labor bus at 4 A.M.—arrive at work at 6 A.M. and arrive back home between 8 P.M. and 9:30 P.M. It meant working 13 or 14 hours per day in the fields in addition to time used for transportation. For this they estimated the average day-haul laborer earns from $12 to $15 per day. It is the usual custom for crews to have a stopping place in New Jersey for the crew to buy wine and possibly food. One of the main stops is on the White Horse Pike. Here Alfie's Bar and Picnic Grounds caters to hundreds of buses a day. There is a huge picnic ground with tables under the trees and take-out windows for people to buy wine and sandwiches. The drivers probably get some kind of a bonus or at least a free meal for stopping their buses there. Many drivers say that the people they take won't go with them unless they let them stop to buy wine "over the bridge." Some workers would manage to still do a fairly productive day in spite of drinking rather heavily. Others would be too drunk to be very productive by the time they arrived in the fields and would struggle to pick only enough to pay for their wine that day.

The majority of the workers on the buses and on the crews for whom our Field Workers worked were men. Some under-age children are used occasionally. We were told that there are some crews leaving from North Philadelphia made up largely of women and teenage children. Here these women often refused to go with the crew leader *if* he stops at the wine stop. . . .

The crew leader or bus driver gets the best of the deal financially. We talked with one woman who was the bookkeeper for a labor contractor. According to her, the crew leader that she worked with was paid 30 cents per basket for each basket of tomatoes. Of this 30 cents, 18 cents went to the picker and 12 cents to the driver. It can be seen that the picker would have to pick close to a hundred baskets per day to make a decent wage. If the picker is productive and the crop is reasonably good, a hundred baskets are possible. But it can be seen that if the driver or the contractor gets 12 cents per basket for each basket that every person on his crew picks, he has considerable income for the day. Of course many of the drivers are not the true entrepreneurs but simply work as drivers on a daily wage for some bigger contractor who may have several buses.

Crews are paid off at the end of each day. There is a great deal of turnover and the same people may not show up two days in a row. When a person does go, he tends to seek out the same driver or crew leader each time he goes. There are, of course, some who get on whatever bus is handy. . . .

Our Field Workers found that in no case that they observed was Social Security being deducted from the worker's pay. The worker would be given a ticket for each basket of tomatoes or flat of blueberries he picked and he would turn these tickets in at night and collect his money. He was paid in cash on the spot. There is no record of his name or the amount of money he was paid.

The farmer usually pays the driver for the delivery of bodies to his field. One crew leader said that he got a "dollar a head" for all those he brought to the field plus his percentage on the crops picked. In addition, he sold wine, beer and sandwiches in the fields on credit which he would deduct when he paid off the workers. . . .

Most of the men traveling on the crews were estimated to be between 40 and 60 years of age. When our Field Workers would question them about the possibility of getting training or getting into some kind of a training program to get new and better jobs, they would all say that they were "too old." This was probably based partly on the reluctance of industry to take trainees who were over 40. It would probably also stem from the feeling of hopelessness on the part of the individuals concerned and the lack of confidence in their ability to do anything better. As far as we were able to determine, most of these people do odd jobs during the winter months, often with the City. They may be engaged in snow removal, garbage pickup, or they may work with truckers, loading and unloading trucks, hauling miscellaneous items about the City.

Institutional and Resort Jobs

Many men from Skid Row accept live-in jobs (Wiseman refers to them as "live-in servants of an institution"),[13] although this practice is apparently on the decline. Interviews with administrators of institutions in the Philadelphia vicinity (the number was small, but we believe that the facts are typical) indicated an increase in hiring trainable mentally retarded persons, conscientious objectors (fulfilling alternative service assignments), and black men with families. Furthermore, the conditions of work have been redefined so that the employees (especially married black workers) do not live in as they did in the past.

A live-in job appeals to Skid Row men because it seems to be a place from which they can stabilize their lives and build a stake for either leaving a Skid Row situation or financing a spree. It provides the security of regular meals, room, and extra money. Live-in jobs are easy to get, either through an agency or through advertisements in newspapers. Jobs such as kitchen help and maintenance work require few skills. These are found primarily in hospitals, nursing homes, country clubs, hotels, and resorts, usually located well outside the center of the city, often in the most distant suburbs.

The men work 40 hours a week and are paid biweekly. In 1970, the hourly wages ranged from $1.12 per hour plus room and board to $2.00 per hour (with room and board deducted from the check). Live-in workers are usually assigned a private room, although they must sometimes share it with another man. One employer reported that labor turnover varies with the kind of person employed—it was highest with the mentally deficient and lowest with blacks. Absenteeism after payday and showing up drunk for work are given as major reasons for firing a man.

Summer camps, mountain hotels, and resorts offer a noninstitutional kind of live-in job that has attracted Skid Row men in the past. They work as porters, kitchen men, operators of dishwashing machines, maintenance men, and occasionally as caddies. Thus, they are doing the same kind of work that they do in the cities.

Many Skid Row men who work in the Poconos come from a few Philadelphia employment agencies, who advance bus fare, supply references, and make other arrangements. The less scrupulous employers seem to accept the employment agency as the reference, knowing that only minimal screening could have been done; some agencies are said to take carloads of men up to the Poconos and then to travel from resort to resort peddling them as they go. On the other hand, one major year-round hotel conducts a careful formal interview, takes mug shots and fingerprints, and, through its contacts with the township police, can arrange to have these prints checked out for a criminal record if this seems desirable.

As in other jobs supplied by Skid Row employment agencies, there is a high turnover in the hotel-resort employment scene during the summer season. The mobility of the men is increased because more are needed to prepare the resorts and hotels for opening than are needed to operate them; the operators use the preparation period to determine the better workers whom they want to keep. The others drift through the region looking for work until they get discouraged or find themselves in jail. There is little housing available in the region for these drifters. There are few gospel missions and no really cheap hotels.

Two pay patterns prevail in the resorts. Some employers pay every two weeks, knowing fully that many men will leave then or soon after. Some other employers try to cope with the high mobility through payment of small sums during the season with a final lump sum at the end. This practice seems reasonable because the individual may indeed want to build such a stake. But there is another factor involved. Resorts borrow heavily from local banks in order to open, and their financial problem is acute until August. If August is cool or rainy, they may be in serious trouble. Therefore they pay out as little money as they can during the season, conserving their resources until the end; in other words, the work force is a partner in the speculative enterprise through a loan that is one of the conditions of the job. However, this is a situation that employees neither understand nor usually agree to.

The composition of the resort work force and work-related practices seems to be changing, with Skid Row men becoming less relevant to it. For example, Hutter, in his discussion of the middle-class, low-cost Jewish resort hotels of the Catskills, observed that there were more poor black and Puerto Rican workers than there were poor whites from the Bowery.[14] Our field observations in Monticello, New York, which is the county seat of Sullivan County and central to the hotel-resort industry of the Catskills tend to confirm this. The general picture was of young people, blacks, Puerto Ricans, and some Skid Row men in the offices. The college-age people are generally hired for jobs dealing directly with the customer; the blacks, Puerto Ricans, and Skid Row whites are hired for the menial work.

In general, we believe that living conditions in live-in jobs help reinforce heavy drinking behavior. There are few provisions for leisure activity. Boredom can be colossal in institutions, camps, resorts, and hotels that are far from active city or community life. Furthermore, the kind of low-skilled, low-paid, and low-status jobs given Skid Row men offer few prospects for promotion. By the time a man has finished paying his fees to the employment agency or soon afterward, he usually quits or gets fired, so that he has to start all over again. Wiseman points out how difficult it is to change one's status when the launching pad is Skid Row; we would extend this to say that Wiseman's observation is probably true for all poor and low-status persons whether living on Skid Row or not.[15]

There is also a trend toward hiring local people rather than outsiders in the Pocono area and to the north of it. This seems likely to be the preferred hiring pattern for year-round luxury resort hotels that are developing and in the franchised motels that are being built in conjunction with the interstate highway system, and it also seems to be emergent for the seasonal jobs. Our information suggests that those who are hired for these jobs are probably people who are marginal in the local population—including those with alcohol problems. This pattern is reminiscent of the old big city hobohemia-transient man-Tenderloin area of the past. At least until the beginning of the 1930s—and even more so before World War I—there were many transient workingmen who lived inexpensively in what we now call Skid Rows on a seasonal basis; these included railroadmen, farm workers, lumbermen and seamen. With unemployment compensation to carry them through the winter, the present local workers in resort areas may have a style of life that is comparable to that of other unskilled workingmen of an earlier era. The relationship of these trends to the decline of Skid Row is not clear; the decline in able-bodied men must certainly constitute a pressure on employers to look to other segments of the population, but we are inclined to think that these trends are manifestations of more general changes in society as a whole—particularly the Social Security system, which was developed in the 1930s. In many ways, the issue of employment of Skid Row men is not easily separated from the larger issue of widespread peripheral employment and its consequence.[16]

Mission Employment

One employment situation merits some attention if only because so many men have had contact with mission work rehabilitation programs over the years.[17] Most mission beds are in dormitories. For those men who join the program, there are usually separate sleeping rooms; these rooms are graded with respect to status, so that a man starts out in a room for three or four, and if he continues in the program long enough and gets promoted to foreman or supervisor, he will probably eventually have a single room.

Housing is only one element in the employment-related status system of the missions. The bottom level is composed of truck helpers, balers, kitchen workers, and porters; within this level, the truck helpers have a slightly higher status. Kitchen helpers, porters, and warehouse workers are paid less than truck helpers. These jobs are generally filled by older men who are not strong enough or intellectually intact enough to do anything else. For Skid Row men, the truck helper's job is the reference point in the mission work program; there is a general belief that younger men who want to stay at the mission must be available as truck helpers.

For the salvage operations of the missions to function effectively, the trucks must be on the road. The drivers are paid the minimum hourly wage plus an incentive bonus based on what they bring in. In the largest mission program in the 1968–70 period, the bonus rates were as follows: for newspapers and magazines, ten cents a hundredweight; for rags, one cent a pound; for furniture and appliances, 15 percent of valuation according to a prepared sheet; bric-a-brac and miscellaneous articles, such as dishes, records, toys, books, are evaluated on a spot basis at low rates. The driver does not get 15 percent of the retail sales value of the furniture; rather, he receives 15 percent of the value according to the valuation sheet. Thus, chairs may be valued at 25 cents (without respect to the kind of chair); a kitchen table and set of four chairs, $3.00; couches, $3.00; refrigerators, $5.00;

gas stoves, $3.00; recent model and working television sets, $7.50; antiques and fine furniture may be double or triple the usual figures.

The experienced, aggressive driver on a good route can make as much as $125 a week; $90 a week is considered good pay for any driver. To make this much money, a driver needs an able-bodied helper. Helper's pay in Philadelphia missions at the present time follows two patterns. One major mission starts a man at a dollar a week and increases it at the rate of a dollar a week to four dollars ("if you come in drunk, you're back to a buck!"). At other missions, the wage varies from $12 to $20 a week. A good driver keeps his eye on the men who come in as helpers. If he sees one on another truck, he may recruit him by "piecing him off" (giving him a piece of the action); he may say, "I'll give you $4 a week and all you can steal, but you got to work." (The reference to stealing is not from householders but from the load that is being brought back to the mission.)

It must be clear that the driver and his helper have an incentive to hustle. Even though routes have been laid out by the mission administration, these are respected only when necessary. In addition, some streets are known to be loyal to one mission or another, but since there is a good deal of floating from mission to mission by drivers and helpers, they will solicit where they are known rather than in terms of their current mission affiliation. They are similar to salesmen selling a service—they help the householders assuage their consciences about discarding things "which still have a lot of use in them, if only they could be repaired a little." In this way the lower income levels of our society benefit by changes in styling and planned obsolescence. (The recent rise of the so-called "ecology movement" has raised the scavenging-salvage activities to a new level of respectability; it is doubtful that this will be accompanied by a correlative rise in the status of the scavengers, however. What is more likely is that the more profitable components of their activities will be taken up by "respectables" who will use the funds they collect for their own concerns about the "good of society" and the missions will need to develop some new sources of support.)

The driver and his helper may start the day by calling at houses where they have left a "we'll be here tomorrow" flyer the day before or by making calls at houses from which someone has phoned the mission. After the planned calls, they may make house-to-house solicitations on the streets starting out cold (the similarity to individual panhandling is striking). In some missions, a truck from the store goes out in response to phone calls, but route drivers will try to steal these calls and make the pickup themselves. When a housewife hesitatingly asks if he will take a Goodwill bag, he will probably say yes and be grateful for it. ("In fact if it wasn't for the Goodwill bag, many helpers would never get nothing.") Similarly, in suburban shopping centers, route drivers will raid the drop boxes; the route drivers see these as a drain on their production and believe that they are being cheated ("to raid one of these boxes you don't need a key, you don't need a hammer to break a lock, all you need is a small helper. You boost him inside and he throws everything out"). "The way they set up the system (the pay, the evaluation sheets, the house calls in response to the phone, the suburban drop-in boxes), you would think they wanted you to steal and their attitude is, 'I know you are going to steal, but this way I can keep it down.'" We are not concerned here with the possible interpretation of these remarks as self-serving but, rather, with the way the work rehabilitation program seems to operate financially. It is this which interests the men.

In an organizational sense, the paper balers, who work in the warehouses, are on a level with the truck helpers. However, they seem to get about two-thirds of what a helper gets (because of the incentive bonus). There are also men who work around the warehouse sorting rags, moving furniture, and working in the bric-a-brac room. Their pay is about the same as that of the baler. We know a man who seemed to be especially good at sorting books and routing them to various mission bookstores where they would most likely be sold: his cash-in-hand pay was $4 a week. He believed that he was being exploited because he also handled sales of books in one of the more active stores, and said that there were sales of from $300 to $600 a day. (Such figures are hard to accept as fact, but even if the sales were only half the amount, the disparity is still large. The case gives us some understanding of the men's perception of the missions as hypocritical and exploitative.) Men with skills such as repairing radios, television sets, washing machines, refrigerators, and similar appliances receive pay somewhere between that of the truck helpers and drivers. Store managers are paid a salary and commission, but their pay is less than that received by a good route driver. If there is a manager of all the stores, his pay is comparable to that of the warehouse boss, who is also a salaried worker. However, it is not uncommon for the warehouse boss to have responsibility for all the stores as well. Thus, below the administrative level of the minister, the warehouse boss is at the top of the mission status system. It is a job to which a Skid Row man might aspire. To do so, he must conform to the religious tenets and the religious behavior expected by the mission director, develop a stable nondrinking work pattern, and have or develop the necessary managerial skills.

The number of men who make it to the top of the mission employment system is clearly limited. It is a strictly circumscribed system that does not really prepare many men to move into the larger community and to solve their problems in terms of the larger community. The mission work rehabilitation program is only one step above the nineteenth-century plan to make vagrants chop wood in order to earn their room and board (a work test rather than a means test to qualify for financial assistance).

7　Skid Row Is an Unhealthy Place to Live

In our 1960 study of Skid Row, we asked the men about their medical histories and disabilities so that we could anticipate possible difficulties in relocating them successfully to decent, safe, and sanitary housing. At that time we believed that an attempt would be made to stabilize the men after relocation through rehabilitation into the active work force. We believed, accordingly, that medical disabilities would be a major obstacle to employability and found, in fact, that such disabilities were substantial among Skid Row men. About 23 percent of the sample of 377 men who answered our more comprehensive interview (the long form) reported a medical history of alcoholism—that is, the men accepted and were willing to acknowledge that a physician or psychiatrist had labeled their behavior in that way. (This was a lower figure than our own conclusions from the interview material that at least 35 percent were pathological or uncontrolled drinkers.) In addition, about 17 percent reported that

Parts of this chapter were derived from reports by Dr. Donald Ottenberg and Dr. Alvin Rosen; Luther Lassiter, Joseph McGillen, and Albert Rosenbaum; and William Hood. We wish further to express our appreciation to: Dr. L. Molthan, Temple University Hospital; Dr. Herbert Colwell, Dr. Joseph Spelman; Stephen F. Barsky, who initiated the blood bank study, and Leonard Moore and Deanne McClain, who continued it. Finally, we want to acknowledge the assistance of Sally Meisenhelder, Martha Blumberg, Paul Miller, and J. Richard Keifer, Jr.

they had a hernia or were ruptured; 15 percent had had arthritis, 12 percent had had a venereal disease, 11 percent had had stomach ulcers, 7 percent had had heart trouble, and 7 percent had had tuberculosis. When asked if they had any present physical disabilities that limited their work capacity, 36 percent reported a wide variety of conditions (excluding alcohol problems). We recommended medical diagnostic and referral facilities within the center on the basis of the substantial number of men with medical incapacities.

THE CENTER'S MEDICAL PROGRAM

Our medical procedures were originally undertaken as a bridge between the purely diagnostic-referral activities of the center and the relocation process. Was a man well enough to be relocated? (As we became progressively able to accept the need for, and to provide, financial assistance rather than work as a means of securing stability, the physician's findings on the nature and degree of incapacity became more important to the work of others on the staff.) Many men were entitled to Social Security benefits, veterans' pensions, or Public Assistance, but were not capable physically or mentally of initiating or following through with the application procedure. Finally, as the physicians accumulated evidence of the high prevalence of serious disease, the medical department of the center became a minor treatment center as well as a place for referral to hospitals for immediate care and to outpatient clinics for further diagnosis or therapy. Further, some of the physicians' time was devoted to short-range therapy to combat alcohol withdrawal symptoms. As the word spread on the Row that there was medical help available, the medical program attracted men to the center who otherwise might not have come; possibly this help was more attractive to some desperate men than was the dining room.

Examination and Diagnosis

The physical setting of our medical department was not prepossessing; a man coming directly from Skid Row, often with the shakes, frequently foul-smelling and in old filthy clothes, need not feel more uncomfortable. If the man was extremely dirty or infested with lice, he was asked to take a shower and was given new clothes before the examination began. Of the 177 men on whom data were available, 52 gave a history of having had lice in the past or were infested with lice at the time that they were examined. If the man was greatly affected by alcohol withdrawal symptoms at the initial visit, he was given medication to last for one to three days and asked to come back.

If a man was so severely ill that he required immediate hospitalization, suitable arrangements were made. The hospitalization of Skid Row men involved special difficulties. If a man had a "legitimate" medical emergency, such as an acute myocardial infarction, pneumonia, or acute thrombophlebitis, hospitalization was usually not difficult to arrange. If, in addition to one of these conditions or some other significant medical illness, he was also suffering from the acute withdrawal symptoms of alcohol or was actually intoxicated, the process became more difficult. Finally, if he did not have a clear medical emergency in the usual sense of the word— that is, if he had a medical condition without the immediate complications of alcohol but was obviously suffering from the effects of alcoholism, it was even more difficult to arrange hospitalization. Hospitals would usually simply refuse to accept such a person as a patient. We would therefore try to find him temporary housing under protected conditions (such as a bed among those reserved for us at the Sally). Failing that, the man would drift back to the Row to fend for himself until his symptoms abated or until he became an acute emergency case and was brought to the hospital by the police.

We began our medical evaluation by acquiring a detailed history done at a leisurely pace while we were also being fully responsive and receptive to the patient. Most of the medical history questions were written in order to insure uniformity among the members of the medical department. The physical examination was detailed and as thorough as it could be with only simple diagnostic tools. (It was interesting to discover that during the winter months the Skid Row men wore all the clothing they owned; undressing for examination took a long time as the man peeled off layer after layer of socks, underwear, pants, and shirts.) A rectal examination, including proctoscopic and, when indicated, sigmoidoscopic inspection, was included in the examination. Admittedly, the prospect of performing a complete physical examination on a Skid Row "bum" is usually faced with little enthusiasm by an admitting resident or intern; nonetheless, the thorough examination by an interested physician went a long way toward cementing a relationship between him and the men. Indeed, three years later, some men were still looking for the doctor who examined them at the center as the only physician who was really interested in them.

After the medical history and physical examination were completed, each man had a chest X-ray taken at the center. This film was developed and read by the Philadelphia Tuberculosis and Health Association, with the results usually available to the center medical staff within a few days. Each patient also had an intermediate purified protein derivative (PPD) tuberculin skin test, which was read within three days at the center. In addition, a paper urinalysis was performed, which included tests for albumin, glucose, pH, and blood. Several tubes of venous blood were collected and sent to the city department of health laboratory, where tests were carried out for hemoglobin, cholesterol, thymol turbidity, and blood glucose, including serologic test for syphilis. When indicated, an electrocardiogram was made. If a patient presented symptoms that indicated the need for other than the routine tests, the required procedure was completed at an outside laboratory.

Only 2 percent of the men were free of organic disease discernible by the examinations of the center's physicians. It should be mentioned that disorders of the eyes and teeth are not presented here (for various technical reasons). Of the 255 men examined, 33 had serious visual impairment or blindness in one or both eyes; another 49 had eye disorders which could for the most part be corrected with glasses. Thus, 32 percent of the men examined had disorders of the eyes. Deafness was present in 17 out of 221 patients, and another four had serious ear diseases. This is to be accounted for in part by the age of the clients who came to the center, many of whom were middle-aged or older, and in part by the hard lives the men had lived both before coming to the Skid Row neighborhood and after arriving there.

Medical Findings

Our tables in this chapter are based upon a total of 255 men.[1] However, complete medical data were not available in all cases; the unavoidable errors involved in collecting data have probably led to underestimation rather than overestimation of the frequency of specific diseases and conditions among the center's client-patients.

Of the 255 men, 51 percent suffered from alcoholism, 22 percent had pulmonary disease other than tuberculosis, 20 percent

were anemic, 16 percent suffered from a disorder of the musculoskeletal system, and 13 percent had active tuberculosis (Table
7-1). We have already discussed the diagnosis of alcoholism and
its significance in the larger Skid Row perspective.

Just as excessive drinking is characteristic of many men on Skid
Row, so is tuberculosis. No other segment of American society
approaches the almost unbelievable prevalence rates of tuberculosis one finds among Skid Row men. As shown in Table 7-1, our

TABLE 7-1   THE FIFTEEN MOST FREQUENTLY OCCUR-
                   RING DISEASES AND ABNORMAL SYSTEMS/
                   CONDITIONS, BY PERCENTAGE

Disease or Abnormal System/Condition	Percentage
Alcoholism	51
Pulmonary disease (no TB)	22
Anemia	20
Musculoskeletal disorder	16
Tuberculosis (active)	13
Skin disease	13
Hypertension (essential)	12
Disease of the central nervous system	11
Tuberculosis (inactive)	8
Prostatism	8
Hemorrhoids	8
Cardiovascular disease	7
Varicose veins	7
Inguinal hernia	6
Cirrhosis of liver	4
No disease found	2
N = 255[a]	

[a] Most had more than one disease or abnormal system.

physicians diagnosed 13 percent of the 255 patients examined as
having tuberculosis—a remarkable rate of 130 per thousand. (Of
the 33 cases involved, 7 were diagnosed by the examining physician on the basis of history and physical findings, 15 were diagnosed from X-ray evidence, and 11 from both indications.) In
1963, Philadelphia had a rate of reported cases of active and probably active tuberculosis of 54.1 per hundred thousand (range:
17.8 to 164.5 within health districts); in 1964, the rate was 48.8
(range: 14.9 to 127.4). Table 7-2 shows that the alcoholic patients
had five times the prevalence of active tuberculosis that the nonalcoholic had. More specifically, 27 of the men were both tuber-

TABLE 7-2   DISEASES AND ABNORMAL SYSTEMS/CON-
DITIONS AND ALCOHOLISM DIAGNOSIS, BY
PERCENTAGE

DISEASE OR ABNORMAL SYSTEM/CONDITION	DIAGNOSIS	
	Alcoholic	Nonalcoholic
Pulmonary disease	32	12
Fractured ribs	25	4
Anemia	24	17
Tuberculosis (active)	21	4
Musculoskeletal disorders	18	14
Disease of the central nervous system	17	5
Skin disease	16	9
Hypertension (essential)	14	10
Varicose veins	11	2
Tuberculosis (inactive)	10	5
Hemorrhoids	10	5
Cardiovascular disease	10	3
Inguinal hernia	8	4
Prostatism	7	9
Cirrhosis of liver	7	2
N = 255[a]		

[a] Some had more than one disease or abnormal condition.

culous and alcoholic; 5 had tuberculosis but no alcoholism; 102 had alcoholism but no tuberculosis; and 59 had neither condition. The chi square is statistically significant. Further, the prevalence of inactive tuberculosis was twice that found in the nonalcoholic; this disease is more likely to become active in the alcoholic than in the nonalcoholic. More striking differences between the two groups are evident in the fact that varicose veins occur more than five times as often among the alcoholics than among the nonalcoholics, and that the incidence of pulmonary disease other than tuberculosis is two and one-half times greater in the alcoholic than in the nonalcoholic. These pulmonary diseases include emphysema, chronic bronchitis, bronchial asthma, bronchiectasis, various forms of pleural disease, neoplasm, and other conditions. In our patient population, the usual correlation with age did not hold, a finding which was corroborated by the results of tuberculin testing using intermediate strength PPD. This may be explained by differences in racial composition, however, since 15 percent of the white client-patients were diagnosed as having tuberculosis, in comparison with 9 percent of the black client-patients. The number of cases is too small to analyze further with these data, although we do know that the black clients were younger than the whites.

The physical examination of the chest revealed other symptoms of disease in a high proportion of those diagnosed as tuberculous. Of 33 tuberculous patients, 21 (64 percent) had abnormal physical findings, as compared with 53 out of 144 nontuberculous patients (37 percent). Most of the abnormal findings were accounted for by rales and impaired excursion of some part of the chest.

Only 14 of the 33 tuberculous cases had been in a tuberculosis hospital, indicating that a significant proportion of the cases identified were newly discovered, especially through the use of X-rays. This impression was borne out by further evaluation of individual patients where more intensive study could be made. (Hospitalization for treatment of active tuberculosis was arranged for 23 of the patients.) Another indication of the high prevalence of tuberculosis was the fact that among these homeless and extremely mobile men, 15 of the 33 diagnosed as tuberculous were aware that they had had contact with a person who had the disease.

Rib fractures are another mark of the Skid Row alcoholic. Because of the high incidence of trauma, either self-inflicted (falling) or produced by other (being rolled), 25 percent of the alcoholics have evidence of rib fractures (healed or recent), whereas the nonalcoholic population has a prevalence of only 4 percent (Table 7-2).

Cirrhosis was three and one-half times more prevalent among the alcoholics than among the nonalcoholics (Table 7-2). While this finding is not unexpected, it is interesting to note that the prevalence among the alcoholic population is as low as 7 percent. There is among the lay population (if not among some physicians as well) the popular misconception that all alcoholics—and certainly all Skid Row alcoholics—must have cirrhosis. The prevalence of enlarged liver, abnormal liver function tests, fatty liver, or acute alcoholic hepatitis is high; but for the most part, this is reversible liver damage that can be corrected with good nutrition, vitamins, and abstinence from alcohol.

Among the alcoholics, such disorders as central nervous system diseases, cardiovascular disease, inguinal hernia, and hemorrhoids were from two to three times more frequent than among the nonalcoholics. Hypertension and musculoskeletal disorders occurred somewhat more frequently among the alcoholics, but there were no striking differences in these conditions between the two groups. Prostatism, accounted for primarily by benign prostatic hypertrophy, was the one frequently occurring condition which was found to be slightly more frequent among the nonalcoholics than among the alcoholics. One can speculate that liver impairment leading to elevated estrogen levels may be protective to the prostate.

Table 7-3 presents the results of the center's laboratory tests on Skid Row men. Of the six men with a positive serologic test for

TABLE 7-3   RESULTS OF LABORATORY TESTS, BY PERCENTAGE

TEST	RESULT OF TEST Abnormal	Normal	TOTAL Percentage	N
Serology	4	96	100	170
Hemoglobin (11.9 gm. or less)	30	70	100	176
Cholesterol (greater than 250)	13	87	100	168
Thymol turbidity (greater than 4.1 Maclagen units)	12	88	100	167
Blood glucose	30	70	100	178
Glucose in urine	6	94	100	164
Albuminuria	18	82	100	164

syphilis, only one stated that he had been treated for venereal disease. However, 32 of the 181 men who responded to the question on treatment of venereal disease said that they had been treated in the past. Most of those who had a history of venereal disease indicated that they acquired it while serving in the armed forces; it was usually gonorrhea rather than syphilis.

Cholesterol was elevated in 22 of the men; 18 of these were alcoholics. Only 4 nonalcoholics had elevated cholesterol. The thymol turbidity was elevated in 20 men, of whom 12 were alcoholic and 8 nonalcoholic. It was impossible to control the timing of venipuncture for blood sugar determination in relation to the last meal or last drink, so that the significance of an elevated blood sugar was clouded. However, we did diagnose nine cases of diabetes in the population, a rate of 3.5 percent; other cases probably went undetected. Of 164 men, 18 percent had albuminuria at the time of the examination. The significance is unknown, since evidence of genitourinary disease other than prostatism was low. The albuminuria may have been related to alcoholism, trauma, or other transitory phenomena.

Our findings underscore the importance of a medical screening as an integral part of any project designed to work with Skid Row men, since 209 men (82 percent) had conditions that required further evaluations or treatment. We estimate that one-quarter of the men examined were subsequently hospitalized. Tuberculosis and alcoholism accounted for the most of these cases.

Many Skid Row men are sick and in need of care; much of the prevalent disease appears to be chronic and remediable, requiring either long-term medical regimens or surgical correction. These men are unlikely to seek out medical care unless pain or some other urgent symptom forces them to do so. It is often not until the police pick up a man who is severely ill or unconscious that contact with the clinic and hospital is made. In the relatively few instances when Skid Row men do take the initiative in seeking medical care, the chances of carrying the treatment through to a successful conclusion are poor. The men discourage easily and are frustrated by the smallest obstacles, such as the need to wait to see a physician or nurse, to register or fill out forms, or to return a number of times for various examinations. Shame about their appearance undoubtedly keeps some men hidden in the Row. The uncertainties and unpredictability of their life also make long-term planning difficult for them.

The overriding impression one gets from the men as they appear in the center is one of quiet, depressed passivity. The most obvious defects were missing or deformed limbs and the stoop-shouldered posture, often associated with pallor and malnourishment. Many of these men showed obvious evidence of alcohol withdrawal, with tremors, hyperirritability, memory defects, and unsteadiness. They were mainly cooperative, although a few balked at such procedures as venipuncture. Few were openly hostile.

Our data make clear that Skid Row is a hostile environment for its residents, who live there at the cost of their health and may even go there as a result of already existing disabilities. One thinks of the disabling musculoskeletal problems as related to alcoholism, for instance. It is clear that tuberculosis frequently develops while a man is living in Skid Row; it recurs with disquieting frequency if the patient who has been adequately treated elsewhere returns to a Skid Row way of life. This may come about through an alcohol-ism-to-malnutrition-to-tuberculosis cycle; or it may be through an alcoholism-to-peptic ulcer-to-gastrostomy-to-nutritional deficiency-to-tuberculosis cycle. In any case, the treatment of alcoholism is a key to the control and prevention of many of the health problems on Skid Row.

Anemia and Polluted Blood. Table 7-2 shows that about 24 percent of the alcoholic and 17 percent of the nonalcoholic patients were anemic. While the majority of patients in both groups undoubtedly suffered from malnutrition to a greater or lesser degree, thus contributing to the anemia, in the alcoholic an additional important factor was present. We were able to trace anemia directly to the sale of blood in 17 out of the 31 alcoholics; we believe that more than one-half of the alcoholics were anemic because they sold blood too often.

There is a common belief among Skid Row men in Philadelphia that the drinking of port wine will build up any loss suffered as a result of selling blood. Most of the men do not eat while drinking; those who do, eat little meat, either because of poor dentition or lack of funds. As a consequence, a man's hemoglobin may drop precipitously in less than two months. The net result is lowered resistance to other disease processes.

There comes a time when blood banks reject the prospective seller. In 1968–69 we undertook a special study of DRC/P clients who reported that they had sold blood. Over 40 percent had been rejected by blood banks at least once for iron deficiency; one major Philadelphia blood bank reported that iron deficiency was the basis for its rejection of over one-third of those who presented themselves as sellers. In our group, 106 men were blood sellers; of these, 83 lived in the Skid Row area and 23 said that they lived elsewhere. In almost all respects, differences in response between these two subpopulations were not statistically significant. Much that we have said about Skid Row men is characteristic of one large segment of those whose blood finds its way into commercial channels.

In the 1960s, excluding military demands, the commercial market for blood in Philadelphia expanded rapidly; for example, in 1959, commercial blood used by one major hospital was only 4 percent of the 7,678 units used, while in 1969, commercial blood was 37 percent of the 7,302 units used. Hospitals prefer blood from the American Red Cross donor program, from public volunteers, who come directly to the hospital, and from professional volunteers, who are well known to the hospitals and who have blood with special characteristics that are occasionally needed. The amount from professional donors is small. The proportion made available to one major hospital by the American Red Cross from volunteers rose from 27 percent in 1959 to 50 percent in 1968;

the proportion given to the hospital by the general public dropped from 69 percent in 1959 to 13 percent in 1969. (This is in sharp contrast to England and Wales, where almost all blood donors are volunteers from the community.[2])

Users of commercial blood face an additional risk, associated with the blood itself—the risk of contracting serum hepatitis from commercial blood is extremely high. It has been estimated that the incidence of serum hepatitis in patients receiving single transfusions from prison-Skid Row variety donors is 10 times that of volunteer donors and the risk of hepatitis is 10 to 25 times higher for commercial blood than for voluntary blood.[3] The term "prison-Skid Row" is hyphenated because it is common for commercial blood sales to be made by prisoners in Houses of Correction. In fact, there was a scandal in Philadelphia in 1969–70 when it was learned that a prison physician, who was a part of a university-related medical service team, proposed to set up a highly profitable blood bank to deal in prisoner's blood; the scandal arose because he was getting an insider contract rather than because the men were being underpaid or exploited.

Serum hepatitis is an infection of the liver that is largely transmitted through blood transfusions, the administration of drugs with inadequately sterilized needles, and similar procedures. The virus has an incubation period of from 50 to 160 days.[4] The condition is especially difficult to treat. It is estimated that from 1,500 to 3,000 deaths occur each year from hepatitis contracted as a result of blood transfusions.[5] Even if the patient recovers, he will suffer severe after-effects.

A less severe form—infectious hepatitis—has an incubation period of 15 to 40 days; this viral infection is easily transmitted through water supplies, infected clothing, and inadequately washed food supplies. It is estimated that about one person in ten in the world may carry in his blood an agent potentially able to cause one form of hepatitis in the recipient of a blood transfusion.[6]

Under these circumstances, a logical procedure would be to establish some system to screen blood before use. Such systems are now being developed, although one reported method for detecting the serum-hepatitis-associated antigen within two hours is apparently only 50 percent effective.[7] Nonetheless the Bureau of Biologics of the Food and Drug Administration has now notified 530 major blood banks in the United States that they must demonstrate an acceptable level of proficiency in screening for the hepatitis virus.[8] These major blood banks collect about 85 percent of the nation's supply of blood that is used for medical purposes. There are an additional 3,000 community and hospital-based facilities that the Bureau has moved to also bring under supervision on the basis of the 1962 Food, Drug, and Cosmetic Act. We believe that this procedure should be supplemented by the development of carefully restricted donor lists. The economics of blood make such restrictions difficult. Blood is a "high value added" commodity—that is, the "donor" sells his blood for a relatively low price, and the "consumer" receives the blood for a relatively high cost. In Philadelphia, the current payment to the commercial donor seems to range from $5 to $8 a pint-unit; about 87 percent of our blood-seller sample reported that they had been paid $5. (This included those who donated whole blood and those who apparently were involved in plasmopharesis, in which the red blood cells are extracted and returned to the body, with the plasma being retained by the laboratory.) It is estimated that it costs the Philadelphia Red Cross Blood Center $6.44 a unit of donated blood; costs are about 25 percent higher in Washington and about 100 percent higher in New York City. Costs in commercial blood centers would presumably be even higher. These costs, along with those of the hospital, are passed on to the patient, so that charges of $60 a unit are not uncommon.[9]

Under these circumstances, what explanation is there for the sharp rise in the demand for relatively expensive commercial blood rather than for relatively inexpensive replacement blood drawn from relatives, friends, and associates of the patient? Apparently there has been a trend away from volunteer (as distinct from Red Cross or commercial) blood for some time. One possible explanation is that the rise in demand for commercial blood is a latent consequence of Medicare legislation. According to this view, Medicare and its supplementary state legislation, which came into being in the period 1966–68, provided that the patient would pay for the first three units and that Medicare would pay the balance of the cost. Pennsycare (the supplementary Pennsylvania state legislation) was designed to cover the costs that Medicare did not cover, and thus paid for the first three units. It has been suggested that low-income patients do not feel under any pressure to solicit replacement blood because they are getting it at no cost. Medicare legislation may therefore tend to raise considerably the risk of serum hepatitis among the poor of our community.

Poverty leads people to sell blood, which is a valuable commodity that is often in short supply. As a consequence, the poor always have one last financial resource—themselves—and the community always has in this resource a potential supply of blood for emergencies. The situation is somewhat analogous to that in animal husbandry, with man himself as the source of life-giving substance. But people sell their blood reluctantly. Thus, almost 40 percent of the Skid Row blood-seller sample said that they did it only out of necessity; another one-third gave a variety of negative responses. Furthermore, such necessity is of relatively long standing. The median period when the men first began to sell their blood was seven to nine years before the interview; about 75 percent had sold blood within the preceding year. Nor has selling blood been a one-time thing for many of these men, for they reported a median of ten times that they had sold blood over the years.

Finally, their poverty was closely related to their use of alcohol. Two-thirds reported alcohol as a major chronic health problem. This report is consistent with their statements that they had a style of daily drinking; four-fifths of the blood sellers reported that they had gone on a binge or spree in the past; 87 percent reported that they took another drink to cure their hangover. They were long-time drinkers also, for two-thirds began their drinking before they were 20 years of age. Thus, these blood sellers fit the stereotype of the Skid Row alcoholic.

These men, while not happy about the situation, clearly recognize their bodies as a final resource. In this, they are similar to men of the classical era, who mortgaged their lives and fell into slavery when they defaulted on their debts. Since slavery is now formally illegal, blood selling has become a substitute. The fact that this supply of blood is partially polluted is a matter for serious concern in the urban communities which draw upon such a source.

The evidence of a large polluted blood supply brings home the gravity of the basic problem of alcoholism on the row in all its ramifications. Skid Row is a matter for concern not only for all urban communities; in view of its relation to public health, Skid Row is clearly a matter for immediate concern for the whole citizenry.

Dying on Skid Row

"Squeeze" is the commercial mixture of wax and alcohol called canned heat, which is manufactured and sold to be used in small camp stoves and under chafing dishes. In the most widely sold brand of canned heat, ethyl alcohol formerly comprised 75 percent of the mixture. To remove canned heat from the category of a beverage, the alcohol was denatured, with approximately 3.75 percent wood alcohol and the balance was ethyl alcohol and wax. However, since Skid Row men continued to drink canned heat even when the alcohol was denatured, in 1961 the manufacturer, with the encouragement of federal officials, adulterated the product still further with a bitter substance known as Bitrex. Indeed, the manufacturer added twice the amount considered intolerably repugnant to human taste. Skid Row men still continue to drink squeeze, usually mixing it with a cola carbonated beverage or with inexpensive wine. (They also sometimes drink bay rum, hair tonic, or paint thinner—"smoke"— either taking it straight or diluting it as they have done with squeeze.)

In our 1960 study of Skid Row, we included among our questions to a sample of

Part of the discussion of the squeeze incident draws upon a memorandum entitled, "Report on Skid Row Fatality Crisis," written by Luther Lassiter and Eugene S. McMelty to Dr. Joseph Spelman, Medical Examiner; we want to express our appreciation to them and to Stephen F. Barsky, Leonard Moore, and Pete Peterson.

377 respondents one on the extent of their drinking of nonbeverage alcohol in 1959. Of the respondents, 16 percent said they did not drink any alcohol, 66 percent said that they did not drink any nonbeverage alcohol; 12 percent said that they drank canned heat or some other nonbeverage alcohol. (The balance of the responses were "don't know," "refuse to answer," or "no answer.")

The differences between the effects of drinking ethyl (grain) alcohol and methyl (wood) alcohol are the following. Ethyl alcohol oxidizes in the liver into acetaldehyde, a substance which is more harmful to the body than alcohol itself. But the acetaldehyde is quickly carried into the blood and throughout the body, where it is oxidized into acetic acid, which is relatively harmless. The acetic acid is further oxidized to carbon dioxide and water. The human metabolism therefore rapidly reduces the harmful chemical properties of ethyl alcohol. In contrast, methyl alcohol oxidizes to formaldehyde, which, like acetaldehyde, is more harmful to the body than alcohol itself. Carried into the blood and throughout the body, formaldehyde oxidizes to formic acid. Formic acid oxidizes much more slowly in the body than acetic acid does, so that the concentration of formic acid persists. Formic acid damages the cells of the retina, causing irreversible blindness; it also causes cerebral edema, a swelling and irritation of the brain; it is toxic to the liver, resulting in rapid fatty degeneration; it causes acidosis, a condition in which the acid-base balance in the body is disrupted, quickly resulting in death. In some cases, death has followed the ingestion of as little as two-thirds of an ounce of methyl alcohol.

When mixtures of these two types of alcohol are drunk, the dangerous effects of methyl alcohol are lessened. Ethyl alcohol inhibits the oxidation of methyl alcohol to formic acid; thus it is possible for the body to ingest small quantities of methyl alcohol with relatively little damage. The ratio of relative safety for such a mixture is about one to ten—which may explain the continued use of squeeze on Skid Row.

During Christmas week in 1963, 33 persons died in Philadelphia's Skid Row from drinking squeeze. The Office of the Medical Examiner began an investigation of the source of the wood alcohol that had caused the deaths. The first hypothesis was that adulterated bootleg whiskey had been brought into the city during the holidays, but there was no evidence of this. Further investigation led to the discovery that those who had died—and some others, still alive—had been drinking an institutional variety of canned heat that was different from the usual type used by Skid Row men. In some cases it had been cut with water, and in others, with cheap wine; but the effects of the methyl alcohol had taken place anyway. This institutional type of canned heat was first put on the market in September 1963. The Skid Row residents were unfamiliar with the fact that it contained 54 percent methyl alcohol, in contrast to the 3.75 percent of the regular, noninstitutional type. Furthermore, the cans were inadequately labeled.

How did this new and dangerous substance, designed for hotels and caterers, get into the hands of Skid Row men? In the Philadelphia area, canned heat is handled by paper wholesalers as part of their line. The police found that only one wholesaler stocked the new product. Later court testimony revealed that the first shipment of 30 cases had arrived in Philadelphia early in September 1963. The wholesale price for the new product was lower than for the regular one. In December four cases were sold to a merchant in the Skid Row area. These were the only cases to reach retail outlets in Philadelphia. At his trial, the retail merchant was convicted of involuntary manslaughter and violation of the pharmacy act (which restricts the sale or distribution of poisonous substances) and sentenced to a term of from 4 to 12 years in prison.

The outcome of the Squeeze Incident in relation to the larger society was the arrest and conviction of the retail merchant. The dead were presumably avenged, and the living warned. But the selling of nonbeverage alcohol on Skid Row continued in other retail outlets after the heat was off, and so we have come to regard both the merchant and the dead as victims of circumstances. The outcome of the Squeeze Incident, as far as the Skid Row men were concerned, was not the giving up of nonbeverage alcohol but a transfer from canned heat to witch hazel. From the public point of view, this was a peculiarly expensive and inhumane way to reduce the risk of death from methyl alcohol in Skid Row.[1]

When a Skid Row man dies in a cubicle hotel or rooming house or when he is found dead in some alley or abandoned house, the police are usually called and the body is taken to the morgue of the Office of the Medical Examiner. (If the body is badly decomposed, the OME staff removes it with their own equipment.) The OME staff is then responsible for disposal of the body. First of all, they seek to establish the identity of the deceased; from this point on, a number of alternative possibilities exist. If identity is established, an effort is made to contact the next of kin for instructions. Many next of kin make burial arrangements with an undertaker in the metropolitan area. A large number of the men are covered by Social Security, which provides minimal burial expenses. Sometimes the next of kin will refuse to accept responsibility—usually for financial reasons, but occasionally family hostility and rejection continue to be manifest after the man is dead. Under these circumstances, the body will be released to a local undertaker—but to which of the many available and equally qualified? When the dead man is known in Skid Row, a "friend" (usually the hotel clerk or rooming house operator) is asked to recommend an undertaker. An examination of records suggests that there are a small number of preferred funeral directors. (We do not infer collusion on the part of the OME.) In those cases where the man remains unidentified, or his next of kin is unable or unwilling to provide burial, the OME turns the body over to a local funeral director selected by the city Finance Department from a list of those who have expressed an interest, with the city reserving the right (which it normally exercises) to refer all intact cadavers to the Anatomical Board. Philadelphia has six schools for training physicians, and there seems to be a continuous need for cadavers. Ultimately such bodies are cremated and buried in Mount Peace Cemetery.

The fact of death results in the same kind of problems and social organization for Skid Row men as it does for others. For some men, the outcome may be little different from what might have happened under more fortunate circumstances, although the mourners may be few. But we have strong reservations about funeral directors who are recommended by a hotel clerk "friend." Although we have no way of estimating the profitability of handling burial arrangements for Skid Row men in comparison with that of other funerals, we are sure that the Social Security allowance of $250 is extremely generous for the minimal attention that these bodies probably receive.[2] All in all, it seems that the Skid Row man may be exploited in death as well as life.

Bogue points out that while the general death rate in the United States in 1956 for white males was 10.8 deaths per thousand residents, it was 70.0 for white males on Chicago's Skid Row in 1957—more than six and a half times larger.[3] Our procedure differed from Bogue's, but we do agree that the death rate on Skid Row is extremely high. We checked the names of 2,333 client-respondents for a period from April 15, 1963, to April 15, 1970, using racial characteristics and addresses as further confirming evidence to minimize errors. In some cases, ex-Skid Row members of our staff viewed the bodies of the deceased at the request of the OME. In a search of the records of the OME and of the Division of Statistics and Research of the Department of Public Health, we found 203 (8.7 percent) cases of deceased men from our population. Thus, in the Philadelphia Skid Row the death rate seems to have been about 90 per thousand. When our data are analyzed with respect to race, we find that about 8 percent of the white client-respondents had died, in comparison with about 2.6 percent of the blacks. (The average death rate for nonwhite males in the United States from 1963 to 1967 was 11.2 per thousand.) We cannot infer trends from these data, but we can safely conclude that whites on Skid Row have a greater immediate likelihood of dying than do blacks.

We made an extensive comparison of the deceased and the survivors with respect to a number of variables: marital status, education, place of birth, father's occupation, length of residence on Skid Row, class identification before moving to Skid Row, work in the past 12 months, source of livelihood, cost of room, how long since visiting relatives, number of nights spent in a jail or police station in the past 30 days, patterns of drinking behavior, number of diseases and medical conditions, and recent hospital experience reported. In terms of chi square scores, we did not find statistically significant differences between deceased and survivors for these variables. The differences that did exist, while not systematic, seemed to suggest that the deceased more closely fit the stereotype of a Skid Row man grown old. This impression is consistent with our finding a significant statistical difference between the deceased and the survivors who had responded to the question of whether they were members of Skid Row or whether they were permanent or temporary residents of the area. Significantly more of those who had accepted Skid Row identification and had seen themselves as permanent residents were found among the dead. We will explore this variable in greater detail in a later chapter.

We differ with Bogue on the details of the cause of death. Table 8-1 presents a comparison of death rates for the United States, Chicago Skid Row, and selected census tracts in Philadelphia. Column 1 gives the death rates per one hundred thousand for males 30 years of age and older in the general population for

TABLE 8-1   A COMPARISON OF U.S. DEATH RATES FOR MALES 30 YEARS AND OLDER WITH SKID ROW DEATH RATES, SELECTED CAUSES, PER 100,000

	1[a]	2[b]	3[c]	4[d]
Tuberculosis (001–019)	11.1	446.7	309.0	192.0
Syphillis (020–029)	3.7	6.7	—	—
Cancer (140–205)	370.8	490.0	689.2	576.0
Diabetes (260)	31.9	20.0	35.7	—
Alcoholism or alcoholic psychosis (322, 307)	6.2	36.7	107.0	96.0
Vascular lesion affecting CNS (330–334)	208.4	320.0	261.4	192.0
Arteriosclerotic heart (429)	777.5	690.0	1022.0	576.0
Pneumonia (490–493)	59.3	440.0	261.4	224.0
Other diseases of the respiratory system (470–483 and 500–527)	69.1	36.7	—	—
Diseases of the digestive system (530–587)	91.5	63.3	392.2	160.0
Cirrhosis of the liver (581)	39.9	156.7	202.0	64.0
Diseases of the genito-urinary system (590–617)	35.5	63.3	107.0	64.0
Accidents, motor vehicle (E810–E835)	42.8	86.7	166.4	96.0
Accidental falls (E900–E904)	20.5	176.7	213.9	32.0
Accidental poisoning by alcohol (E880)	0.2[e]	—	285.2	192.0
Other accidents (E800–E802, E840–E962)	38.2	76.7	71.3	160.0
Suicide (E963, E970–979)	28.0	80.0	83.2	32.0
Homicide (E964, E980–E985)	13.9	30.0	47.5	192.0

[a] Vital Statistics of the United States, 1967, Vol. II—Mortality: Part A, Tables 1–25 and 6–2, and Part B, Table 7–5. The numbers after the causes of death are category numbers of the Seventh Revision of the International Lists, 1955.

[b] Chicago Skid Row, 1955–57 (Bogue, Skid Row, p. 228).

[c] Philadelphia Skid Row census tracts 10A, 12B, and 13B; white males 30 years old or older; data averaged for 1963–67.

[d] Philadelphia census tracts 12B, 13B, black males, 30 years or older; data averaged for 1963–67.

[e] Unpublished table, "Deaths from each cause by age, color, and sex, United States, 1967," courtesy of Robert A. Israel, Acting Chief, Mortality Statistics Branch, Division of Vital Statistics.

1967. We have deviated from Bogue in excluding the younger men from the general population statistic because they do not appreciably contribute to the Skid Row death rate. Column 2 gives data from Bogue which reports deaths in cubicle hotels from 1955 to 1957. Our data on the deceased client-respondents discussed above were taken from records of OME and of the Department of Public Health of Philadelphia[4]; we were not able to derive comparable rates with respect to cause of death. However, rates are available by census tract for selected diseases and by race for Philadelphia. Column 3 presents this material for census tracts 10A, 12A, and 13A (the three principal Skid Row tracts) for white males; column 4 is for tracts 12A and 13A for black males (most of the nonwhites in tract 10A were Chinese). While column 3 is almost exclusively Skid Row, column 4 includes both black Skid Row residents and blacks from the surrounding slum. Columns 3 and 4 are based on the average number of deaths for 1963 through 1967. We recognize that a variety of errors in these data do not make them exactly comparable. Nonetheless, the magnitudes of the rates can be relied upon.

A general comparison of column 1 with the Skid Row statistics indicates that Skid Row men die of vascular lesions that affect the central nervous system, of arteriosclerotic heart, and from many different kinds of accidents more often than do the general United States male population 30 years old and older. (But note the relatively high rate of deaths from miscellaneous accidents for black males in Philadelphia.) The rate of death from cancer in the general population is higher than that for Chicago's Skid Row and at about the same level for the Philadelphia white male Skid Row population. It seems likely that the differences between the Philadelphia and the Chicago rates are due to the somewhat younger median age of the Chicago Skid Row population. The extremely high Skid Row rate of death from tuberculosis looms frighteningly out of the table, and echoes our earlier medical discussion. Almost as grave are the high rate of death from pneumonia; and the rates of death from motor vehicle accidents, accidental falls, suicide (among white Skid Row men), and homicide (especially for blacks in Philadelphia) are notably higher than those for the entire United States.[5] The high Skid Row rates of death from these causes are more directly attributable to the environment in which men live rather than to organic conditions. Obviously Skid Row is a dangerous environment.

Significant diagnostic and recording problems related to the conditions connected with alcohol consumption make it difficult fully to believe statistics on death from alcoholism and alcoholic psychosis. Nonetheless, the Skid Row rates are high, although we cannot explain the differences between the Philadelphia and the Chicago data. Perhaps a better measure of death from the effects of alcohol is cirrhosis of the liver. There is little doubt that in cirrhosis death is caused by malfunction of the liver. And there is good reason to argue that the liver is damaged considerably by nutritional deficiencies which may or may not be associated with heavy drinking as well as by hepatitis. Nonetheless, Terris concludes, after examining national data with respect to long-term trends, age distribution, sex, race, urban-rural differences, social class and occupation, and national alcohol consumption, that "cirrhosis mortality is directly related to per capita consumption of alcohol from spirits and wine."[6] The relatively high rates in Chicago and among white Philadelphia Skid Row men for death from cirrhosis of the liver corroborate Terris's conclusion.

Finally, a word about "accidental poisoning by alcohol." We included figures for these deaths even though comparable data from Bogue are not available. The rates reflect in part the drinking of squeeze and other nonbeverage alcohols.

9

Identification with Skid Row

Early in our discussions of the 1960 survey, we were confronted with the question of a possible Skid Row community. Is there a distinctive Skid Row way of life? Is there a set of relationships and related practices that binds the Skid Row population together in some special way?[1] Much that we have already said suggests that there is a distinctive way of life among Skid Row men. However, as we have argued elsewhere, the differences between impoverished men who live in the Skid Row locality and impoverished people who live in other parts of our big cities have been exaggerated.[2]

IS SKID ROW A COMMUNITY?

Another approach argues that Skid Row men are a community not so much because they participate in Skid Row institutions but because they have "objective interests." They have been shaped by others into an oppressed and exploited class, whether they recognize it or not, and whether or not they have acted in concert to free themselves from their oppressors.[3] We believe that this approach has some basis, and have intimated as much in our discussions of the police and the local courts, housing, and employment. However, as a single approach, we reject it as too simple a basis for understanding the Skid Row vagrant, his way of life, and his problems. Furthermore, we do not believe that this approach alone will yield the useful recom-

129

mendations that we have labeled "alternatives to Skid Row." We can also approach the matter on the basis of attitudinal reports of the people concerned. Do the men consider themselves members of Skid Row?[4] Are they willing to identify themselves with a Skid Row community? From the point of view of policy formation and subsequent action, including relocation, we believe that it may make a difference if the men themselves identify with the neighborhood to the degree that they regard it as their own. In an era rife with the rhetoric of community self-determination, why should Skid Row men not have a voice in the determination of the future of their own community—if such a community is thought to exist in the eyes of the Skid Row men themselves? Without regard to any argument from the perspective of an emerging concept of the democratic ideology, can this form of social affiliation (if it is found to exist) be a basis for an alternative to vagrancy? In view of the tenuous nature of most of the other direct interpersonal relationships of these men, this might be a source of security and emotional warmth that they are not able to get in the larger community. It may be argued that some social roots are better than none.

There is good reason to argue in this subjective sense that there is a Skid Row community. In a sample of the 1960 study population, a little more than one-third said that they were members of Skid Row. At the time we asked them about their identification with Skid Row, we also asked them questions which called for some evaluation of their living conditions. Their answers may be closely related to whether or not a man identified himself as a member of Skid Row. Table 9-1 shows that the relationship between identification with Skid Row and whether the man said he liked or disliked the locality is not strong although it is positive. Many men who admitted to being Skid Rowers nonetheless dis-

TABLE 9-1   RELATIONSHIP BETWEEN IDENTIFICATION WITH SKID ROW AND ATTITUDE TOWARD NEIGHBORHOOD, BY PERCENTAGE

INDENTIFICATION WITH SKID ROW	ATTITUDE TOWARD NEIGHBORHOOD				TOTAL	
	Likes	Dislikes	Indifferent	DK, RA, NA	Percentage	N
Identifies	29.7	50.5	18.7	1.1	100	91
Does not identify	19.6	61.6	18.1	0.7	100	138
DK, RA, NA	14.3	0.0	14.3	71.4	100	7

liked the locality; in our subsequent presentation, we will give considerable attention to both Skid Row identification and a like/dislike attitude toward the locality, both as separate variables and taken together. The population included in the table is limited to those living within the boundaries of the 1963–64 demonstration study area. (Later tables omit the "indifferent" attitudes and the Don't Know, Refuse to Answer, and No Answer Categories for simplicity and because the number is so small.)

But I Like It Here

One might reasonably consider the man who identifies with Skid Row, likes the neighborhood, and wants to relocate to this or another Skid Row as the "pure" type Skid Rower in Wallace's terms.[5] However, they represent only one-twentieth of the total sample. This is a pitifully small proportion of the total Philadelphia Skid Row population who "ask for nothing more." Table 9-2

TABLE 9-2   RELATIONSHIP BETWEEN IDENTIFICATION, ATTITUDE TOWARD NEIGHBORHOOD AND RELOCATION PREFERENCE, BY PERCENTAGE

IDENTIFICATION	Neighborhood Attitude	RELOCATION PREFERENCE This Neighborhood	Another Neighborhood	TOTAL Percentage	N
Identifies with Skid Row	Likes neighborhood	46	54	100	26
	Dislikes neighborhood	9	91	100	46
Does not identify with Skid Row	Likes neighborhood	26	74	100	26
	Dislikes neighborhood	1	99	100	84

shows that almost half of this small proportion of the men who both identified with Skid Row and also liked the neighborhood preferred to be relocated in this neighborhood (that is, into this or another Skid Row locality). By comparison, almost none of those who rejected both Skid Row membership and the locality preferred relocation to a Skid Row neighborhood.

This is probably a more extreme position than Wallace would take, but it does suggest that we should take a systematic look at the issue. For example, we asked all the men what they liked (as well as disliked) about living in the neighborhood. The reason for liking the neighborhood was systematically different for those who liked it and for those who did not like it. Those who liked the neighborhood stressed that they liked it because they liked the people; those who did not like the neighborhood said that the best reason for living there was that it was cheap. This relationship holds for both those who identified and those who did not identify with Skid Row. Similar findings with respect to attitudes toward housing are shown in Table 9-3. Those who liked the neighbor-

TABLE 9-3   RELATIONSHIP BETWEEN ATTITUDES TO-
WARD THE NEIGHBORHOOD AND HOUSING
FOR DIFFERENT IDENTIFICATION GROUPS,
BY PERCENTAGE

| IDENTIFICATION | Neighborhood Attitude | ATTITUDE TOWARD HOUSING | | TOTAL | |
		Likes	Dislikes	Percentage	N*
Identifies with Skid Row	Likes neighborhood	88.5	11.5	100	26
	Dislikes neighborhood	39.5	60.5	100	43
Does not identify with Skid Row	Likes neighborhood	92.3	7.7	100	26
	Dislikes neighborhood	32.1	67.9	100	78

* 12 DK, RA, NA omitted from "Attitude Toward Housing."

hood emphasized that they liked the men with whom they lived; economy was emphasized by those who did not like the neighborhood. This was true for both those who said they were members of Skid Row and those who said they were not. Few of those in any grouping were willing to say that they liked the men in general.

It is evident that identification as a member of Skid Row and a like or dislike of the neighborhood were related to a limited extent. In many respects, a man's like or dislike of the area was more strongly related to what differentiates him as a "Skid Rower" than to his identification with a Skid Row community. Thus, identification was not clearly related to residence patterns or length of residence on Skid Row; but, for example, attitude toward the neighborhood was related to length of residence. The longer a man had lived in the neighborhood, the more likely he was to say that he liked the neighborhood. (We chose five years in Table 9-4,

TABLE 9-4   ATTITUDE TOWARD THE NEIGHBORHOOD AS A FUNCTION OF LENGTH OF RESIDENCE,** BY PERCENTAGE

| LENGTH OF RESIDENCE | ATTITUDE TOWARD NEIGHBORHOOD | | TOTAL | |
	Likes	Dislikes	Percentage	N*
Less than five yrs.	19	81	100	74
Greater than five yrs.	38	62	100	104

* 22 DK, RA, NA on residency question omitted.
** Chi square = 7.72, 1 df, p < .01.

because this was roughly the median length of residence.) This finding must be kept in perspective, however, for, even among those who had lived in the locality for five or more years, the majority said that they disliked it. Of course there are a number of reasons why the probability would increase with increased length of residence. Other kinds of persons—even other poor ones—would move if they did not like the locality. However, there are many pressures that bind a man to Skid Row.

Different kinds of housing also separated those who liked and those who disliked the neighborhood. About one-half of those who lived in rooms in comparison with about one-fourth of those who lived in dormitories or cubicles liked the neighborhood. Although the relationship is significant, there were only 21 men who lived in rooms. We also found that about two-fifths of those who liked the neighborhood paid for their room on a weekly basis or less frequently, in contrast to about one-fifth of those who paid for their room more frequently. This relationship is also significant (chi square = 7.11, 1 df, p < .01). Considered together, these three results are undoubtedly correlated. That is to say, those who lived on the Row longer were more likely to live in rooms and to have more stable rental arrangements. In addition, rooms are more desirable than cubicles or mission dormitories. Thus, those who had a more stable life style were more likely to report approval of the neighborhood and better housing. It seems reasonable to expect that as a man learned to live under Skid Row conditions and came to share the life style with others who had moved into the area before him, the probability would increase for him to say that he liked the neighborhood. The data also suggest that being a real Skid Rower seems to have less to do with willingness to accept the label of or awareness of the existence of the community than with living the life and the attitudes that support it.

SOCIAL RELATIONS AND COMMUNITY

One would expect different kinds of relationships within and outside Skid Row among those for whom the area is a community. One might expect, for instance, that identification (or lack of identification) with Skid Row might be correlated with the existence of familial ties in the broader community. Among our sample, about one-half of those who rejected the Skid Row community reported that they had relatives in other parts of Philadelphia, in comparison with about one-third of those who accepted membership in the community—a significant finding (chi square = 6.05, 1 df, p < .02). On the other hand, their reports of the number of times that they had seen their relatives did not seem to differentiate the identification or attitude groups.

Of course we are not sure why there are no differences in visiting behavior between the identifiers and the nonidentifiers. Tentatively we suggest that for men living on Skid Row relatives are much like gospel missions—they are reserves to be drawn upon in emergency. One might argue from what we have presented in earlier chapters that living the Skid Row life involves a perpetual emergency, but most Skid Row men have been cast out (or, depending on the point of view, have cast themselves out) from close family ties. What familial duties and obligations remain are likely to be residual. The men have lost almost all their social credit, and can draw upon it only in the most extreme circumstances. (Our concept of "social credit" is similar to Wiseman's "social margin."[6])

One might also expect that there would be a difference in the reported pattern of friendships inside and outside Skid Row. In this case, although there is no significant relationship, there is a tendency for those who identify with Skid Row and who like the neighborhood to report more—and also closer—friends in the neighborhood. For adults, friends may of course be pseudo-kins-men, and it is tempting to think along those lines. We do not have good interview data on the depth or quality of friendships on Skid Row—how long they have existed and how intimate they actually are. Stable relationships, indeed, do develop, as the biographies in Chapter 2 show. However, ex-Skid Row members of the center's staff tell us that these relationships are usually limited to: showing a man the ropes when he first arrives (where to find housing, where to get free food, where the employment agencies are); taking him to a hospital when he badly needs medical care (but ducking out before questions are asked); getting him to a place of shelter when he is drunk, so that he will not be picked up by the police or freeze to death; and giving him a drink when he has the shakes.

Finally, one might expect that sexual relationships would differ-entiate those who do and do not consider themselves members of the Skid Row community or those whose attitudes differ toward such a community. There is relatively little systematic information about the sexual relations of Skid Row men, and we certainly did not have time to explore the matter in the 1960 survey. But our data do show that Skid Row men range in their attitudes toward homosexuals from the most liberal to the most hostile in equal measures. One would expect greater homosexual contact in such a predominantly male society; the fact that one of the authors was propositioned while he was engaged in a participant observer study of a bar on Skid Row suggests that such contact is not uncommon. Of greater importance, however, are the heterosexual contacts of the men; the reported recency of last heterosexual contact, while not related to Skid Row identification, was significantly related to attitudes toward the neighborhood. A little more than one-third of those who liked the locality, in comparison with a little more than one-half of those who disliked the area, reported sexual inter-course with a woman within the past year (chi square $= 4.58$, 1 df, $p < .05$). It is of some possible interest that there were differ-ences in the nature of the relationship within which this sexual activity took place. One-third of those who identified with Skid Row, in comparison with about one-sixth of those who did not identify, reported that their most recent contact was with a prosti-tute (chi square $= 6.73$, 1 df, $p < .01$). We may conclude from these data that those who identify with the Row and who also like the neighborhood tend to have fewer ties of family and friendship within the larger community outside Skid Row. They have fewer heterosexual contacts, and those that they do establish tend to be more ephemeral than those established by those who do not identify with Skid Row.

CORRELATES OF COMMUNITY IDENTIFICATION

We believe that, taken together, the data on family, friendship, and sex support the belief that for some men there is a Skid Row community in Philadelphia; we believe that this is true also for all the large cities of the United States. What are the characteristics of the men who are probably the most committed to the Skid Row community? Black men tended not to identify with those who liked the Skid Row neighborhood, although there were a few who did consider themselves as members of Skid Row. Since the Philadelphia Skid Row abuts a black ghetto, we would expect the black respondents to identify more readily with the black community than with the Skid Row community. While the age of the men was not related to Skid Row identification, it was related to their attitudes toward the neighborhood. Table 9-5 shows that the rela-

TABLE 9-5   RELATIONSHIP AMONG SKID ROW IDENTIFI-
CATION, NEIGHBORHOOD ATTITUDE, AND
AGE, BY PERCENTAGE

SKID ROW IDENTIFICATION	Attitude Toward Neighborhood	AGE < Median	> Median	TOTAL Percentage	N*
	Likes	25.9	74.1	100	27
Identifies with Skid Row					
	Dislikes	66.7	33.3	100	45
	Likes	25.9	74.1	100	27
Does not identify with Skid Row					
	Dislikes	63.5	36.5	100	85

* 1 DK, RA, NA for age omitted.

tionship was marked, regardless of Skid Row identification; this was significant for those who did identify (chi square = 11.28, 1 df, p < .001) as well as for those who did not (chi square = 11.66, 1 df, p < .001)—that is, the older man was more likely to identify. Although Skid Row identification was not significantly related to the men's participation in the job market there was a tendency for those who did not identify to report having had a more prestigious job; there was a similar tendency for those who did identify with the Row (two-thirds, in comparison with about one-half). In addition, more than one-fifth of those who liked the neighborhood reported relatively high prestige jobs (prestige ranks 1–4) in contrast to more than two-fifths of those who did not like the neighborhood who reported such high prestige jobs as their longest jobs (chi square = 7.65, 1 df, p < .01). The evidence suggests that those who had been downwardly mobile in terms of occupational prestige class were more likely to reject the locality. Our data suggest also that those who did not identify with Skid Row were more active in the job market—i.e., more reported that they worked during the week just before the 1960 study, and more reported applying for work.

Throughout this book we have stressed the significance of alcohol for the men on Skid Row. Alcohol is the cement of Skid Row relationships, even though it may also be the solvent of other relationships in the larger community. This is Wallace's position when he argues that Skid Row has a deviant status system which stands the normal criteria for prestige and respect on their heads through the centrality of alcohol.[7] Consequently, one would suspect that alcohol would be an important characteristic and criterion for differentiating life styles in the Skid Row locality between those who belonged to or enjoyed the Skid Row community and those who do not. We found that about nine-tenths of the spree drinkers disliked the neighborhood whether they identified with it or not. Table 9-6 shows, however, that there was a significant difference among heavy drinkers (who reported "daily and off and on during the week"). Table 9-6 also shows that for those who identified with Skid Row, the spree drinkers disliked the neighborhood more than the other heavy drinkers did; the same pattern holds also for those who did not identify with the Row. (chi square = 11.78, 1 df, p < .001; and chi square = 5.53, 1 df, p < .02.) Furthermore, those who disliked the neighborhood were more likely to report that they had used nonbeverage alcohol, such as squeeze; this finding is also true for those who did identify with Skid Row, although the relationships are not significant.

Along with the fact that those who disliked the neighborhood tended to be spree drinkers were a number of correlated characteristics. Those who disliked the neighborhood tended to report that they had been drunk more often during the past year and that

TABLE 9-6   RELATIONSHIP OF DRINKING PATTERN TO
                   NEIGHBORHOOD ATTITUDES FOR THOSE WHO
                   DO AND DO NOT IDENTIFY WITH SKID ROW,
                   BY PERCENTAGE

IDENTIFICATION	Attitude Toward Neighborhood	DRINKING PATTERN Spree Drinker	Daily and Off and On in Week	TOTAL Percentage	N*
Identifies with Skid Row	Likes	13	87	100	15
	Dislikes	70	30	100	37
Does not identify with Skid Row	Likes	29	71	100	14
	Dislikes	69	31	100	42

* Others with different drinking patterns and indeterminate patterns omitted.

they had had more serious symptoms from drinking than did those who liked the neighborhood. Of those who identified with Skid Row and liked the neighborhood, only one-third reported serious symptoms from drinking; of those who disliked the neighborhood, more than one-half so reported—significant relationship (chi square = 4.02, 1 df, p < .05). In addition, reported convictions for a felony or misdemeanor were consistent with the reported drinking style. Thus, more than one-half of those who liked the neighborhood, in comparison with over one-third of those who did not like the neighborhood, said that they had never been convicted. This relationship is again statistically significant (chi square = 5.42, 1 df, p < .02), and is more striking for those who did not identify with Skid Row than for those who did.

In general, we may conclude that those who do not like the neighborhood are in greater personal and social difficulty because of their drinking. At the same time, they show some recognition of this by their activity in Alcoholics Anonymous. Whereas the report of attendance at AA meetings does not significantly differentiate those who do and who do not like the neighborhood, they are consistent with the data we have already reported, since those who report that they do not like the neighborhood report more frequent attendance at AA meetings.

Although the numbers in Table 9-6 are small, they are representative, as much as we can determine, of the men living in an East coast Skid Row. They are at least suggestive that there are a significant number of men who are driven to Skid Row by their spree drinking and who find it hard to take; whereas there are others, approximating blood-level drinkers, who have adapted to a neighborhood which suits their life style. These latter epitomize Wallace's characterization of the "completely acculturated" Skid Row man.[8] Differences in life style, attitude toward the locality, drinking behavior, and law enforcement experience should have different motivational and public health consequences for relocation and rehabilitation.

Our initial approach to the existence of a Skid Row community has been different from that of other recent studies. Bogue emphasized the isolation of the men on Skid Row, and ignored the possibility of a Skid Row community; Bahr gave his attention to homelessness and "disaffiliation" rather than to the possible dimensions of a Skid Row community.[9] On the other hand, Spradley argued: "There is a 'brotherhood of the road' in this culture which is often entered while in jail so that the 'urban nomad' learns to live as a part of 'A World of Strangers Who Are Friends.' "[10] Wallace also seemed to adopt the position that there is a community on Skid Row and, furthermore, that the detection of this community depends on one's becoming a part of it. Thus, one must become an "insider" before one can appreciate the extent of the community or the values held within it.[11] Wallace presents a warm and sympathetic approach to Skid Row as a way of life, in which "Beggars, law evaders, and alcoholics drifted into homelessness; and some finding it an attractive and natural way of life simply stayed there."[12] Wallace believed that he had been accepted as an insider and that he could therefore speak for the Skid Row men. He commented on the historical changes that had taken place over the years, and then went on to say:

In only one major respect is the Skid Rower still true to traditional form. Throughout the years he has remained both destitute and single. For the most part he claims no kith or kin. Outcast by all accepted standards, degraded and facing an ever-widening gulf between himself and society, the Skid Rower has nevertheless managed to survive for almost a century. More than that, he has managed to evolve on his own behalf a community of sorts, a community which shelters, clothes, and feeds him, and even keeps him supplied with drink. He asks for nothing more.[13]

We cannot accept this viewpoint. Skid Row men can—and do—ask for something more. The issue is, rather, that they have few expectations of getting it.

Part III

Alternatives to Skid Row

10 Experiments in Rehabilitation Procedures

We believe that the larger community can provide the basis for a better life for Skid Row men—decent, safe, and sanitary housing; adequate and nutritious food; ready access to health services, especially during periods of personal crisis. Furthermore, we believe that these are elements of a national policy that is already enacted by the Congress and that is applicable to all citizens.

Our problem has been to develop alternatives that are acceptable to the men themselves, and to try to make these alternatives feasible in terms of the resources of the larger community. The center has been oriented to help whoever will accept help. The limiting factors have been the size of the staff, and whether the men wanted to continue with us. We have deliberately created another resource for these Skid Row men, all the while hoping that we could encourage and assist them to leave the debasement of the Skid Row style of life. In so doing, we have not thought that we have a panacea for all their problems. We see our efforts in terms of a theory of optimal goal discrepancy in which programs must be de-

Dr. Irving Jacks coauthored this section. We wish to express our appreciation also to the following who helped in the administration or the collection and analysis of the data: Mr. Edward J. Hendrick, Dr. Francis Hoffman, Dr. Victor LoCicero, Dr. Herman Niebuhr, Dr. Alfred Wood, Dr. Donald Cole, Dr. Ali Aydin, Dr. Sheila Scott, and James Rooney.

143

veloped that are not widely divergent from the individual's present level of achievement and geared to provide wider opportunities for achievement through an appropriate sequence of small intermediate steps.

We have made a series of efforts over the years to develop alternative procedures—that is, to provide alternatives to vagrancy on an experimental basis. It is the task of this section to discuss these efforts and to provide an assessment of them.

GROUP THERAPY IN THE HOUSE OF CORRECTION

Our first effort actually predates the establishment of the Diagnostic and Rehabilitation Center/Philadelphia, having been conducted from 1960 to 1962 under the auspices of the Department of Psychiatry of the Temple University Medical School and of the Department of Public Welfare (of which the Philadelphia House of Correction is an administrative unit). The focus of assessment and group therapy was the alcoholic offender.

Relatively few studies of Skid Row men or of alcoholics have included systematic assessment of their personalities. In general, these studies reported a Minnesota Multiphasic Personality Inventory (MMPI) profile which was high on the Psychopathic Deviancy (Pd) scale and also high on the Depression (D) scale, although some interpretations of these facts have differed radically.[1] In addition, we know of no systematic studies of therapy with Skid Row alcoholics which have included adequate controls or described the differential effectiveness of therapy with members of this population who possess different personality characteristics. (It would somewhat simplify the problem if psychotherapy could be shown to have differential effectiveness with men of different personality characteristics.) Wallerstein describes a study of four different therapeutic approaches to the problem of alcoholism and demonstrates the differential effectiveness of these therapies with different diagnostic categories.[2] However, the characteristics of his population differed from the present one, and replication of the personality assessment procedures would be difficult because these relied on clinical diagnosis. Several studies demonstrate that alcoholics may be induced to enter therapy by systematic efforts to establish relationships at general hospital clinics and prisons, but they do not demonstrate the efficacy of therapy once contact had been established.[3]

The Treatment Program

Following acceptance into group therapy, the inmate was reinterviewed by the group therapist-psychiatrist in order to prepare him for the group experience, to answer additional questions, or to allay doubts and anxieties which might have arisen during the assessment procedure. Following this initial, individual, therapeutic contact, each inmate joined a group, with whom he met once or twice a week for a 90 minute session throughout the remainder of his sentence, which usually ran for 10 to 12 weeks.

The group therapy procedures were problem-centered, being neither completely nondirective nor completely directive in general orientation.[4] Often the therapists selected one critical problem for an individual inmate and concentrated on exploring that problem and its ramifications for the remainder of his sentence. This procedure was adopted partly because of the limited time available and partly because it had the advantage of concreteness and the possibility of giving the inmate feelings of accomplishment.

During the final weeks of group therapy, social service interviews were held with each participant. These interviews were oriented toward solving whatever problems the inmate would face upon his return to the community. Usually this involved setting up interviews with the Pennsylvania State Employment Service and the Department of Public Assistance. Also, appropriate living quarters were located and clothing provided when possible and necessary. The man was urged to continue with group therapy provided for him at Temple University Medical Center. Counseling and social service were available to the man at all times after he had been released. Outpatient facilities at Temple Hospital were also available for emergency service; for instance, drug therapy was frequently instituted when appropriate.

Selection of Samples

Potential candidates were selected from the files of the House of Correction on the basis of several criteria. Heavy alcohol drinking must be a significant factor in his style of life. He must have been sentenced to prison for at least three months and have been due for discharge at the end of the following three-month period; this limitation was imposed to guarantee that the man would have about three months in group therapy while in prison. He must be under 60 years of age.

All potential candidates were given an intelligence test (Otis) and a personality test (MMPI). The long form of the MMPI was administered to most candidates, but occasionally the short form was used when the inmate did not finish all items in the allotted time.

A personal interview was then conducted with all candidates with an Otis IQ of 60 or higher. A few men refused to participate in the program, but the number was small because the program had been carefully explained to all the men, and because they were excused from their regular work assignments during the therapy period but were nonetheless paid the regular hourly rate for their participation. The usual reason for refusal was a denial of alcoholism. The interviewer also collected further information about the candidate with respect to degree of alcoholism, medical history, psychiatric problems, prison record, work record, education, family involvement, and prospective location of residence following release.

Following the interview, the case histories of all candidates were reviewed and a determination was made regarding appropriateness for inclusion into the group therapy program. All men were excluded from further consideration who denied problem drinking or who obviously had no such problem, who were overtly psychotic, who had recent and dangerous criminal records, or who did not plan to live in the Philadelphia area following release. No men were excluded from consideration because of a poor prognosis based on the severity of their alcoholism.

All who had previously passed the selection criteria were randomly assigned to therapy or control groups. Consequently, only those candidates judged appropriate for the group therapy were included in the therapy or control groups, and this final assignment was made on the basis of chance.

Of all the men in the House of Correction with sentences terminating at appropriate times, and who could have been selected at any given time for the therapy program, between 10 and 20 percent met the criteria as outlined above. Most of those who were rejected for therapy were rejected because they did not have a significant problem with alcohol. A sizable minority were rejected because of age or because verbal and conceptual ability was not judged appropriate for group therapy. The Otis test was the primary criterion used, although men were occasionally permitted to join a therapy group despite a low score if we believed that their score was spuriously low by reason of illiteracy or poor eyesight.

Characteristics of the Samples

Age. The ages of the men in the therapy and control groups were similar (therapy, 44.5 years; control 46 years). The median for the total sample was 45 years. This may be compared with the median age of 49 years for spree drinkers in the Philadelphia Skid Row in 1960.

White and Black. Whites comprised about 86 percent of the therapy groups and about 89 percent of the control groups. These proportions were similar to the proportions of whites and blacks in the Skid Row population at the time.

Marital Status. About 21 percent of each type of group were married and living with their wives immediately before they were sentenced to the House of Correction. In addition, there were about 23 percent who were "separated" from their wives and an additional 21 percent who were divorced. These proportions closely approximated those found for spree drinkers in the 1960 Skid Row study, in which 24 percent were divorced and 21 percent were separated.

Education. The median number of years in school was 10.5 years for the therapy group and 10.4 years for the control group. These values are higher than the median of 9.4 years for the spree drinker in Philadelphia's Skid Row in 1960. This discrepancy is probably explained by the selection procedure, which includes the age and IQ of the inmate among the criteria for selection.

Prior Convictions. Table 10-1 shows that the number of prior convictions was similar except for those who had had no prior convictions or those who reported one previous conviction. Despite this discrepancy, for which we have no explanation, the groups did not differ significantly with respect to the median number of convictions.

Otis Intelligence Test. The difference between the median intelligence scores for the two samples was not significant (therapy group, median IQ 86; control group, IQ 83). The absolute value of these scores should not be taken too seriously; the scores of early therapy groups were checked by individual testing with the Wechsler Adult Intelligence Scale, and the Otis IQ scores signifi-

TABLE 10-1   NUMBER OF PRIOR CONVICTIONS FOR THER-
                APY AND CONTROL SAMPLES

Number of Convictions	Therapy	Control	Combined Samples
0	21.3%	39.2%	26.8%
1	23.3	8.7	18.8
2	10.7	13.0	11.4
3	10.7	10.9	10.7
4	8.7	8.7	8.7
5–9	14.6	10.9	13.4
10–19	6.8	4.3	6.1
20–29	3.9	0.0	2.7
No answer	0.0	4.3	1.3
Total percentage	100.0	100.0	99.9
N	103	46	149

Therapy Sample Median = 2.5.
Control Sample Median = 2.0.
Combined Sample Median = 2.3.

cantly underestimate the Wechsler IQ's. The average discrepancy
was about ten IQ points.

MMPI Code Distribution and Mean Scores. Table 10–2 shows
that the distribution of high points for the therapy and control

TABLE 10-2   COMPARISON OF DISTRIBUTION OF HIGH
                POINTS IN THE MMPI CODES OF HOUSE OF
                CORRECTION SAMPLES WITH BRANTNER SAL-
                VATION ARMY AND "NORMAL" MINNEAPOLIS
                MALE ADULT SAMPLES

MMPI Code	HC Therapy Sample	HC Control Sample	HC Total Sample	Brantner Salvation Army Sample[a]	Brantner "Normal" Minn. Sample[a]
?	3.3	0.0	2.3	2.8	3.9
—	0.0	0.0	0.0	1.0	23.6
1	4.9	1.4	3.9	6.4	10.6
2	15.2	8.3	13.3	13.1	6.7
3	0.5	4.2	1.6	1.3	7.1
4	54.3	65.2	57.4	46.6	11.6
6	3.8	5.6	4.3	4.6	7.9
7	4.9	0.0	3.5	6.1	6.8
8	1.1	2.8	1.6	5.9	5.2
9	12.0	12.5	12.1	12.3	17.6
Percentage	100.0	100.0	100.0	100.0	101.0
N	94	42	136	296	258

[a] J. B. Brantner. *Homeless Men, A Psychological and Medical Survey*, Ph.D. Thesis,
University of Minnesota, 1958, Table XL, p. 159.

samples was similar. As shown in Table 10-3, the percentage distribution of high point scores was similar to each other and remarkably similar to the Minneapolis Salvation Army sample. Table 10-3 shows that the mean scale scores for the therapy and control groups and the combined samples were obviously and significantly raised above the mean of 50, which is the norm for the standardization sample. The most outstanding is scale 4 (Pd), in which the mean for our total sample was more than two standard deviations above the mean for the normative population. This scale was developed to aid in the clinical diagnosis of the psychopathic or sociopathic personality and describes a style of life that includes "social maladjustment." It is not possible to determine from the scale alone whether it indicates antisocial or merely asocial tendencies. However, if, as is generally believed, this scale has importance for therapeutic prognosis, then this fact is of special consequence because, as Brantner warns, "they [Skid Row men] are frequently interesting and charming people, but they are generally incapable of forming durable, satisfying, or, in a psychotherapeutic sense, useful personal relations."[5]

TABLE 10-3   COMPARISON OF MEANS ON MMPI SCORES FOR HOUSE OF CORRECTION SAMPLES AND OTHER STUDIES

MMPI Code	HC Therapy Sample	HC Control Sample	HC Total Sample	Hewitt Sample[a]	Button Sample[a]	Brantner Sample[b]	Hill Alcoholic Sample[a]	Hill Addict Sample[a]
L	4	4	4	—	5	4	4	4
F	6	7	6	—	5	6	7	6
K	14	14	14	—	15	12	13	14
1	56	54	55	52	57	55	58	61
2	64	65	64	60	58	62	66	68
3	57	58	57	57	56	58	59	60
4	73	73	73	67	69	70	69	74
5	56	57	57	56	57	54	55	58
6	56	59	57	59	53	53	59	57
7	58	55	57	57	56	60	59	60
8	56	56	56	57	53	60	58	60
9	61	60	61	—	55	59	58	62
0	52	52	52	—	51	53	—	—
N	94	42	136	37	64	296	184	192

Note: All scale scores have been converted to nearest whole T score value, L, F, and K scores have been converted to nearest whole raw score when necessary.
a See note 1 to this chapter, p. 285.
b J. P. Brantner. *Homeless Men*, Table XXXIX, p. 148.

The next highest profile peak, and the second largest percentages of high point scores, was that of scale 2, the depression scale. In conjunction with a high Pd scale, this is generally taken to be an indication of the sociopath's reaction to an unfortunate set of circumstances in which he finds himself. Certainly most of the men were resentful of their incarceration, and might be expected to reflect this resentment with depressive concern on such a test as the MMPI.

There is a third elevation on scale 9, the hypomania scale. Brantner believes that a comparable peak in his own sample was consonant with the elevation on scale 4 and contributed no new information about this group.[6] In our own data, a peak on scale 9 was almost always accompanied by a secondary high on scale 4.

Table 10-3 also gives the mean profiles and high point distribution of our sample in comparison with those obtained in other studies we have already cited. There is a remarkable similarity, amounting to almost an identity from scales 1 through 5 and patterns of similarity in scales 6 through 9 that are all within the same range although not so similar. A comparison with Brantner's "normal" adult Minneapolis population in Table 10-2 suggests that most of the variance is accounted for by a gross measure of general pathology (MMPI code, —) and on scale 4, the measure of psychopathic or sociopathic personality.

Post-therapy Criterion of Success

Our criterion of success or failure was whether the man was arrested or convicted within a two-year period after leaving the House of Correction. The rate of recidivism and arrest presents problems. This rate is a function of factors which vary from time to time. For instance, if the local police and judges zealously clean up the neighborhood during conventions or other special occasions, a man's chances of rearrest will rise. On the other hand, those men who leave the city and state for hotel and farm jobs during the summer thereby reduce their probability of arrest. Nonetheless, the rate of recidivism and arrest does have the distinct advantage of being objective. Likewise, a report of arrest and conviction of all members of both groups is more easily obtained than interviews with the men themselves, since they are notoriously mobile. The Philadelphia prison system has a record of all returns or new admissions to any of the three city prisons as well as reports from the FBI on all those incarcerated in cooperating institutions; our data are taken from these records.

Results of the Therapy Program

Table 10-4 presents the means and percentages of men arrested and convicted from both the therapy and control samples for two years before and after the period of imprisonment during which the therapy took place. Our analysis in Table 10-4 is limited to the first two therapy groups (Therapy I and II, Control I and II). These are the groups for which it was possible to allow a sufficient post-treatment time to elapse for results to be meaningful. Table 10-4 shows that the post-therapy mean of arrests-convictions for the combined therapy groups was lower than for a comparable period before the therapy period. Also, it may be seen that the mean is lower for the therapy groups than for the combined control groups after the therapy period, even though the therapy groups had a slightly higher mean before the critical period. These differences suggest positive effects of therapy. Since neither difference is statistically significant, we cannot conclude from these data that group therapy had a consistent, pervasive influence on the men's immediate rehabilitation as a group. Table 10-4 further shows that the reduction in percentage for the therapy groups is almost exactly paralleled by that for the control groups. This reduction is not statistically significant in either group. The fact that both groups showed a comparable reduction in percentage underlines the importance of the use of appropriate control groups in the

TABLE 10-4   RECORD OF ARREST AND CONVICTION FOR THE THERAPY AND CONTROL SAMPLES FOR TWO YEARS PRIOR TO AND FOLLOWING THE THERAPY PERIOD

GROUP	N			PERCENTAGE	
		Mean Yearly Prior to Therapy Period	Mean Following Therapy Period	Prior to Therapy Period	Following Therapy Period
Therapy I	14	.82	.57	64	57
Therapy II	13	1.08	.75	92	54
Control I	6	.92	1.42	67	67
Control II	8	.86	.50	75	50
Total Therapy	27	.95	.74	78	56
Total Control	14	.89	.89	71	57

assessment of therapy in this kind of study and when using such criteria of success.

We do not conclude from these data that the group therapy program will have no effect with Skid Row men. The recidivism measure was collected for a relatively short time, and is limited with respect to changes in life style in other ways. Nonetheless, considering Spradley's discussion of the significance of the jail experience, it seems questionable that group therapy alone can be effective, and it seems doubly doubtful that it can be successful if it is conducted only in a jail context.[7]

Can the MMPI Predict Recidivism?

Our study had a twofold purpose. In the first place, it was designed to assess the effectiveness of the group therapy program undertaken in the House of Correction. In the second place, it was designed to determine whether recidivism may be predicted with customary biographical data or with new personality measures. To explore this problem, a rating was developed for each individual based on his scale 4 score on the MMPI. The following rules were established: a rating of 5 was given if scale 4 was the highest and was equal to a T score of 70 or more; a rating of 4 was given if scale 4 was not highest but was equal to a T score of 70 or more; a rating of 3 was given if scale 4 was highest and there was a T score between 54 and 70; a rating of 2 was given if scale 4 was not highest and it fell between a T score of 54 and 70; a rating of 1 was given if scale 4 was highest and fell between a T score of 45 and 55; a rating of 0 was given if scale 4 was not highest and it fell between the T scores of 45 and 55. (There were no ratings of 1 or 0 for the groups in the therapy program.)

Ratings of scale 4 (Pd) yield consistent and significant predictions of post-therapy arrest and conviction. Table 10-5 compares the number of men of the therapy groups I and II rated high and low on scale 4 who were arrested or convicted following the therapy period. The trend of the data is clear: those who were rated high on scale 4 were arrested or convicted significantly more often than those who were rated low. Table 10-5 indicates also that the same trend holds for those in the control groups. If the data from both groups are combined, the trend is highly significant (p < .001). Rank order correlations indicate that the magnitude of the relationship between rated degree of psychopathic traits

TABLE 10-5   COMPARISON OF THE NUMBER OF MEN RATED HIGH AND LOW ON SCALE 4, ARRESTED OR CONVICTED FOLLOWING THE THERAPY PERIOD FOR THERAPY GROUPS I AND II AND CONTROL GROUPS I AND II

RATING ON MMPI SCALE 4	ARRESTED OR CONVICTED	NOT ARRESTED OR CONVICTED	TOTAL
Therapy groups			
High	8	1	9
Low	4	10	14
p < .01, Fisher's exact test			
Control groups			
High	5	0	5
Low	3	3	6
P ≅ .12, Fisher's exact test			

and the incidence of arrest and convictions for the therapy and control groups after the therapy period is moderate, consistent, and statistically significant (therapy groups I and II, rho = .58; control groups I and II, rho = .56).

The question remains whether those who are relatively low in psychopathic traits do relatively better following therapy than those who are relatively high on this scale. Table 10-6 gives the pertinent data. It is apparent that those who are low in rated psychopathy in the therapy sample do relatively better after therapy than those who are rated high on this trait. However, it may be seen that the control group men show the same trend; consequently, it may not be concluded on the basis of the present data that there is an interaction between therapy and rated psychopathy. Never-

TABLE 10-6   PERCENTAGE ARRESTED AND CONVICTED PRIOR TO AND FOLLOWING THE THERAPY PERIOD FOR THOSE HIGH AND LOW ON SCALE 4 IN THE THERAPY AND CONTROL SAMPLES

RATING ON MMPI SCALE 4	THERAPY SAMPLE			CONTROL SAMPLE		
		PRIOR TO THERAPY PERIOD	FOLLOWING THERAPY PERIOD		PRIOR TO THERAPY PERIOD	FOLLOWING THERAPY PERIOD
	N	Percentage	Percentage	N	Percentage	Percentage
High	9	89	89	5	80	100
Low	14	62	23	6	75	50

theless, there is a possible interaction, which will need to be examined in further research.

Our study of arrests and convictions during the two-year follow-up showed no sizable difference in recidivism between treated and untreated groups. However, those offenders rated highest on sociopathic traits, according to the MMPI from both the therapy and control groups, were arrested and convicted more frequently than those rated low on these traits. In addition, those offenders rated low on sociopathic traits tended to respond differently to group therapy than those rated high on sociopathic traits.

ASSESSMENT OF A GENERAL COUNSELING PROGRAM

Chapter 1 describes the activities of the anchor counselor as the coordinator of services for the Skid Row men who came to the center; this included X-ray screening for tuberculosis, medical examinations and referral, psychiatric screening, and liaison to the Department of Public Assistance and to the Pennsylvania State Employment Service. As a part of the entire process, those men who agreed to be relocated from the Skid Row area were referred to a representative of the Centralized Relocation Bureau (CRB), which had a staff group working in the center and which was charged with the responsibility of assisting the man in making his new housing arrangements. Finally, as a part of the total program, we developed, during the 1963–64 period and under the Section 314 demonstration grant, a series of follow-up procedures: What became of the men? Were the services of the center effective? Could we develop a procedure which would reduce the high dropout rate from the program? We later used these procedures in the NIMH-sponsored study, which did not involve the relocation services of CRB but did use the same anchor counselor casework model as its central feature. We now discuss data from the NIMH study.

Follow-up Procedures

Follow-up work with Skid Row men is extremely difficult and time-consuming. Success depends a good deal upon the nature of the relationship that has been developed not only between the man and the agency but between the follow-up worker and the Skid Row population conceived as a community. It also depends upon the circumstances under which relocation has taken place—

if it has taken place at all. Thus, if a friendly, helping, and trusting relationship was achieved, and if the man went to an alcohol treatment program within an institution, then the interview was relatively routine; on the other hand, if the relationship was relatively superficial, and if the man moved from Skid Row to an isolated rooming house, then follow-up interviews were often difficult or impossible to complete.

The following is a composite of procedures which have been used: The caseworkers were supposed to notify the follow-up staff at the time that the case was closed—either the man broke contact with the agency or he went to a hospital or treatment center. (It was necessary to review the files regularly to take up the slack.) Just before the first follow-up interview, three months after the case was closed, the counselors were asked if they had any additional information on the man's current address. If indications were that he had moved, a certified letter was sent to the last known address asking him to come to the center or to let the center know if he could be interviewed where he now lived. If the letter was returned as undeliverable, the man's name was forwarded to the Department of Public Assistance (many were receiving Public Assistance aid through the intercession of the center), and a call was made to the House of Correction. These were the two most readily available additional sources of information. The constant circulation of men in and out of the center and into several neighborhoods might have been expected to yield some leads. The most effective person in getting this sort of information from clients of the center was a mature caseworker who had had some years of experience with the men and who had taken a direct personal interest in them.

The follow-up worker went out to seek an interview. Some of these workers were thoroughly familiar with Skid Row because they had lived in the area in the past. The interviewers made three or four attempts to find a man at his last known address. They would make inquiries of friends, former center clients, and other acquaintances in and around Skid Row, call on AA groups, and so forth. The effort to secure interviews took place several times during the day; however, experience had suggested that a good time was after six o'clock in the evening. Finding a man required some ingenuity, however, for dwelling entrances were sometimes on a side alley or reached from a basement. Then too, a client might not always answer his door, even though it was known from his neighbors that he was in his room; the hotel clerk might not give the necessary information (unless he was offered a small bribe); protective neighbors might deny that they knew the client (they might know him only by another name or nickname). Given these conditions, the cooperation of landlords and landladies certainly needed to be secured.

A monthly lost list was circulated to such agencies as Department of Public Assistance, Social Security Administration, Veterans Administration Domiciliary, House of Correction, and the largest of the gospel missions (when we were on good terms with them). From time to time, other center staff workers who were familiar with the local bars, restaurants, cubicle hotels, and rooming houses would circulate through the Row in search of "lost" men. From time to time, checks were made with the Office of the Medical Examiner to see if the man had died. Furthermore, all counselors at the center were notified through the lost list; men do come back to see these counselors, and some even have written letters of greetings and appreciation from other cities. Contrary to procedures used in St. Louis, there was no tie-in with the Police Department.[8]

Follow-up interviewing took place in the center and on the street. Men often returned to the center some months after they had left the effective caseload (cases were considered inactive—not closed—during this period of the center's work).

Follow-up Success and Failure

Not all men who came to the center and who received some service there were Skid Row men in the sense that they actually lived on Skid Row. Members of the staff came to recognize that there were clients who in almost every respect were like Skid Row men—drinking habits, marital status, age, occupational activity, and residential instability—but who did not say they lived in the stereotypically defined Skid Row locality. Rather, they lived in one of the other deteriorated or deteriorating neighborhoods of the city. We therefore coded them "Skid Row-like men." There were also a number of men who did not live in the Skid Row locality and who were not Skid Row-like; these were coded simply as "non-Skid Row men."

The follow-up program was designed to interview Skid Row men, non-Skid Row men, and Skid Row-like men at three different times: three months, one year, and two years after the man had moved out of the Skid Row area or when the case was closed. We will concentrate on the one-year follow-up of the Skid Row men, although some additional comparative statistics for the non-Skid Row men will also be presented. For example, in Table 10-7, we will give most of our attention to Skid Row men who only received a one-year follow-up interview (N = 133) and those who received both the one-year and the two-year interviews (N = 160).

Table 10-7 shows that a little less than two-fifths of the Skid Row men and a little less than one-half of the non-Skid Row men

TABLE 10-7 FOLLOW-UP CONTACTS

TIME OF CONTACT	SKID ROW MEN Number of		NON-SKID ROW MEN Number of	
	Men Contacted	Percentage	Men Contacted	Percentage
Never contacted	225	37.3	203	47.5
One year only	133	22.1	63	14.8
Two years only	84	14.0	92	21.5
Both one and two years	160	26.6	69	16.2
Total Eligible for Contact	602*	100.0	427*	100.0

* Total eligible for contact does not include those who died before contact appointment (N = 48 for Skid Row men). Contrast of these men with the living has been made elsewhere in this book.

were never interviewed again after their initial casework contact with the center. Within these two populations, a significantly higher proportion of Skid Row men than non-Skid Row men were reached again during the follow-up program (chi square = 10.63, 1 df, p < .01). Although this result is difficult to interpret because there was no obvious discrimination between the groups, we shall see later that this result is consistent with the finding that, in general, those men from the Skid Row group (who were more typically long-term and stable habitués of Skid Row) were also more frequently contacted in the follow-up. In view of this general result, it is not surprising that we found more Skid Row men than non-Skid Row men.

Finally, we conjecture that the way we have ordered the timing of contacting a man, in Tables 10-7, 10-8, and 10-9, represents a reasonable ordering in terms of the apparent ease in contacting. This is to say that those who were contacted on both occasions were surely more stable in geographical or other terms than were those who were never contacted. Furthermore, it is arguable that those who were contacted at two years only were more stable than those contacted at one year only. Consequently, the next section, which considers factors favoring contact in a follow-up program, will also consider some of these factors in relation to this ordering, as well as the simpler contrast of never contacted versus contacted at both one- and two-year follow-ups.

Factors Related to Follow-Up Contact of Skid Row Men

Finding the Skid Row men one and two years after the initial contact was difficult, time-consuming, and consequently expensive. Because it was expensive, we think that the issue of whether these men can be contacted is of some systematic interest. Are there factors which will predict success of contact one and two years after the initial casework?

In general, the answer is that not many factors predict success in follow-up contact. However, a number appear to be reasonably related to successful contact, and a few are clearly related but do not make any obvious sense in terms of the variables that we have found most helpful.

Demographic variables. Age is significantly related to follow-up contact. A significantly higher proportion of older men (over 50) were contacted on both the one- and two-year follow-ups in contrast to those (under 50) who were contacted on neither follow-up. Religion and race also appear to be related to successful follow-up contact. We were much more successful with Catholics than with Protestants (Table 10-8). It is clear that there is a trend in the data; indeed, the differences between "neither" and "both" are highly significant (chi square $= 17.14$, 1 df, $p < .001$).

There are clear trends for age and religion which in themselves

TABLE 10-8   Success of Contacting Catholics and Protestants

Religious Orien- tation	Percentage Contacted			
	One Year Only	Two Years Only	Both	Neither
Catholic	53.9	62.0	66.2	44.3
Protestant	46.1	38.0	33.8	55.7
Number	128	79	154	212
Percentage	100.0	100.0	100.0	100.0

are not suggestive of meaningful implications but may be consistent with trends reported later. These suggest that we were best able to contact the habituated Skid Row man who was older and Catholic. There also appears to be a relationship between success of follow-up and race, in that relatively fewer blacks were contacted at one *or* two years than were whites. This finding is probably related to age and religion as well as other factors. Thus, Skid Row is historically primarily a white neighborhood with white institutional linkages. Consequently, following these linkages, we may have been more successful in contacting the whites. (These linkages include many of the missions as well as the welfare offices and labor hiring halls.)

Residency variables. Clearly, the most obvious variables related to ease of follow-up contact are various residency variables.

The beginning point for our analysis was the birthplace. Table 10-9 shows that almost two-thirds of those who were never con-

TABLE 10-9   BIRTHPLACE OF FOLLOW-UP CONTACTS, BY PERCENTAGE

| BIRTHPLACE | FOLLOW-UP CONTACT | | | |
	One Year Only	Two Years Only	Both	Neither
Metropolitan Philadelphia	40.4	47.6	56.6	35.0
Non-metropolitan Philadelphia	59.6	52.4	43.4	65.0
Total N*	131	84	159	223
Percentage	100.0	100.0	100.0	100.0

* Five were excluded because of no information.

tacted were born outside the metropolitan Philadelphia area, whereas over one-half of those contacted on both attempts were born within the metropolitan area. This result is highly significant (chi square = 17.66, 1 df, p < .001). The same general results were obtained for the non-Skid Row sample, although the trend was not so striking. The outcome was roughly significant at the 5 percent level of confidence. Thus, a higher percentage of the metropolitan area birthplace sample (64 percent) was found on both follow-ups than for the nonmetropolitan birthplace sample (51 percent).

Other residency factors were also significantly related to success of follow-up for the Skid Row men, including type of residence, how the men paid for their accommodations, and their length of

residency. Table 10-10 presents the results for these three factors.
All these results are highly significant (p < .01 by chi square test),
and tend to show that we were most successful in locating the
relatively stable Skid Row men.

TABLE 10-10   RELATIONSHIP OF FOLLOW-UP SUCCESS TO
                   TYPE OF HOUSING, RENTAL ARRANGEMENTS
                   AND FIRST MOVE TO NEIGHBORHOOD, BY
                   PERCENTAGE

| | FOLLOW-UP SUCCESS | |
	Neither Interview	Both Interviews
Type of housing		
Cubicle hotel	44.2	67.1
All other types	55.8	32.9
Total N*	224	158
Percentage	100.0	100.0
Rental arrangements		
Paid money	44.1	62.5
All other arrangements	55.9	37.5
Total N**	220	160
Percentage	100.0	100.0
First move to neighborhood		
Less than 10 years ago	67.5	51.3
10 or more years ago	32.5	48.7
Total N***	194	154
Percentage	100.0	100.0

* 3 excluded (DK, RA, NA).
** 5 excluded (DK, RA, NA).
*** 37 excluded (DK, RA, NA).

This outcome of course has implications for the evaluation of
the success of our rehabilitation program. Thus, if we can most
easily locate the long-term Skid Row residents, we are apparently
biasing the results. Although the direction of the bias is not totally
clear the following arguments could undoubtedly be made: that
we have found the more stable and economically affluent or, alternatively, that we have found those who were less stable and who
could not make it successfully off Skid Row.

Furthermore, a significantly higher percentage who received
both interviews indicated that they had close friends both within
and without the neighborhood. This underlines their acculturation
both to the Skid Row neighborhood as well as to the metropolitan
area, and makes it more understandable why a successful contact
is more probable.

Economic factors. There were no striking economic factors characteristic of those men whom we were able to contact over the two years. Thus, such factors as work the past week, type of best job, longest job, or type of job that their fathers held were not related to success of contact. Of course the fact that a higher proportion of successful contacts were paying for their living accommodations is relevant to this variable, but no other factors that we investigated yielded helpful clues.

Drinking patterns and health. We were not able to detect many factors related to drinking pattern or health at the time of initial contact which would also predict successful follow-up contact. Thus, none of our consistently most important variables—drinking pattern, spree drinking in the past year, or difficulties resulting from drinking—was related to success of contact; neither were questions about health or job handicaps.

However, there were a few clues in this general area. For instance, a higher percent of those who received neither interview (62 percent) indicated that they came to the DRC originally because of a drinking problem. This contrasted to 48 percent of those who received both interviews who came to the center for a drinking problem. This difference is statistically significant (chi square $= 5.81$, 1 df, $p < .05$). We may possibly infer from this that those we were not able to contact in the follow-up had a greater problem with drinking. However, we also found that a higher proportion of successful contacts at both interviews (63 percent) had attended an AA meeting in the past than unsuccessful contacts (53 percent) had. From these data at least, the answer to the question of which group had a greater problem with alcohol is uncertain.

We considered also jail records and other factors such as union membership. None of these proved helpful in predicting successful follow-up contact. Nevertheless, we believe that, for an Eastern city, we have a significant bundle of variables and factors that predict who will be contacted in a conscientious follow-up to a Skid Row rehabilitation program. In general, these factors are related to stability on a Skid Row and in a metropolitan community. Such factors as birthplace, age, length of residence within a community, number of close friends, community identification, and type of residence are all related to successful contact in a Skid Row follow-up program.

The One-Year Follow-Up

The data on the one-year follow-up are relatively elementary. However, they represent important areas of function, and at least the residency and economic adjustment data are relatively objective for interview material. We shall present one-year follow-up data relevant to four areas: residency, economic adjustment, physical health, and drinking pattern.

Residency. From Tables 10-11 and 10-12, it may be seen that the follow-up adjustment showed somewhat improved accommodations and somewhat more stable rental arrangements. Thus, as shown in Table 10-11, the follow-up group had far fewer men

TABLE 10-11   PRESENT SLEEPING ACCOMMODATIONS AT
                TIME OF INITIAL CONTACT AND AT TIME OF
                ONE YEAR FOLLOW-UP, BY PERCENTAGE

Sleeping Accommodations	Initial Contact	One Year Follow-up
Walked streets	7.8	7.2
Mission	19.5	8.2
Cubicle hotel	51.9	35.9
Hotel	2.4	4.4
Rooming house	1.4	22.5
Hospital, other	15.0	20.8
DK, RA, NA	2.0	1.0
Total N	293	293
Percentage	100.0	100.0

living in missions and cubicle hotels and a much larger percentage living in rooming houses. The rental arrangements showed comparable shifts over the one-year period. Thus, there was a large decrease in free beds for the one-year follow-up. There was also a large number of longer rental periods, indicating a more stable economic adjustment with respect to residential accommodations. Although those who were without any accommodations did not shift much following the casework and one-year follow-up, this group may represent a group which needs much more intensive casework or more appropriate institutional accommodations. They may also of course like to sleep out, at least in the summer.

We asked a number of other questions relevant to community identification and friendships within the neighborhood. These

TABLE 10-12   RENTAL ARRANGEMENTS AT TIME OF INI-
TIAL CONTACT AND AT TIME OF ONE YEAR
FOLLOW-UP, BY PERCENTAGE

Rental Arrangements	Initial Contact	One Year Follow-up
Walked streets	8.9	7.5
Free bed	33.5	1.0
Daily rental	20.5	20.8
Weekly rental	17.4	24.3
Twice a month	5.8	21.5
Monthly	6.1	13.3
Other pay	2.7	3.4
Worked for it	1.4	1.4
Other	2.7	6.1
DK, RA, NA	1.0	.7
Total N	293	293
Percentage	100.0	100.0

indices did not appear to shift much as a function of casework and/or relocation.

Economic adjustment. We have seen already from the residency data that those contacted at one year appeared to show greater stability in their economic ties following casework than at the time of the initial contact.

Additional economic indices are ambiguous with respect to the casework and follow-up results. Table 10-13 indicates that relatively fewer reported a job at the one-year follow-up and relatively more reported Public Assistance as their main source of income;

TABLE 10-13   SOURCE OF "MONEY TO LIVE ON" AT TIME
OF INITIAL CONTACT AND AT ONE YEAR
FOLLOW-UP, BY PERCENTAGE

Source of Money	Initial Contact	One Year Follow-up
DPA (relief)	15.7	32.8
Social Security	8.2	13.3
VA or other pensions	4.1	4.4
Other sources (gifts, etc.)	11.6	5.8
Job	51.9	30.4
No other	8.5	4.4
DK, RA, NA	.0	8.9
Total N	293	293
Percentage	100.0	100.0

this appears to be an important shift in the type of economic support following casework. However, this is not an easy table to interpret. If we examine those (N = 152) who had a job at the time of initial contact, we find that a significant number (N = 45, almost 30 percent) reported Public Assistance at the time of the one-year follow-up; another group (N = 62, approximately 41 percent) still reported a job as the principal source of income. One of the principal effects of casework seems to have been to move the men from jobs to Public Assistance. However, Table 10-14 indicates that there was little difference between the two

TABLE 10-14   HOURS WORKED DURING THE PAST WEEK AT INITIAL CONTACT AND AT ONE YEAR FOLLOW-UP, BY PERCENTAGE

Number of Hours Worked	Initial Contact	One Year Follow-up
None	73.5	71.4
1–32	17.3	10.2
33 or more	8.6	17.1
DK, RA, NA	0.6	1.3
Total N	293	293
Percentage	100.0	100.0

groups in the percent of those working during the prior week. There was perhaps a slight indication of a higher proportion working a full week at the time of follow-up. Of primary interest, however, is the fact that at the time of initial contact, in contrast with the one-year follow-up, a larger percent reported a job as the major source of income, even though a slightly smaller percent actually reported working in the prior week. One possible conclusion is that placing on Public Assistance the men who had marginal jobs had increased their economic stability. Certainly, the data for the residency rental arrangements would support such a conclusion.

With respect to the type of work that the men were engaged in, there did not appear to be many differences. There was a slight indication of upgrading, since roughly 15 percent reported semiskilled or skilled occupations at the time of initial contact, in contrast to roughly 23 percent who reported such jobs one year later. This is clearly not a significant difference. Other job classifications did not show many differences either, although service occupations dropped (from 41 percent to 34 percent) and unskilled occupations dropped (from 32 percent to 26 percent).

Physical health. Of course a questionnaire is no substitute for a medical examination, but we did ask about illness and handicaps at the time of follow-up, as we had at initial contact. With respect to physical health, there was little to distinguish the follow-up group from the same group at point of initial contact. Approximately the same number reported handicaps which were serious enough to interfere with their employment. This was approximately one-third of the men for each point in time. With respect to present illness, a slightly smaller proportion reported illness at the time of follow-up (37 percent) than at the time of initial contact (44 percent). Reports of hospitalization during the past 12 months were consistent with the above, and also did not show marked differences. Thus, 55 percent at the time of initial contact reported no hospitalization, whereas 62 percent reported none at the time of follow-up. These are obviously very gross measures of physical health. A related but more specialized issue is that of drinking pattern.

Drinking pattern. To study changes in drinking patterns, we relied most heavily upon two questions: How often do you drink? Did you go on a binge or spree in the past 12 months?

Our results with respect to drinking pattern are encouraging in that at the time of follow-up a smaller proportion reported daily drinking (45 percent) than at initial contact (58 percent); also, more than one-quarter of the men reported that they were not drinking currently at all. This was more than double the proportion at the time of initial contact (although the recording of the answers to the question was not exactly comparable for the two periods). Other comparisons between frequency categories did not show an appreciable shift.

With respect to reported spree drinking, however, there was a marked shift in reporting sprees during the past 12 months. Thus, almost three-quarters (73 percent) of the men at the point of initial contact reported sprees, whereas slightly less than one-half (47 percent) reported sprees during the past 12 months at the time of the one-year follow-up. In general, the men reported somewhat more restrained drinking habits at follow-up.

Outcome of Follow-Up

In summary, the results of the follow-up pointed to the modest success of the casework program. Although there were few large shifts, the results indicated that some of the men could take advantage of the services offered. At least at one year following the initial casework contact, they reported somewhat better living arrangements; even if their reported employment seemed to have dropped off, their economic stability seemed to have increased. Finally, their health was as good, and indications of present problem drinking showed some abatement. These conclusions, though encouraging, must remain tentative because of the nature and possible bias in the group that we were able to follow. As pointed out earlier in this chapter, we seem to have been able to follow most successfully those men who, by and large, had a more stable adjustment to Skid Row. It is not clear how such a sample bias would influence the results. It is of course the nature of such sampling problems that we are left with conjecture. However, we have tried different kinds of follow-up studies in other projects within the general program, and we will discuss these in the next chapter.

11　The Halfway House Experiment

The experiment in rehabilitation was designed primarily to study the efficacy of a "halfway house" in the rehabilitation of Skid Row men. The program was directed to men who, except for an alcohol problem and a marginal unemployment problem, might be expected to live elsewhere in the community. All these men were physically capable of getting full-time employment and of achieving independence. However, any hope of successful relocation out of Skid Row was likely to be disrupted by a return to drinking. Referrals to existing programs in the community seemed to bring few tangible results, because either the men never arrived at their destination when they were referred or they would soon drop out of the program and, once more homeless, drunk, and without funds, would return to their counselor. It appeared that they needed more than the community had to offer—greater support, better follow-up to engage them in rehabilitation programs, and, most important, someone or something to keep them off Skid Row.

THE RESEARCH PLAN

The Halfway House (HWH) program, sponsored by the Vocational Rehabilitation Ad-

The material in this chapter has been edited from a much longer report by Dr. Walter Stanger, director of the project. The program was supported by the Vocational Rehabilitation Administration under Grant RD-1611 P. The VRA is not responsible for either the data or the interpretation.

ministration, was planned to provide this kind of service to Skid Row men. It was also to provide for an assessment of its effectiveness in comparison with the anchor counselor procedures, on the one hand, and with a more intensive casework procedure, on the other. In other words, we were studying two major facets: efficacy of treatment under residential versus nonresidential conditions, and the importance of continuous and intense interpersonal relationships.

The center's anchor counselor model of organization is an example of a nonresidential outpatient alcoholism treatment program, (such as general psychiatric and alcoholism clinics and AA groups). These programs are available in a community more often than are residential programs, if for no other reason than that the former are less costly than the latter. In addition to the anchor counselor approach, we also developed a more intense personal relationship between the caseworker and the men from Skid Row. Steps in the rehabilitation program were always discussed thoroughly and agreed upon between the client and the intensive counselor, although there may have been strong pressure by the counselor on the client to relinquish his right to drink. While the anchor counselor tended to be desk-bound, the intensive counselor sometimes pursued a man into the Skid Row residential area in order to guarantee that he would meet clinic appointments, that he would adhere to an agreed upon program, that he would attend employment interviews arranged for him, and that he would get to work once he had obtained a job. In a sense, the intensive counselor was similar in function to the sponsor in an AA group who, although sympathetic to the man's alcohol problem, furnishes external controls for the regulation of drinking behavior when internal controls appear to be absent in the man. We felt that an appeal based upon a highly individualized, directive approach to rehabilitation might be particularly appropriate with those individuals who were passive, dependent, and low in interpersonal skills.

In addition to these strategies designed to assist the Skid Row alcoholic in his rehabilitation, there was consideration given to the major barrier to rehabilitation: Skid Row itself. The temptations for a man who is attempting to go straight on Skid Row are enormous; not the least of these are his buddies, who constantly remind him that tomorrow is another day and that they are all bound together in a common need for alcohol—someday he may need them when he has the shakes. HWH was a voluntary residential program; in it we endeavored to establish a new atmosphere in which old ways could be unlearned and new feelings about oneself could be developed. HWH housed a maximum of twelve men and a resident manager in a three-story residence located in a working-class neighborhood. We argued that, for the men who lived there, the pressure to find lodging, to depend upon the missions or friends for meals, and so forth could be temporarily alleviated, so that the men could then concentrate upon themselves, upon their work, and upon entry into a non-Skid Row style of life.

We recognized that there would be some persons who, because of the severity of their alcohol problem or their inability to respond to the types of programs offered, would require greater restraints than HWH residential treatment. In this program, our counselors offered the clients the opportunity for treatment at Norristown State Hospital (NSH), a psychiatric institution. NSH accepted people with a drinking problem and prevented them from getting alcohol while undertaking treatment at the institution. We were prepared to recommend NSH as an ace in the hole for men who seemed unable to respond to a treatment program requiring less stringent external controls. Upon successfully completing the program at NSH, however, a man returned to that part of the program to which he was originally assigned and which his hospitalization had interrupted. Finally, for those who were unable, despite their repeated efforts, to control their drinking and return to independent living, referral was made to a domiciliary institution.

Briefly then, we set out to compare the following kinds of treatment programs: nonresidential—the anchor counselor group or the intensive counselor group—and residential—HWH group.

THE POPULATION SAMPLE

Selection

Once the center's diagnostic procedures were completed, men who met the criteria established for acceptance into the study had their names entered into the sample pool by their anchor counselor. In general, men were eligible if they met these initial qualifications: a diagnosis of alcoholism by either a physician or a psychiatrist; physical capability of immediate employment by the center's medical staff; less than 60 years of age; no communicable disease; no obvious homosexual problems (which might create special difficulties in an all-male group-living situation). Assignment was made to the various treatment conditions on a random basis. Statistical analysis of the various independent variables thought to be relevant to outcome showed that the three groups did not differ substantially from each other.

The flow of subjects into the study was governed by the availability of beds in HWH (there were 12 beds in all). When all these beds were filled, no additional clients were accepted into the pool. If a subject was assigned to HWH and he did not reappear at the center within two weeks, his name continued to be entered on the sequence list until that bed was filled. Of course many subjects were given treatment assignments but never returned to the center for further help during the period of the study. They were eventually dropped from any subsequent analyses that were made relating to treatment or outcome.

Characteristics

The men finally selected for the program tended to be younger than the 1960 group; they were also better educated; a higher proportion said that they had been married at some time in their lives; a higher proportion of the alcoholics had lived on Skid Row for less than a year; a higher proportion were without a night's lodging or had stayed in a mission the night before the interview; a smaller proportion of the alcoholic sample had worked during the week before the interview, and, of those who worked, fewer had for a full week; the alcoholic sample had more daily drinkers and fewer weekend drinkers. The mean IQ score of the alcoholic sample (Quick Test) was 103.0, which does not differ significantly from that of the general population. A high proportion of the alcoholics reported a chronic illness. The present sample is more similar to the self-avowed spree drinkers of the 1960 survey than to the whole sample of Skid Row men.

We have already discussed the MMPI and the special significance of the Pd and the D scales in Chapter 10. The mean Pd scale score for the alcoholic sample was 78.5, a score surpassing those obtained by 99 percent of the original standardization group. The D scale mean score was 76.5, which surpasses scores obtained by 95 percent of the general population. Both these scores are typical for alcoholics.

The Social Alienation and Self-Alienation scales are subscales developed from the Pd scale of the MMPI by Robert E. Harris and James C. Lingoes.[1] The Social Alienation scale describes attitudes concerning "feelings of isolation from other people; lack of belongingness, externalization of blame for difficulties; lack of gratification in social relations." The Self-Alienation scale describes persons characterized by a "lack of self-integration, avowal of guilt, and exhibitionistically stated 'despondency.'" Harris and Lingoes indicate that alcoholics who refer themselves for treatment often score high on these scales. Our alcoholic sample had scores that were high on both these scales, suggesting a deep sense of alienation and isolation.

The Socialization and Self-Control scales were adapted from the California Psychological Inventory, which is itself taken partly from the MMPI. The Socialization scale "indicates the degree of social maturity, integrity and rectitude which the individual has attained." The Self-Control scale assesses "the degree and adequacy of self-regulation and self-control and freedom from impulsivity and self-centeredness."[2] Our sample was considerably less socialized and had less self-control than the general population in terms of these scales. In fact, the alcoholic sample obtained lower Socialization scores than any other group of persons reported, including prison inmates and delinquents.

FOLLOW-UP

Initially we had planned to obtain follow-up interviews at six-month intervals on all subjects in the study, but there were significant problems in the follow-up of Skid Row men. We found that a more feasible plan was to try to get one interview on each subject at least one year after the man had entered the study. We believed that this interval gave each subject sufficient opportunity to demonstrate his ability to change his life style.

As soon as the follow-up files were processed, out of the original sample of 209 men, follow-up interviews were completed on 152 of the men, or 73 percent of the original sample. The application of the criterion of success and failure, which will be discussed below, required that there be a complete special anchor counselor rating schedule and a follow-up interview. Of the 152 men with whom we had follow-up interviews, we could accept only 117 because of insufficient information which the anchor counselors had provided on the other men. Thus, of the 209 men admitted to the study, the criterion sample consisted of 117 men, or 56 percent of the original sample.

It is of some interest to note that all treatment groups were not equally represented in the final follow-up sample. Thus, only 39 percent of the anchor counselor group met the criteria for inclusion in the final criterion sample, whereas 65 percent of the intensive counselor sample and 57 percent of the HWH sample met the criteria. We believe that the intensity of the interpersonal relationship established in the course of the intensive counselor and HWH programs accounts for the relative difference in the success of the follow-up. The fact that there was a relatively higher turnover of anchor counselors than of intensive counselors also partly accounts for the difference.

THE CRITERION OF SUCCESS AND FAILURE

Walter Stanger, the director of the program, who cooperated with us in its evaluation, made a considerable effort to develop rating scales based on a large number of variables. These were made available in the several interviews of the men, but the rating scales developed were, for a variety of reasons, unsatisfactory. Finally, and with some reluctance, Stanger turned to the one factor that appeared to have a direct and pervasive bearing upon outcome: drinking behavior. He had been disinclined to use this criterion because periods of sobriety were extremely difficult to verify and because he did not wish to become entangled in speculations as to whether these men could or could not drink—whether they should or should not.

It seemed reasonable, nevertheless, to postulate that continued dependence upon alcohol would be correlated with a man's losing his job or otherwise disturbing his source of income and his housing and compelling him to return to Skid Row. On the basis of a three-point scale, the DRC/P counselors had been asked to estimate the longest continuous period of sobriety of the men on their caseload: more than one year, less than one year but more than two months, and less than two months. When each man's sobriety was described in these terms and correlated with his place of lodging at the time of follow-up, a strong relationship was found to exist between sobriety and residence (Table 11-1)—that is, alcoholic men who moved away from Skid Row could not hope to resist its attraction if they returned to drinking. The one man who had been sober for a year and who was living on Skid Row at the time of the follow-up was on a binge at that time. However, he recovered in a short time and returned to treatment and eventually to independent living, away from Skid Row.

TABLE 11-1 RELATIONSHIP BETWEEN SOBRIETY RATING
AND RESIDENCE RATING, BY PERCENTAGE

| SOBRIETY RATING | RESIDENCE RATING | | | TOTAL | |
	Independent	Dependent	Skid Row	N	Percentage
Long-term	39.0	55.5	5.5	18	100.0
Medium-term	42.8	23.8	33.4	42	100.0
Short-term	17.5	26.3	56.2	57	100.0

The abbreviated criterion scale, then, represented different periods of sobriety. For this variable, three sobriety levels were chosen to describe the longest period of continuous sobriety achieved by a subject while in the study: long-term—one year or more; medium-term—more than two months but less than one year; short-term—less than two months.

SUCCESSES, SURVIVORS, AND FAILURES

In view of the small size of the sample, analysis was limited to three outcome groups, which were labeled successes, survivors, and failures. The nomenclature reflects our lingering concern with factors other than sobriety, but reflects also the fact that drinking pattern is demonstrably related to other facts of life style (Table 11-1). The successes were persons who had at least a year's continuous sobriety during the period of this study. Survivors were those who demonstrated moderate periods of sobriety. Failures had periods of sobriety of less than two months. We have of course a greater degree of confidence in the reliability of our extreme groups: those persons labeled successes to a large degree maintained this status after completion of the study, as did the failures, who continued in their drinking and dependence on Skid Row. These labels appear to describe a relatively fixed or permanent condition, at least as a function of our continued rehabilitation efforts.

If we consider the failures to be those alcoholics who are relatively attached to Skid Row, the survivors are probably a more mobile population that is able to obtain seasonal, temporary, or live-in employment off Skid Row. It should be noted that the survivors had the highest proportion of men living independently at the time of follow-up—a tribute to their resourcefulness and tenacity. From this group ultimately came a handful of persons who might now be considered successes. On the other hand, a

large number have dropped into the failure category as continued
alcohol abuse has lessened their ability to maintain themselves.
Table 11-2 illustrates the relationship between the success-

TABLE 11-2   RELATIONSHIP OF OUTCOME TO TREAT-
                  MENT GROUP, BY PERCENTAGE

| TREATMENT | OUTCOME | | | TOTAL | |
	Success	Survival	Failure	N	Percentage
Anchor counselor	7.7	53.8	38.4	26	99.9
Intensive counselor	23.3	44.2	32.6	43	100.0
Half-way house	12.5	18.7	68.8	48	100.0

Chi square = 16.90, 4 df, p < .01.

failure criterion dimension and the major treatment conditions.
Although the chi square test indicates that there is a significant
relationship between outcome and treatment condition, there is no
simple interpretation of the significance. Although there was a
higher proportion of successes in the intensive counselor and HWH
groups than in the anchor counselor groups, the advantage of the
former two groups does not appear to be very striking.

The overrepresentation of the HWH group in the failure category is more striking. We will discuss the implications of this
surprising outcome below.

A large number of demographic and behavioral variables were
examined with respect to their relationship to outcome; most of
these turned out to be not significant. It seems most economical of
time and space for us to report only those which were significant;
even for those, the implications were not always readily evident.
For example, no relationship was found to exist between outcome
and prior hospitalization for drinking, or between outcome and
prior attempts to give up drinking. The theory of residual effects
of earlier treatment is therefore cast into question.

While there was a significant relationship between success-
failure and the type of previous treatment, the greatest contribution to the differences in outcome may be attributed to the treatment conditions in interaction with AA involvement and with
short-term institutionalization. However, a high proportion of men
with prior AA involvement were more likely to be survivors at the
conclusion of the study, while an even higher proportion with previous short-term hospitalization were judged to be failures. If there
is any basis to a theory of residual effects, it would therefore

seem to be in terms of some element in AA—probably the close personal interest of the sponsor—rather than in short-term institutionalization.

The single psychological variable upon which outcome was found to be dependent was the score from the Social Alienation subscale of the MMPI (chi square = 8.5; 2 df, p < .02). Successful outcome was associated with a high score on the Social Alienation scale. Another example of the surprises in the data is the finding that success was more often related to an absence of recent work stability, which will be discussed below.

In the analysis of success-failure, we found considerable confirmation of the importance of the counselor, both in his ability to assess the motivation of the man and in his relationship with the Skid Row man. Thus, the single alcohol-related item upon which outcome was dependent was the anchor counselor's estimate of whether the man was motivated to do something about his drinking problem. There was a significant relationship between the counselor's assessment of poor motivation to deal with a drinking problem at the outset and to failure (chi square = 9.7; 2 df, p < .01).

The counselors were asked to rate the men on a dimension that we call conning-sincere. Conning, a behavior pattern common to alcoholism and to the Skid Row way of life, is a deliberately dishonest and manipulative approach wherein the client tells the counselor what the counselor wants to hear in return for something the client needs. In our particular situation, promises of making rehabilitative efforts were exchanged for services offered by the counselor; there would be no intention on the part of the man to carry out his part of the deal. There was a direct relationship between success and rated sincerity (chi square = 7.5; 2 df, p < .05). It should be noted further that of the total population, 44 percent were rated by their counselors as conning—testimony to the difficulty of the counselor's task in attempting to work with these men. (Whether the counselor liked or disliked the man was not significantly related to outcome.)

Men were also rated on their dependability in keeping appointments at the outset of the treatment experience. The smallest proportion of the failure group were rated as "very dependable"; the success and survival groups were not significantly different from each other in this respect (chi square = 9.4; 2 df, p < .01).

Counselors were asked to provide a judgment on the depth of

involvement of all men who remained in continuous contact with their counselors. Deep involvement with counselors was more often related to success; a lack of involvement was more frequently related to failure (chi square = 12.4; 2 df, p < .01). In short, it was found that the quality of the relationship was related to outcome—sincerity, dependability, and involvement were associated with success; a lack of these elements in the relationship was associated with failure.

It seems evident that the development or reestablishment of close relationships may be important to the success or failure of rehabilitation efforts with Skid Row men who have an alcohol problem. Thus, while we did not find that outcome was dependent upon earlier relationships with some family member, we did find that new (or renewed) relationships were related to the criterion. Thus there was a direct relationship between success and the fact that the counselor had contacted a member of the client's family; a lack of contact was associated with failure (chi square = 9.17; 2 df, p < .02). More important than mere contact by the counselor was what developed out of such contact or out of independent attempts at reconciliation by the man. We found that the success and survival groups did not differ in this respect, but that a high proportion of the failure group did not establish a relationship with some family member (chi square = 8.35; 2 df, p < .02). Family members were able to supply the reinforcement and support that a man needed after leaving the Skid Row life style.

One might reasonably expect that a participation in an alcoholism treatment program would be related to success. We found that the highest proportion of failures did not attend AA meetings at all, and that none of those who attended regularly were considered failures (chi square = 6.6; 2 df, p < .05). We explored this further by asking counselors to rate those who attended AA meetings. These ratings were related to outcome in the sense that the highest proportion in the failure group were described as not having made a personal commitment to the AA program (chi square = 11.88; 2 df, p < .01). In short, we were unable to demonstrate any relationship between successful outcome and attendance at AA; our data indicated only that those who did not make a deep AA commitment were least likely to be successful. Furthermore, admission to Eagleville Hospital and Rehabilitation Center (a 60-day institutional program that began in July 1967 and was therefore really only in its shakedown period during the program) was unrelated to outcome. On the other hand, long-term treatment in the Norristown State Hospital, a psychiatric institution, was related to outcome. Outcome was significantly dependent upon admission to the institution (Table 11-3), and entry into the Center for Alcohol Studies and Treat-

TABLE 11-3   RELATIONSHIP OF ADMISSION TO NORRIS-TOWN STATE HOSPITAL AND OUTCOME, BY PERCENTAGE

HOSPITAL ADMISSION		OUTCOME		TOTAL	
	Success	Survival	Failure	N*	Percentage
Admitted	28.6	34.7	36.7	49	100.0
Not admitted	7.7	36.6	55.7	52	100.0

Chi square = 9.70, 2 df, P < .01.
* 16 Anchor Counselor protocols failed to indicate Norristown State Hospital status.

ment (CAST), an intensive program into which a patient must be invited by his fellow patients at NSH, was likewise significantly related to success. Of the 18 men rated as successful by our criteria, 14 had been residents of NSH. Since such a large proportion of our clients of immediate concern entered the CAST program, that program may be a significant factor. Thus, it may be important for others to explore not only long-term hospitalization but also special programs within the hospital.

We had anticipated that there would be differences between outcome groups with respect to their recreational and social activities. Successes were more likely to limit their participation to groups where alcohol did not play some part (chi square = 7.15; 2 df, p < .05). They were also more likely to meet with some type of organized groups (church, union, AA, therapy, social) than were survivors or failures (chi square = 7.25; 2 df, p < .05). Outcome was independent of the nature of such groups—whether they were therapeutic or nontherapeutic.

We have reported significant results at some length because we believe that our study provides an important basis for the discussion of the alternatives to Skid Row. We want to emphasize that in this research we did not see the objective of rehabilitation of Skid Row men as imposing middle-class values upon them. Most of these men came from the working classes, as we have already reported, and our modest criteria of success were to have them live independently (outside an institution) and under less degraded conditions than Skid Row provides. Our study tends to support the thesis that once a man is committed to a Skid Row style of life (in which alcohol is a central feature), it will take heroic efforts to bring him back into the larger community's style of life. Wallace's explanation of this thesis lies in the acculturation of the men to Skid Row values and a status system that is hostile to that of the larger community. Once a man becomes a real Skid Rower, he has acquired a style of life that has its own satisfactions, even though these are radically nonconforming with respect to the larger community.[3] What has the larger community to offer as a substitute? Wiseman points out that the alternative world views of the Skid Rower and those of the larger community are so radically different that, at least perceptually, there are two different realities in the same situation. The rehabilitation services offered by case-workers from the larger community are not necessarily attractive in rehabilitative terms to the Skid Row man. Rather, he sees them as resources to be used for survival. The road into the respectable community is cold and lonely, while Skid Row provides instant warmth and friendliness for some. Small wonder that after exposure to a rehabilitation program and some efforts to continue in the new direction, the Skid Row man is likely eventually to call it quits—"and then I decided to hell with it, and started drinking again."[4]

What looms as important under these circumstances is that our program was successful with some men and that some of our results need further explanation.

SHORT-TERM TREATMENT

The total treatment experience before the man entered the program was important in the subsequent results. Failure was found to be related to previous short-term institutional treatment, and survival was related to prior involvement with AA, but with neither related to success. Short-term programs are geared to help the man who needs little help: the alcoholic with an existent family, community ties, friends, and probably an employer who will welcome him back after treatment. For the man who is without these social and vocational resources but who has not yet become a vagrant, such treatment offers only a brief respite from a life style that is already deteriorated. Upon discharge from an institution and without strong financial or emotional supports, such a man will usually suffer a relapse into drinking in a short time, together with loss of job and often lodging. Post-institutional referral is often made to other outpatient programs or to AA groups with which the client is unfamiliar. Thus, for the alcoholic who is rapidly losing his supports and who is Skid Row bound, the short-term treatment program that is initially unsuccessful can even have a deleterious effect in that it sets up an expectancy of failure and a tendency, on the part of the alcoholic, to see subsequent programs not as opportunities for rehabilitation but as temporary havens between binges. A new revolving door has therefore been created.

Early AA experiences which reward self-helping attitudes and behavior patterns are probably crucial in setting up expectancies in these persons of intermittent periods of sobriety and drunkenness and of alternating phases of independence and dependence. It is not surprising, then, that the survivors in this study—those men with modest periods of sobriety and independence from Skid Row—had had prior AA involvement.

We believe that prior treatment programs have the effect of locking in many men in such a manner that they repeat earlier mistakes but do not make any serious change in their total life style. Programs that offer intermittent support do, in fact, perpetuate a status quo, since they offer the client an opportunity to maintain a pattern of existence that, despite its great ups and downs, is tolerable to him. Such programs usually suffer from two major defects: they are often unable to discriminate between clients they can help and those whose illness is being supported; they usually fail to refer the client to some other, more appropriate treatment service.

SOCIAL AND VOCATIONAL SUPPORTS

Tiebout has described the AA concept of hitting bottom, and has indicated that, along with several other attributes (humility, surrender, ego reduction), this is a necessary prelude to recovery. He describes this final stage of the alcoholic's emotional and social deterioration in these terms:

At last he hits what might be called an emotional bottom. The pattern of his life is changing for the worse, his attempts at control, often concealed even from himself, have regularly failed, and the prospect ahead is frightening. He begins to despair, to see nothing but hopelessness ahead, with pain and misery his lot for the rest of his life. He is shaken, desperate, sunk in depression. He has hit a low, he has hit bottom. At that point, he wants help.[5]

Is there a bottom lower than Skid Row? There, men have lost friends, families, jobs, self-respect—seemingly everything. By this standard alone, they should be prepared to do anything to become rehabilitated. And yet, only about 20 percent of the men were described by counselors as highly motivated to do something about their drinking problem, and only about one-half were described as sincere in their efforts to change. The "hitting bottom" theory seems questionable. What has prevented these men from throwing every ounce of effort into freeing themselves from Skid Row?

We believe that social and occupational factors are involved. When a man comes to Skid Row, he has lost the social and vocational supports that have helped to maintain him in the community; even after he has been rejected by kinsmen and friends, he may continue to hold a job. But there comes a time when he loses his job and, in the absence of alternative supports, he becomes a vagrant and moves into the Skid Row locality. There, drinking is accepted. (Trice suggests that his process of alcohol-related changes in relationships has been going on for a long time.[6] If this is so, then Skid Row is the extreme case—the end of the line.) A man's failure to work is lauded by many of his new companions. One works only to get money for drinks; food, clothing, and lodging are residual items rather than primary concerns, especially when a man is on a spree. Although this acceptance hardly takes the place of family and the friends of the larger community, it is much more readily obtainable and with little effort expended. The newcomer to Skid Row is now on the threshold of shifting from the socially accepted to the socially outcast, and in this new world the values of the rejectors are, in turn, rejected. Thus, those persons who before treatment had the best potential for rehabilitation could be identified, in part, by their high scores on the Social Alienation subscale of the MMPI. These were the men who hungered the most for society, despite their acceptance of Skid Row. Since they had the most to gain by turning their backs on Skid Row, they were the most willing to reject the Skid Row ethos.

The second major obstacle to rehabilitation of the Skid Row alcoholic is the matter of vocational independence. For many men, the ability to work is the yardstick by which manhood is measured. When this ability is severely diminished or lost, deep feelings of despair and helplessness set in, unless one's misfortune can be blamed upon persons or circumstances outside oneself.

But what of the man whose drinking behavior alone appears to be the reason for his occupational failure? It would appear that men who recognize—or are helped to recognize—this relationship between their drinking and their inability to work are ready to change their life style and are motivated to do something about their alcoholism. In the two years prior to treatment 64 percent of the success group either had not worked or had worked only spot jobs, while 80 percent of the survival and failure groups had been able to keep a job for at least two months. There is strong evidence to support the belief that rehabilitation candidates who have exhausted their vocational resources have a greater need for change.

Thus, some Skid Row men seem willing to begin to alter their life style when they have exhausted both their vocational and social resources. It is in this sense that we believe "hitting bottom" should be interpreted. These men wish to escape from Skid Row but find themselves imprisoned there by their inability to work with any sustained effort. They are lonely. The shallow camaraderie that they find in the bars and flophouses is not sufficient to dull their need for people. It is perhaps this need for people, more than any other, that characterizes the motivation of the alcoholic finally to seek help. So long as he finds the comradeship of Skid Row satisfying and accepts other Skid Rowers as a substitute for family, he may have little reason to seek for other, closer relationships. A final example of the importance of new social roots lies in the major difference between ratings of success and failure with respect to the kinds of recreational pursuits in which clients engaged between our working with them and the follow-up interview. As would be expected, successful persons engaged in recreation of a largely nonalcoholic nature—movies, bowling, spectator sports, TV. They also met more frequently with organized groups— therapy, AA, church, union. We could find no relationship between attendance at therapeutic meetings and success; regular association with any active group appears to have been sufficient. As we have suggested, securely relating the Skid Row alcoholic to a group which does not tolerate deviant alcoholic behavior is an important precondition for his success.

COUNSELOR INVESTMENT

Factors associated with the treatment experience were more important than any others in their contribution to success and failure. These factors can be divided into those associated with the client-counselor relationship and those associated with the treatment program.

When the relationship between the man and the anchor counselor was a good one, the likelihood of rehabilitation increased. As in any relationship, this had a two-way basis—requiring dependability and sincerity on the part of the man and real involvement on the part of the counselor. Usually, the man would seek evidence from the counselor about the latter's sincerity and if he really wished to help. The counselor might be forced to prove himself by doing more than his job, by performing time-consuming, difficult, and personal services for the man. Sometimes, only after the counselor had appeared in court as a witness or intervened with an employer, family member, or welfare worker, did the man feel that he could count on his caseworker. In terms of what is currently called "exchange theory" in the social sciences, the counselor now made an investment of his own in the relationship and therefore could be trusted. A bond of trust was thereby possible between the two as part of an implicit bargain—"You invest in me, and I'll stop conning you and really listen to your suggestions," one the one hand; on the other, "I'll invest in you from my own personal resources if you stop conning me and permit us to get on with helping you." In those cases in which the counselor believed he was being conned (for example, when the Skid Row man made vacant promises or failed to keep his appointments), a poor relationship existed between the pair, and a feeling of involvement and trust between them failed to develop. This, in turn, blocked most avenues to rehabilitation.

The real implication of our study, as it relates to the efficacy of the three treatment approaches, points to the relative failure of the HWH as a treatment condition. A significantly lower proportion of survivors and a higher proportion of failures were in HWH, as compared with those in the other treatment conditions. We believe that these differences may be better understood if we make a more specific and detailed comparison of the clients' experiences in the intensive treatment condition and those in HWH. These were the treatment approaches with the highest and lowest proportions of failures and the least variability with regards to number and replacement of staff. Many counselors participated in the anchor counselor approach, whereas there were only three intensive counselors and four other counselors in the HWH.

It should be kept in mind, however, that the intensive approach was not the most effective technique for helping men into permanent independent living. Those men who were able to achieve this goal usually did so only after they had been institutionalized at NSH. The intensive approach was effective in persuading men to enter the facility and to remain there until they were ready to return to the community. For a man who was not rehabilitated in this manner, the intensive technique alone often yielded moderate improvement in his pattern of life. He continued to drink, but perhaps with longer intervals between bouts and with longer periods of independence from Skid Row. His dependence was transferred from Skid Row to his counselor. The tremendous support offered by the counselor was able to raise the man's level of subsistence for longer—but still brief—intervals. The intensive counselor invested some of his own social credit in the situation in place of the exhausted social credit of the Skid Row alcoholic. Both the HWH and the intensive approaches had the same immediate objective: to remove the man from Skid Row and to make him independent of its supporting services and its contaminating influences as quickly as possible.

A major difference between the two approaches developed around work expectancies. In the intensive procedure, stability came only gradually. A man might require months before he could seriously consider working at a job. In the meantime, he must learn to trust his new counselor, become comfortable with his new lodgings, pay for his room in advance, budget his welfare check, find a restaurant with reasonable prices. Often, before this point was reached, the man had experienced so many relapses that, rather than seek employment, he accepted institutionalization for help with his drinking problem.

In HWH, on the other hand, with all his basic needs provided for, the alcoholic achieved—so it appeared—instant stability. There was little testing of client and counselor, and this relationship was often diffused by the group-living experience. What we could not fully appreciate was the unrealistic attitudes that men held concerning work: their fears of being rejected by a potential employer or being fired from a job, and the inappropriate sense of accomplishment they attached to obtaining a job or to holding onto it. Few men obtained employment; fewer still obtained work of a non-Skid Row nature. If men lasted until their first pay day, this was often the occasion for leaving the program and getting drunk. Only one man at HWH held the same job for more than two months.

Despite remonstrances by HWH counselors that men take their time and be selective about employment, many clients would rush blindly into any job. Others would drag their feet interminably about seeking work, holding back until the time was right to visit a previous employer whom they had not seen in ten years. Both the joy at finding acceptance and the fear of being rejected pointed to the inability of these men to put work in its proper perspective as well as to the inability of counselors to help them do so.

Only slowly did we come to recognize, as they did in the long-term therapy program at NSH, that employment or the expectation of it is an unrealistic early goal for the Skid Row alcoholic. What was required first was immense emotional support and a considerable period of protection from facing ordinary life situations before the matter of employment, even for the sake of obtaining pocket money, was broached. The ability to hold a job comes only after successfully dealing with smaller frustrations. Success is the consequence of correlative smaller achievements. In other words, success is a rehabilitative process rather than an outcome.

HWH had perhaps the least effective methods available for dealing with the problem of drinking. Initially, it was felt that drinking behavior should not be punished, that residents who drank should be kept in the program. Within a short time, everyone in the program was drinking. Various attempts were subsequently made to restrict drinking in some manner short of removing men from the program, but all these efforts ended eventually in the men returning to Skid Row and failing to come back to the agency for further help in rehabilitation. The most effective system, in the sense of reducing drinking activity while keeping men engaged in the rehabilitation process, was initally to require sobriety in HWH and to offer Antabuse to new residents as they were admitted into the program. It was explained that we were willing to accept an individual's estimate of his ability to control his drinking; however, if he had a slip, he could remain only if he would take Antabuse daily. If a man still drank while taking Antabuse, he was demonstrating his inability to remain in the community, with its temptations to drink. This approach was eventually effective in preparing men to enter NSH and to impress upon them the need to remain there for a relatively long time. We were, in effect, teaching the men that they required additional external controls instead of rejecting and punishing them.

The intensive treatment counselor worked with his clients in much the same manner on an individual basis, supporting his client in his realistic efforts to achieve independence but requiring that the man examine his unrealistic promises. For example, if a man strongly wished to take a full-time job, even after the counselor had pointed out that he was not ready for this step, the counselor might find him a job and lodging. But if the man soon quit the job, went on a spree, and returned broke to the agency, requesting help to try it again, the counselor would withhold further similar assistance until the man became engaged in at least one outpatient type of treatment—for example, AA or clinic. If the man failed in his next attempts, he might then be ready for the final step (entering an inpatient program), usually at NSH.

The technique of teaching the client that he needed external controls and ultimately long-term hospitalization appeared to work better on an individual basis. In HWH, the men saw the staff reject members by dismissing them from the house (whenever the men voted on similar matters, they always would offer another chance), even if the excluded member accepted his fate gracefully. On an outpatient basis, men were never so fully rejected in this manner— they were never really deprived of treatment, room, and meals by their counselor. Thus it was easier for them to recognize the role they had played in their own defeat. At the same time, it was easier for them to accept the subsequent advice of their counselor, since he would be the helping friend or uncle more than the punishing father.

Another of the major distinctions between the two approaches lay in the degree to which men continued to be "contaminated" by the Skid Row ethos. This influence was rarely absent from HWH. It was the protective chain that linked these men together, protecting them from further hurt, humiliation, and failure in the eyes of the outsiders—the staff. The men brought Skid Row into HWH, with its secretiveness, lack of real involvement, disdain for do-gooders, and the need to con in order to demonstrate to themselves and others their indifference to their need for trust. The highest proportion of men described as having a conning relationship with their counselor were in the HWH group. When such feelings were strong, there was a high rate of turnover in HWH. At other times, a different attitude existed in HWH, one that was more trusting and less resentful of help. This feeling was usually present when some of the leaders among the men began to trust a counselor and openly to admit to this relationship in front of new members. At such times, stability within a small core group would develop, and these men would remain as sober residents for a moderate period of time.

The approach of the intensive counselor was better suited to reducing the danger of Skid Row contamination. Often, after a man had been relocated to a privately operated rooming house that specialized in alcoholics, he was no longer seen at the center, where it was possible for him to mingle with other Skid Row men waiting for service. Instead, he was visited in the community—for example, at his lodgings or in an AA group. At times, several of the men were brought together for counseling, at an AA meeting, or for some recreational activity; however, in any of these situations the value of strict sobriety and pursuing rehabilitation goals was stressed. Once a man reached this stage in the rehabilitation process, he had few legitimate reasons or opportunities to be in touch with other Skid Row men who still held drinking as a desired value.

A large majority of the men who were rated successes had been at NSH. There, many became rehabilitated, while others had their initial period of sobriety. Since the Skid Row men represented a minority of the alcoholics being treated at NSH, for most residents of the program were of middle-class origin, the likelihood of contamination with Skid Row values was minimized. When a man finally broke with the program and returned to drinking, he usually went directly to Skid Row, where he could feel more comfortable.

We noted earlier in this chapter that the Skid Row men with the best potential for success also felt socially alienated despite their living in an atmosphere of acceptance. It would seem that the optimal time to reach these men is when they felt most hurt by the rejection of the community but had not yet surrendered to the acceptance which Skid Row could offer. Before a man moved into the Skid Row locality or during the first few months after he had moved there was probably the most crucial period in his life with respect to rehabilitation. If at this time a man could be given help to return to the community and to those who once cared for him, he might never become acculturated to the Skid Row way of life.

In this last connection, we found that there was a relationship between failure and the inability to reestablish family ties. Examination of this variable in greater detail by treatment group shows that the intensive counselor was much more successful in this endeavor than HWH counselors were. The relative with whom a relationship was established occurred most often in this order: father, mother, sibling, child. Although 63 percent of the men had been married at one time, no man in the study, to our knowledge, was reunited with his wife. The pain between husband and wife seemed too great to overcome; nevertheless, reunion was often a fervent hope, particularly among those men who never solved their alcoholic problems. It appeared that individual counseling, rather than the group approach often used at the HWH, was a more appropriate method for dealing with the problems of reestablishing ties with a family member. Often when the Skid Row man himself made the initial overture with his family, he was either rejected or mistrusted; his relatives had listened to empty promises as a prelude to a touch many times before. But when a counselor would contact these same relatives and describe the client's sincere efforts toward rehabilitation, many would indicate a real desire to help once more. Thus, they accepted the man in terms of the intensive counselor's social credit rather than that of the client's which had long ago been exhausted. Those few men who were rehabilitated without institutionalization were all accepted into some family group, invariably with strong admonitions against their drinking. The value that these men placed upon this relationship was sometimes sufficient to motivate them to control or to stop their drinking. Having regained what they had thought was completely lost, they did not wish to endanger themselves once more. When the question of family reunion was discussed in group situations, the advice of other Skid Row men in HWH was invariably unrealistic. Since nearly all the men had hopes of quickly reestablishing family ties themselves, they would enthusiastically support such efforts in other group members. The ideal first step, many believed, was to appear at the doorstep of the long-lost wife, mother, or child in a new suit of clothes and with arms laden with presents. They unrealistically expected that the prodigal son's return would dissolve all the old hurts and create a new relationship wherein everyone would live happily ever after.[7] Our men were too socially inept to give effective advice to others in the handling of social situations; instead, our HWH groups supported impulsivity, denial of reality, and their belief that close relationships could be reestablished between persons on the basis of simple gestures and new promises.

The Intensive Counselor:
A More Detailed Analysis

It should be evident by now that we have not casually approached the rehabilitation of Skid Row men. Chapters 10 and 11 have made it clear that rehabilitation is not easy and that it should be seen in terms of ability to live off Skid Row and to maintain sufficient sobriety to be able to live independently —outside an institution in a manner similar to that of the general citizenry. We concluded in Chapter 10 that group therapy in a prison setting is of little value. This did not of course resolve the question of whether group therapy in some other setting would have been of value. We also concluded from our presentation of follow-up data, from our NIMH sample population, that the anchor counselor style of casework is modestly successful. There were no major therapeutic activities associated with this procedure, although, it may be argued that the very relationship between the man and his counselor had some rehabilitative potentialities. Even though this approach had modest success from a rehabilitative point of view, we believe that it was helpful in the daily crises

The data reported in this chapter are based on a larger project done under Grant RD-1611 P, Vocational Rehabilitation Administration; the VRA is not responsible for either the data or the interpretation. We wish to express our appreciation to Dr. Walter Stanger, director of the project; to William Hood, the author of this chapter; and to Jack Flounders, who assisted with some of the data analysis procedure.

188

of the men it was developed to assist. At the same time, we have had our share of bitter denunciations from those who said we did not do enough; nonetheless, we believe that this kind of crisis service to Skid Row men is worthy of continued community support. In Chapter 11 we analyzed at some length the HWH program, in which the anchor counselor procedure was used as a basis for comparison with an intensive counseling procedure, on the one hand, and a halfway house program, on the other. The emphasis was on: the development of a social and job-finding experience to ease the transition from Skid Row to the larger community; the generally greater effectiveness of the intensive counseling procedure; and the importance of the CAST program in NSH in conjunction with the intensive counseling procedure. The present chapter will serve to emphasize the reinforcing and supportive significance of the intensive counseling. That is, NSH was not helpful enough for the Skid Row alcoholics in the program; the intensive counseling was an integral element to the rehabilitative process, not merely an optional addition.

In this chapter, we describe and report on the intensive counseling procedure in greater detail. It will readily become apparent that we are convinced that the style of relationship which we will discuss is in the direction that we must proceed if we are to assist Skid Row men in making a transition to a more healthy relationship with the larger community.

The intensive counselor had a caseload of 60 Skid Row alcoholics during a three-year period. He spent many more hours in individual counseling than the anchor counselors did. Much of this counseling, along with other types of relationships, was developed and performed outside the center. He met clients at lunchtime or after work in a Skid Row restaurant, in a public park, or frequently at an AA meeting. Every week he visited clients in detoxification units, long-term inpatient alcoholism facilities, general hospitals, and jails.

The men in the program were sometimes seen in the community while they were on an alcoholic binge; hospitalization was arranged for them if they agreed to it. An evening group therapy program met weekly for three months in a public library. The counselor scheduled social, recreational, and cultural events; personal services were performed, such as helping clients move their personal belongings to new living quarters. In addition, there was a $100 revolving fund, to assist clients when they had emergencies.

There were immediate payoffs in this close interest in the men. For example, arrangements were made to reduce the sentence of one man in the House of Correction, and it was then possible to get him admitted to NSH, for a long-term inpatient alcoholic treatment program. Admittedly he went from one locked program to another, but the mental hospital was not punitive and it boasted of a number of successful cases—some of which are on our own staff. In another case, the counselor was able to get public defenders for two of his clients while they were in the Philadelphia Detention Center (a holding prison for persons not yet brought to trial and not permitted bail). These men were held on serious charges; the counselor assisted in some pretrial investigation for the public defender, appeared on the witness stand, and was able to arrange bail for one man.

CAUSE OR SYMPTOM

One cannot do such intense casework without asking if alcoholism is a symptom of underlying problems or the cause of problems. We doubt that a person without severe life problems will develop into a chronic alcoholic. Such problems were indicated in the histories of all our clients. Heavy and uncontrolled drinking seems only to aggravate the alcoholic's problems and create new ones. Little can be accomplished through casework when a client is drinking in an uncontrolled way. In such a situation, a counselor works so as not to harm the relationship, and directs the alcoholic toward detoxification, back to a hospital that he has left against medical advice, or to the center when he has stopped drinking. Early in the relationship, the man's drinking must stop.

CRISIS

An important emphasis was intervention during crises that the men faced. The counselor-client relationship can best be strengthened through such intervention, and the greatest personality and behavioral change can be effected. Many clients first come to the DRC/P during a crisis: just off a binge with the shakes, malnourished, with no money and no bed. If the man is met with warmth, empathy, and genuineness, with basic needs promptly met, the best relationship is established. In a number of cases, crisis intervention can be effective only outside the office—nine-to-five casework is not good enough, nor is office-bound counseling.

The counselor visited one man in the House of Detention who

had been arrested on his way back from a pass to NSH on a dubious charge of "resisting arrest and assault and battery on a police officer." The counselor arranged for a public defender, got support from an AA sponsor, took the witness stand for the defense, with a sentence of two years' parole and return to NSH. The client, a black man raised in a Baltimore ghetto and extremely distrustful of whites, began real communication with the counselor only following this intervention. His comment: "Nobody ever backed me in court in my life before."

One man had failed three times to appear for admission to NSH. Over a year later, the counselor learned that he was in a hospital with peripheral neuritis from drinking and was able to walk a few steps only after six weeks. The counselor visited him several times and brought in a former drinking companion from a long-term inpatient program to help convince him to agree to joining the same program. The man later returned to his family in another state, has been sober for more than four years, and has been a house painter for the same employer for almost three years.

DEPENDENCE

Social workers and other professionals often warn that the caseworker should not get deeply emotionally involved or develop too close a personal relationship. We believe that these warnings are directed more toward protecting the professional than toward helping the client.[1] A chronic alcoholic is dependent on alcohol, and this dependence must be shifted elsewhere immediately—to the caseworker and/or the indigenous worker, if available, and then gradually to other interpersonal relationships. As self-confidence and specific interests and goals are revived or developed, so should more autonomous behavior and decision-making be encouraged. Autonomy, however, is always relative. Social relations and social interdependence are analytically separable, but rarely so in the real world. Strong dependency upon the counselor was therefore encouraged from the beginning, with an immediate emphasis on other interpersonal relationships not related to drinking. Gradually more responsibility and autonomy were developed, with timing based on the client's expressed confidence as well as on the counselor's estimate of the man's readiness to take the next step.

MOTIVATION

Testing motivation for therapy is another casework rationale. If

the Skid Row alcoholic satisfies the terms laid down by caseworkers, he is served; if he does not, he is often told that the
service is not appropriate for him. How much thought is given to
the responsibility of the caseworker for the encouragement of
motivation? It may be that some men want much more than the
minimum of food, clothing, shelter, and medical care, but they
cannot conceive of making any substantial change through their
own efforts; certainly they do not realize that the tremendous
amount of help they need will be available. For example, Ed (a
volunteer counselor referred to in the "Operation Bumblebee" section of this chapter) had an equalitarian style that seemed to raise
the motivation for therapy. He began as an AA sponsor and developed this relationship into a friendship. Ed and another counselor
arranged a home dinner for clients; they sat with a group of clients
at a table at the annual AA breakfast; during the Christmas season (when drinking is most likely) Ed invited a group of clients
to his apartment for breakfast; a New Year's Eve party at the
intensive counselor's home involved 13 clients. During the course
of this extended relationship, Ed invited all the men to his apartment; there they worked out a drinking chart for each one for
recent years, which was invaluable in assessing progress in sobriety.

SUPPORTIVE CASEWORK

The crucial question is what to support and what not to support.
Skid Row alcoholics usually present patterns of behavior which
have repeatedly led them to uncontrolled drinking. We have
already indicated some of the things the caseworker had painfully
learned not to support: drinking of alcohol (even beer), live-in
jobs, trying to work too soon after a binge, an upward jump in
job status too soon, an early job-training program, an early effort
to restore family ties. In one instance, a man's periodic decisions
to return to live with his mother were discouraged because they
seemed damaging to him. All the men were fully supported in
meeting such basic human needs as housing, food, clothing, and
other aspects of health and welfare. Much of the counseling was,
however, directed toward change, with the emphasis on living differently, which is never easy, not on doing what comes naturally.

One almost illiterate man in his early forties, with a tested IQ
of 65, had been a dishwasher for 15 years. His eyesight was poor,
but he had no eyeglasses. He was a very suspicious man. With
great difficulty, he expressed his dream of wanting to read, get a

better job, and learn to have fun with other people. But after receiving from his caseworker a few simple suggestions, he panicked and shipped out of a Skid Row employment agency to another live-in dishwasher job. Several months later he returned with a laminated disk condition, which required immediate surgery. It took much time and assurance to convince him to go to the hospital. The caseworker made repeated visits to the hospital to build a relationship and to discuss simple postdischarge plans, since the man would not be able to work for some time. When the client was abruptly discharged soon after surgery, with no back brace, money, Public Assistance, or a place to live, the caseworker took him home for the weekend. A DRC/P secretary volunteered to tutor him in reading and arithmetic during her lunchtime, after he had been persuaded that he was not "too dumb to learn." Since his greatest motivation to read was job-oriented, his tutor brought him help-wanted ads and concentrated on the words he could not read. He studied several hours every night; after several months, the caseworker persuaded him to enroll in an Operation Alphabet adult literacy program. His experience in four schools as a child had been so traumatic that he could not sleep the whole night before enrollment in the adult program; so the caseworker arranged to pick him up at his rooming house, take him to school, and introduce him to the teacher. (He said that all that night he had imagined a huge woman with a ruler waiting for him in the hallway of the school.) Fortunately, this was a good school experience; he studied hard, and learned how to use the public library. He went on for several months to a work adjustment program, which included remedial arithmetic, and was placed in a small factory as a shipping and receiving clerk. He has been there over three years, has learned every operation in the factory, and has received periodic raises in pay. This whole process leading up to his current job took one and a half years. Meanwhile, he has continued to receive support as a participant in most of the group recreational-cultural activities of the program.

ADVANCE AND RETREAT

The transition from dependence to substantial autonomy and the development of motivation for change can be achieved only through a long series of small, laborious steps.

It was important to discourage many men from taking precipitous leaps for which they were not ready. Many of these men argued that environmental circumstances alone accounted for their uncontrolled drinking, and they impatiently insisted upon returning immediately to a former higher-level job skill, immediately entering a training program to acquire a new skill, or making an early effort at reconciliation with family members. Such early impatient leaps had not been successful in either the large Skid Row caseload that the counselor had earlier carried or the intensive counseling project.

It sometimes happens that what we regard as a small step is too big for the Skid Row alcoholic at the time, then we found it best to encourage or support a temporary retreat. For example, one man in his early fifties was unable to tolerate a work adjustment program. The casework team concluded that the man was on the verge of an alcoholic binge, and agreed that he quit the program. The client, an amputee, had maintained long-term sobriety; several months later, with help, he was better able to tolerate a job, and has been employed most of the time since then.

EQUALITARIANISM

The Skid Row alcoholic lives in an exploitative, dehumanizing, authoritarian relationship in almost every social institution. Whatever dignity he may still possess is often under attack by the so-called helping agencies. An equalitarian rather than an authoritarian approach helps develop self-confidence in the client. Furthermore, in an equalitarian approach, the counselor can benefit from the ideas and talents of his clients. Our clients and caseworkers were on a first-name basis. The clients developed friendships among themselves and helped each other. Often we learned from a Skid Row alcoholic that another man was depressed or anxious, was about to quit a job or a rehabilitation program, planned to leave an inpatient program against medical advice, had started to drink or was planning to. With this client feedback, we were often able to move promptly toward helping a man meet his crisis.

In summary, then, out of the acceptance of dependence, although always with an eye to increasing autonomy through small steps with a recognition of a critical importance of crisis for change in patterns of life style, we believe supportive casework can facilitate the client's maximum opportunity for self-responsibility. Clients are able to play an essential part in their own recovery and that of other clients. This is an essential goal of group therapy and of AA, and is an essential function of ideal close interpersonal relationships in other real life situations, which the Skid Row alcoholic must learn to develop for successful rehabilitation.

GETTING INTO RELATIONSHIPS

Men usually came to the center after a spree or even while they were still drinking. Often they were physically ill. They wanted a place to sleep, a shower, clean clothing, food, a DPA check, money for a drink, or hospitalization for detoxification or another acute medical problem. They often showed severe depression, anxiety, guilt, remorse, and suspicion; they felt helpless—and we believe that in their condition they were. Some of them said that they wanted to return to a former trade or to their family or to get a better job, or that if they could only get into a job training program their problem would be solved. All these were unrealistic hopes at this point in their relationship to the center. So great was a chronic alcoholic's dependence on alcohol at this early stage, that we did not think that he was strongly committed to giving up booze for the rest of his life. Nor, at this stage, could he plan ahead very well.

The intensive counselor met the man with a warm, empathetic, nonjudgmental, nonpunitive, and nonmoralistic attitude. He tried to give as much time as the man needed to begin a close relationship. Thus, the counselor tried to give as much of his time as the man wanted at this stage; waiting time was minimized; a conference with another man was interrupted long enough to greet the new client and explain clearly how soon they would be able to talk; medical emergencies (including detoxification) were given priority, so that sometimes the first long interview would be in the hospital to which the man was referred.

The first emphasis was to help the man meet his immediate material and medical needs. He was encouraged to stay sober until the next appointment, which was usually the next day; long-term sobriety was not stressed. As the counselor continued to see the man, a new combination of approaches to the man's activities was tried in which the basic philosophy was to take small steps in the direction of a different pattern of living: a low-cost room, preferably one off Skid Row and near an AA meeting place (where the man could go in the evening and on weekends when the center was not open); an outpatient clinic; or possibly hospitalization (but with an alternative program urged if this was not accepted). Often clinic appointments for other medical problems were necessary; arrangements for eyeglasses were made; Public Assistance was usually necessary, and the caseworker strongly encouraged money management. Skid Row employment agencies and live-in jobs were strongly discouraged, because such jobs usually removed the man from sources of help, and because the man was often living with other drinking alcoholics. When he insisted on a live-in job, the DRC/P employment counselor placed him in a better than usual situation, and the intensive counselor made weekly visits to each client or group of clients in the same place.

HOSPITALIZATION

In the beginning of the project, long-term hospitalization was recommended early in the relationship. Practically speaking, this meant the alcoholism unit at NSH, since little else was available at that time. Later in the project, the emphasis shifted away from early pressure toward inpatient treatment: the reluctant patient on voluntary admission was less likely to remain in the hospital. Often it took the man's failure in a less controlled, less intensive outpatient program, with substantial counselor support, to convince him that he needed an inpatient program. Also, it was more difficult—or impossible—to get a client readmitted to a program if he had earlier "bombed out," so that long-term treatment was a resource to be used carefully.

Regardless of variations in approach, however, long-term hospitalization was an unvarying emphasis, and stress was placed on persuading a client to remain in the program until a staff plan for discharge was effected. The man was always told the truth about the program, including the rules, practices, and conditions that he would probably dislike. This meant that the counselor needed to examine in depth not only the alcoholic treatment program but other institutional routines, facilities, and practices that the client would likely confront. The Skid Row man was therefore better prepared to deal with the unpleasant features as well as to maintain confidence in the counselor's integrity. Further, the counselor regularly visited hospitalized clients; when the number of clients in one institution made it necessary, they were seen in groups. Thus there was a continuity in inside-outside relationships which helped convince clients to stay in the program; this also made it possible for the caseworker to detect and help in crisis situations and with discharge planning and to assure follow-through with aftercare programs.

AFTERCARE

Relapse rates for chronic alcoholics following hospitalization are very high. The transition from the therapeutic, inpatient community to the problems of the real world is traumatic: getting or returning to a job; managing an income and other affairs; reestablishing family relationships on a changed basis; returning to the old neighborhood, where the earlier heavy drinking companions lived and where the man has few other friends; or starting out with no roots in a new neighborhood. This was particularly difficult for the Skid Row alcoholic, whose way of life required a much more drastic change if sobriety was to be maintained and developed.

The change was easier to manage if the hospital's exit procedure extended over a prolonged period—at NSH, up to one and a half years. Where hospitals had a policy of hiring patients for hospital jobs upon discharge, and where unattached employees frequently lived on the grounds, a gradual transition was also possible. But unless a future change of jobs and living arrangements was carefully planned for, the trauma might merely be delayed. Thus the periods before and immediately after discharge required strong social and emotional support. Continuation of group therapy in some form was an important aftercare procedure. The development of interpersonal relationships that were not based on drinking was also important, as was the use of AA on a regular and frequent basis. Intensive counseling was gradually tapered off as the participant in the program found other sources of social and emotional support. The older the man, the longer he had lived on Skid Row, and the more central alcohol had been to his style of life, the longer the intensive casework needed to be continued.

OPERATION BUMBLEBEE

During the second year, a two-man intensive counseling team was tried. The second person was Ed, a volunteer, a compassionate man who had attained nine years of sobriety with the help of a psychiatrist and AA. He met every new client as soon as possible, had access to agency diagnostic findings, and, with the caseworker, agreed upon a rehabilitation plan for each client. When it was practical, indoctrination into AA was one objective. Ed facetiously named this phase Operation Bumblebee, after the aerodynamic engineers who concluded that bumblebees cannot fly according to any scientific principles but, being too dumb to know it, fly anyway. The casework team was flying in the face of the overwhelming opinion that Skid Row alcoholics could not be rehabilitated. Over a one-year period they worked with some 20 clients.

One of the advantages to this team approach was that a recovered alcoholic (like other indigenous workers) could speak from experience, could relate wtih clients more easily, was more attuned to feelings and defenses, and served more readily as a role model. If active in AA, the recovered alcoholic could better solicit the help of other recovered alcoholics and provide a wider base for social relationships as well as roots in a group rehabilitative process.

A team approach can also provide 24-hour coverage. Evenings and weekends are the periods when clients are most likely to drink. Loneliness can be relieved; personal crises are more likely to be detected; prompt intervention is feasible. The professional caseworker is aided by this regular consultation with an indigenous worker, assuring sounder plans, more effective use of time, and higher caseworker morale, which is especially important when working with clients who require unusually large amounts of time.

A THREE-YEAR FOLLOW-UP

While the HWH-VRA follow-up program reported in Chapter 11 was based on a one-year follow-up, we had the opportunity to complete a three-year follow-up on the intensive counseling cases (occasionally our knowledge is for more than three years). Therefore the data reported in this chapter are not strictly comparable to those in Chapter 11.

The group of 60 men who were in the intensive counseling part of the program were located through the DRC/P records, the DRC/P follow-up team, and personal contacts. We were able to obtain information on 48 of the 60.

This group of 60 clients was not a homogenous collection of Skid Row men. They were roughly categorized as: 8 transient non-Philadelphians; 6 long-term, non-Skid Row Philadelphians; 19 who were periodically on and off Philadelphia's Skid Row, but who spent much time away on jobs or in other localities; and 27 who spent most of their time on Skid Row, although they might leave periodically for short-term or seasonal summer jobs. The first two categories were clearly distinct; the latter two seemed to be on a continuum with respect to residency.

Improvement

Our discussion will be in terms of improvement over a three-year period. By this, we mean a life pattern over the three-year period of: being entirely or almost entirely off Skid Row, and maintaining sobriety or obviously better control of drinking. If the client was fully employable, job stability and quality of jobs were considered in determining the quality of social function. A man was considered not fully employable if he was receiving Public Assistance, Veteran's Administration or Social Security disability, and/or Social Security retirement payments. (Although originally all men were considered employable, the status of some changed during the ensuing years.) Clearly Skid Row-like employment—such as mission work, seasonal work, farm truck jobs, muzzling, or spot jobs obtained through a Skid Row employment agency—did not qualify as better social functioning. The judgments were made conservatively by the counselor and checked for reliability.[2]

Transients

In Chapter 10 we pointed out that there was a good chance of reaching men who come from metropolitan Philadelphia. The style of life adopted by the transients made casework difficult and also interfered with the follow-up program. Four of the eight men functioned substantially better for two to four months, but they eventually left town. We suspect that this was at the onset of a period of spree drinking, although we are not sure. There is no evidence that any of the transients sustained better social functioning over a three-year period.

Long-Term, Non-Skid Row Non-Philadelphians

These six men were generally the youngest of the four categories, with a median age of 37. We considered them potential Skid Row alcoholics. One of them died from an accident associated with drug use; one has not been heard from in four years; the other four have shown no better social functioning over a three-year period, although three have done so for periods of from two to six months.

Periodic and Regular Skid Row Men

We grouped these 46 men together because outcomes were similar for both categories. Over the three-year period, we had useful information on 37; 3 died; we could follow up the balance. Of the balance, 20 were better and 17 were not.

Variables Related to Social Functioning

Age was not significantly related to better social functioning. Furthermore, sobriety as a variable by itself was rejected because a report of sobriety frequently depended on the client alone, and hence could be unreliable. In any event, we felt that we did not have reliable data about drinking patterns for all the men, and consequently we will not report them in detail. It was clear, however, that our available data tended to confirm our main findings. The variable of work pattern was included as an integral part of the outcome variable—social functioning—and consequently will not be discussed separately.

TABLE 12-1   LIVING ARRANGEMENTS, PARTICIPATION IN AA, AND HOSPITALIZATION BY SOCIAL FUNCTION AFTER THREE YEARS

| | SOCIAL FUNCTIONING | | | | |
	Better	No Better	DK	Deceased	Total
Lives alone	12	23	12	3	50
Lives with family or friends	8	1	0	1	10
Regular participation in AA	7	0	1	0	8
Not regular participation in AA	13	24	11	4	52

Table 12-1 gives data relating to the three-year follow-up with respect to social functioning, living arrangements, and participation in AA. The table suggests that participation with others in living arrangements or therapeutic activity was related to better social functioning at the end of the three-year period. The two variables were highly but imperfectly correlated. Taken together, they were even better predictors than when taken separately. It is likely that other forms of socialization played an important role, but there are insufficient data to include these in the tables. For instance, of six men who showed better social functioning for three years and who lived alone without AA, two had steady women friends, three had close relationships with employers and other employees on steady jobs, while the sixth visited his sister almost daily. We believe that the importance of some kind of participation in the social life of a community cannot be underestimated in its relationship to therapeutic outcome. This is in line with Myerson's results, in which he reported a strong relationship between failure and solitary living.[3]

Thirty-eight of the 60 men went to a state mental hospital and/or a private hospital for alcoholics. There was no clear relationship between better social functioning and hospitalization. However, there was a significant relationship with outcome for men hospitalized for six months or more. Table 12-2 shows the

TABLE 12-2   RELATIONSHIP BETWEEN SOCIAL FUNCTIONING AND HOSPITALIZATION

HOSPITALIZATION	SOCIAL FUNCTIONING				
	Better	No Better	DK	Deceased	Total
No hospitalization	6	5	10	1	22
Hospitalization less than 6 months	3	12	1	1	17
Greater than 6 months	11	7	1	2	21

relationship between outcome and hospitalization. Although it is clear that the relationship was significant for those who were hospitalized, the relationship was not so clear if one includes the non-hospitalized. While the relationship was blurred by the number of unknown cases (DK), we assume that the majority of those who were lost to the follow-up did not make a better adjustment. Many of them came from the younger transient group. Nonetheless the fact remains that we know little about this group. In any event, the factor of hospitalization and the length of hospitalization are reminiscent of the regularity of AA attendance. The same motivational factors may be operating in both cases.

Operation Bumblebee, with 20 men, involved a more active participation of the counseling team, although this factor was of course mixed to some degree in hospitalization, socialization, and participation in AA. Nine men showed a better social functioning over the three-year period, in comparison with 11 of those not in the program—not a statistically significant difference. However, there was only one man in Operation Bumblebee who was not contacted during follow-up, in comparison with 11 in the other group. Thus, one either had a better chance of success or a better chance of continued therapeutic contact, given the highly intensive casework of Operation Bumblebee. Of those involved in Operation Bumblebee, 75 percent agreed to hospitalization, in comparison with about 50 percent who did not. In addition, almost 60 percent of those in Operation Bumblebee remained in the hospital six months or longer, in contrast to only 35 percent of those not in the program. Intuitively one suspects that a continuous contact with a friend outside the hospital must be an important motivational and therapeutic influence. Operation Bumblebee also appears to have been an important influence on the socialization of the men. Thus, 40 percent of those in Operation Bumblebee lived with family or friends or attended AA regularly, in contrast to 22 percent of those not in the program. Again, we see that the intensity of the casework is related to a variable which is significantly related to outcome.

We do not suggest that the three-year intensive counseling project or even the one-year Operation Bumblebee are the only possible, or even the best, models for rehabilitating Skid Row alcoholics. However, we are strongly suggesting that a sharp break with traditional casework is essential for effective rehabilitation of Skid Row alcoholics.

The caseworker needs to show warmth, empathy, and genuineness; to get emotionally involved; to keep waiting time at a minimum; to help meet clients' most urgent, immediate needs as soon as possible; to encourage temporary dependency of client upon caseworker, and to allow it for a prolonged period while working to have dependency needs adequately met elsewhere, along with the development of greater autonomy; patiently to encourage the client to take a realizable succession of small steps toward realistic goals on a long-term basis; to help the client develop more motivation through these many specific accomplishments; to move into crisis situations to help effect greater gain; to develop an equalitarian relationship with the client; to help the client develop interpersonal relationships to enhance his feeling of self-worth, power, and enjoyment of life; and to promote close relationships with nonprofessionals or groups which can devote time to helping the Skid Row alcoholic work toward these goals.

13

Policies, Programs, and Principles

Each metropolitan area should establish a comprehensive service center oriented primarily to people who live a Skid Row style of life.

What is needed is a comprehensive diagnostic, referral, and treatment facility. The center should be able to arrange for adequate care for men with communicable diseases not only because they should have that care but because every effort should be made to insure that a policy of dispersal does not lead to the spread of those diseases. The facility should be a health center in the broadest meaning of the term. That is, the center should be concerned not only about communicable diseases but about chronic disorders such as alcoholism and disturbed behavior. These chronic disorders are related to the loss of social credit of participants in the Skid Row way of life. The reestablishment of that credibility in the larger community should be one of the responsibilities of the comprehensive center. Services should be planned on the basis of "hurts," and Skid Row men hurt in many ways. We believe that the data show that many of these men will come to such a comprehensive service center. Not only will they come but persons living outside Skid Row who have similar hurts will also come. Such a comprehensive service center can facilitate a program of Skid Row prevention.

In the main, our experience leads us

clearly to believe that those who hurt most from use of alcohol—
the spree drinkers—will be prominent users of such a diagnostic
and rehabilitation center. An example of another kind of hurt is
the older persons who are nondrinkers or who drink relatively
little. Why these people move to Skid Row is not always easy to
determine. Some of them may have been heavy drinkers in their
earlier years; they may have been originally referred to housing
in the Skid Row area by social welfare agencies; they may have
been marginal workingmen who used Skid Row housing during
the slack period as a base of operations. In any case, it seems
reasonable to argue that the principal obstacles to their leaving the
Row at this time lie not in their drinking behavior but in their
health and in their poverty. In this respect, they are probably little
different from many people with health and income problems elsewhere in the metropolitan area. What seems to be the major factor
is that they probably now have few family and friends outside the
area. It would seem desirable for social welfare agencies to encourage the relocation of these people to other housing, to undertake to see that they secure reasonable medical care, and to
encourage them to participate on the same basis as others in the
activities of elderly people. If this is not possible because of mental
illness or brain damage, they should be encouraged (but not compelled) to live in a domiciliary facility or sheltered boarding home
where they will get the care and protection that they need. We will
return to a discussion of such facilities later in this chapter.

Public agencies and concerned private agencies should adopt
the position that they will seek to create conditions which will
encourage the abandonment of the Skid Row life style as well as
the elimination of Skid Row localities, whether these are recurrent
major or smaller secondary areas.

We see Skid Row as a special kind of slum—one of persons
living outside family life, in poverty as a consequence of their
inadequacy, age, chronic illness—especially alcoholism and tuberculosis—and whose ties with the larger community have shriveled.
The Skid Row way of life is a dangerous and unhealthy one, and
Skid Row localities are unfit for human habitation. Skid Row people are related to the metropolitan economy as producers through
the menial jobs that they perform. They are among the most powerless residents of our cities both with respect to their vulnerability
to exploitation from all directions and from the point of view of
their inability to express their protest in some meaningful and

effective way. They are accorded no respect—in our litany of pejoratives, "Skid Row bum" is close to the bottom in terms of dignity and respect. (To be black and to live in the Skid Row area is truly to be at the bottom of the American prestige scale.) We are not relativistic about this, although in later recommendations we are realistic—we are willing to accept a compromise when it comes to housing Skid Row men. However, we see their continued degradation as a measure of the inability of our society to solve its problems.

Adequate and easily available detoxification facilities should be established to assist those with alcohol problems.

We have based most of our analysis on the concept of spree drinking loss of control as central to the concept of alcoholism, although we recognize that alcohol addiction, as evidenced in blood-level drinking, may also represent a different form of loss of control. Indeed, we found that the spree drinkers differed in major respects from the daily (blood-level) drinkers. We have given most of our attention to spree drinkers rather than to blood-level drinkers. Our data suggest that, for obvious reasons, the spree drinkers hurt more than the blood-level drinkers and are the ones who are most likely to need and use detoxification facilities and are more amenable to treatment of their alcohol problems. We have no way to accurately estimate the volume of need for such facilities at the present time. In our ten-day study of men who were brought into a Philadelphia police station, we found that slightly more than 10 percent had been picked up by the police two or more times. There seems little doubt that they were on a spree. But this would seem to be an unrealistically low estimate of the volume of need. A more probable figure might be based on the fact that over 50 percent of the men who were entered into the sample by the police during the course of the study said that they were spree drinkers. Then too, it is necessary to add some beds for the heavy drinkers in the general population. All things considered, it is our estimate that Philadelphia (or a city of comparable size) should have from 75 to 100 beds for detoxification purposes. (This happens to be just slightly more than the number now available in Philadelphia.) The availability of detoxification facilities is of course not a solution to the Skid Row problem, but should be seen as a public health measure. Furthermore, the detoxification facility offers a positive situation from which a man may proceed to other types of treatment for his alcohol problem.

Alcoholic beverages should be legally available on a seven-day, 24-hour basis.

We do not want to be misunderstood in this. We regard alcohol as a dangerous chemical which should be used with caution. Nonetheless, if it is the citizen's right to use this chemical at all, it is his right to have it available when he wants it. If drinking places are noisy and disrupt the peace of a neighborhood, that is a police problem and should not be confused with protecting a person from vice by limiting the hours when beverage alcohol is available. We also see this as a partial answer to the problem of the speakeasy. One way or another, the alcohol is made available and is consumed. We believe that it would be better to make it available legally rather than illegally. The other part of the speakeasy problem, with its direct and indirect exploitation of the men, should be solved through changes in law enforcement practices.

In policy and practice, the law enforcement agencies should be committed to a protective approach to Skid Row men.

There are the beginnings of such an approach in police sponsorship of detoxification facilities in St. Louis and in the careful treatment apparently accorded to Skid Row men in the local courts of Chicago. Extensive changes in current practices will be necessary to achieve a protective approach. Thus, rather than taking a drunken person to the station, the police should take him to a detoxification facility. At that point, those who are considered out of danger to themselves and to others might be taken home by a member of the family or someone else. For this purpose, we regard a Skid Row hotel or rooming house as a man's home— that is, we do not regard a man who regularly lives in the same Skid Row hotel or rooming house as homeless, even if he pays on a daily basis. Another illustration of what we mean by a protective approach is the elimination of police roundups as a technique of Skid Row control. It may well be true, as police administrators say, that the day of the foot patrol officer is over; police densities are relatively low, even in our major cities, and many crimes are committed with the aid of automobiles. However, two patrolmen on a Skid Row beat could together get most drunken men off the street to where they live or arrange for transportation to a detoxification facility with little more difficulty than is entailed in the present system. Insofar as they knew the men personally, they might also be more effective in their control function. Similarly, when a drunken man offends the sensibilities of passersby with his vulgar behavior, it would seem to make greater sense to have his current alcoholic condition treated rather than to use his behavior as an excuse for jail. Furthermore, many Skid Row men live alone in the sense that there are few who care about them personally. We recognize that the police are engaged in law enforcement rather than social work, but both these activities are concerned with the welfare of the citizenry. The policeman on the beat is indeed the representative of the larger community, and as such he may well be a very important social tie for Skid Row residents. Another example of this protective approach is the elimination of the petty thievery and cruelty that characterize the behavior of some officers toward Skid Row residents. As we have said, this is hard to prove, but our interviews with Skid Row men indicate that it does happen. In practical terms, we believe that it will take a change in attitude on the part of the officers who patrol the area as well as on the part of their immediate supervisors in the station house. We do not believe that this is simply a matter of misunderstanding—a course of lectures and discussion is probably not sufficient. A special investigative arm of the police force should be created and expanded to keep Skid Row under its surveillance. This same team of special investigators could also be used to bring in evidence against bootleggers, once the question of availability is resolved. Finally, the protective approach to Skid Row men would seem to preclude mass trials of these men. The establishment of adequate detoxification facilities should eliminate the necessity of trials; but if there are to be trials, it would seem desirable that they be conducted after the person has been detoxified, when the dignity of both the court and the accused might be raised rather than denigrated. Lovald and Stub have found that monetary fines have a greater deterrent effect than workhouse sentences with respect to public drunkenness offenses.[1]

The practice of sending heavy drinkers to jail on the basis of failure to satisfy court family support orders should be discontinued.

It is doubtful that such procedures are effective in bringing support money to the family, and there is good reason to believe that the experience speeds up whatever tendency there might be for the transformation of the nonsupporter to the Skid Row man.

As a policy of punishment, the procedure is questionable; it does not uphold the dignity of the court and, insofar as alcoholism is recognized as a chronic debilitating condition ("disease"), it would seem to be within the gray area of legality. Furthermore, insofar as the judge's support order and the threat of jail are used by the wife as a means of revenge for past or present injuries, it seems questionable as well. It might be better to arrange for some other way of supporting the family or of assisting the mother to learn to support herself and her children. In saying this, we do not want to suggest that fathers should not be expected to support their children, which is a separate issue. It may be that the solution might be found in a direct attachment of the paycheck, but, here again, it may be that the resulting take-home pay would be so small as to remove any work incentive and tend to drive the man toward a Skid Row or vagrant style of life. Thus, it would seem that court orders would be appropriate for the middle- and upper-income groups and not for the lower-income groups in the population. However, it is our impression that it is the lower-income groups that are at present most likely to be hit with the "pay or jail" policy, although they are least likely to be able to make adequate payments while continuing to live outside a Skid Row style of life.

Decent, safe, and sanitary housing should be developed as a first step in the rehabilitation of Skid Row men and the prevention of the Skid Row condition.

We have already indicated the desirability for a comprehensive service center. One of its responsibilities would be to organize and supervise the housing complex that we recommend below. As for the enforcement of housing standards, the center would work closely with the Department of Licenses and Inspections. Insofar as the establishment of additional housing is required, it would work closely with the Housing Authority and the Department of Public Welfare. Insofar as there are public health features implicit in all Skid Row housing operations, the Department of Public Health would need a close liaison. Insofar as housing is a locus for cheating Skid Row men, a close working relationship with the District Attorney's office as well as with the Police Department would be necessary. We do not believe that decent, safe, and sanitary housing can now be provided in the private sector at a price that Skid Row people can or will pay. Rather, we believe that some facilities can best be operated by private operators (transient facility, rooming houses, and supervised boarding homes), but that these will need to be subsidized to provide the quality of housing necessary. Furthermore, such subsidization might help reduce overt political exploitation and intimidation by rooming house and hotel operators. It would make possible periodic inspection of the facilities, and it would encourage remedies for fire hazards, vermin, rats, and the like.

A domiciliary facility should be established.

Various kinds of housing are clearly needed. We suggest four major types, not very different from the kind of typology of care for "inept persons" suggested by Lamb and Goertzel.[2] We recognize that there will be some Skid Row residents who may require psychiatric or nursing-type care. Clearly this is a residual category, although we discuss it first here. We assume that the more vigorous and restless will not want to remain in such a facility. The institutional arrangements should allow for as much individual autonomy and for as little stigmatizing as possible. Men should be permitted to leave if they wish—and they should be welcomed back. The emphasis should be that this is their home, and that the staff wants them to stay. The facility should be sufficiently away from the action of the city to pose some difficulties in getting to any Skid Row area that may continue to exist or to recur, but it should also be accessible to public transportation—for example, at the end of a long bus trip, possibly involving a single transfer. We see the desirability of striking a balance between an open institution and its relative isolation. Clearly such a facility should be attractive to the residents. In addition to adequate nursing care, careful attention should be given to recreation. While this should be true for the other housing arrangements that we recommend, it seems to be especially true in the present case. Boredom can be especially oppressive when 24-hour residential care is involved, and the residents are less likely to "deteriorate" if the passage of time can be adequately organized. (In the other housing facilities that we will discuss below, the residents are less likely to turn to heavy drinking if well-planned recreational plans are implemented.) In planning recreational facilities, we recommend that a beer bar be included within the domiciliary. Alcohol is a normal part of a workingman's way of life as well as of a Skid Row man's. Can we successfully make the domiciliary into a home for these men if we deprive them of what is readily available to most workingmen? An additional benefit may be that if alcohol is available within the domiciliary the men will be less inclined to leave the premises; the use of alcohol may be more easily monitored—if a man has had enough, it should not be difficult to persuade him of that fact or to cut off the supply. In other words, the beer bar should make it possible for a man to drink but make it relatively difficult to get drunk.

While we see the facility as the end of the line in a residential-treatment complex, we want to leave open the possibility of some rehabilitation. It may be that some of the residents will improve to the point where they can move to the less controlled and protective living conditions of a supervised boarding home.

Supervised boarding homes should be developed.

We recognize that, for a variety of reasons, many Skid Row men are what might be called dependent persons—at the present time they cannot manage their affairs completely. This is a part of the basis of the exploitative landlord in the Skid Row hotels and rooming houses. At the same time, these men are not completely inadequate. What they need is a protected situation which permits them to be as free as they are able. As we conceive it, such a facility would be managed by a landlady or a wife-husband team. Meals could be made available in the building, or arrangements could be made at a nearby restaurant. While nursing skill might not often be needed, it is likely that there would be a significant number of situations in the course of the management of such a facility to suggest that the resident manager be a licensed practical nurse. Further, we think that it would be desirable for a physician regularly to call on the facility at least once a week. For those who need it, employment, legal, and financial counsel would be available on an on-call basis. One of the major problems with the existing housing situation for people who cannot make it alone is the matter of money management. We have no easy solution for this. It seems likely that special arrangements will need to be made with a bank to permit each man to have his own account and to be able to withdraw his money as he sees fit. Whatever system is adopted, it is clear that each man's financial affairs will need to be reviewed with him regularly by someone whom he trusts.

Rooming houses should be encouraged for persons who are acculturated to the Skid Row way of life.

We recognize that some men like the Skid Row way of life and the social relationships they have developed in conjunction with that way of life. These men tend to be blood-level drinkers, to be marginally employed in muzzling and similar jobs, and to be residentially stable. Many are long-time residents of the area. Of all the Skid Row men, these are the most intact and best able to care for themselves. While they subscribe to some deviant values (especially with respect to alcohol), they are rarely homeless. Their homes are the Skid Row hotels and rooming houses; they usually have a visible means of support. When they are caught drunk on the street and are swept up in the police roundup, charged with vagrancy, and sent to the House of Correction, they are therefore indeed being victimized. We believe that these men should be encouraged to move out of the inadequate housing now available to them and to stay together in what might be roughly termed friendship groupings. We realize that many of the friendships may be perceived by others as superficial—indeed, we ourselves see them that way—but the men place some value on them and so they are therefore important as the basis for a rehousing program. We hope they will retain the best of that relationship in a new and more homelike residence. Such facilities should be subject to inspection and supervision to insure their remaining up to standard, to reemphasize the continued interest of the general community in their welfare, and to encourage men to move to a more protected setting as they get older or as their use of alcohol has greater debilitating consequences. We see the change in housing quality as the kind of rehabilitation that these men need. Furthermore, we view them as workingmen who have a pattern of alcohol consumption that is not presently amenable to therapy because the men themselves do not generally perceive that they have an alcohol problem. We believe that, rather than concentrating the rooming houses in one section of the city (provide them with a community of their own), these should be located in various parts of the ctiy where there are already other rooming houses. In this way we hope to preserve the essential features that the men like in Skid Row while seeking to prevent the development of a new stereotypical slum area.

Temporary housing should be developed for transient Skid Row men.

For some time to come, there will be a need for housing for men who are presently living in their home neighborhoods but who have adopted a Skid Row style of life. These men are likely to become residentially mobile after a number of visits to the House of Correction, during which time their neighborhood roots and their employment ties become more and more tenuous. In addition, while we believe that the number of migratory Skid Row-type men is much less than in the past, we must recognize that there are a number of such men who will come into the city and who will need housing. In view of the fact that Skid Rows are declining generally in the East and the Midwest, there should be no basis for the fear that we will make it so attractive to them that we will be flooded by Skid Row men coming from other cities. Transient housing, which would be designed to replace the cubicle hotel and the mission dormitory housing, should provide clean and adequate toilet facilities, delousing arrangements, laundry service, and at least two meals a day of simple but nutritious food high in protein. The model might be a college dormitory with single rooms, group shower room and toilet facilities, and a central dining hall. We have already mentioned the importance of recreational planning. Certainly there should be no problem about television, playing cards, newspapers, and popular magazines. More controversial might be the installation of a simple tavern, where draft beer could be bought by the glass; men might be encouraged thereby to remain off the streets during late night hours and thus be less vulnerable to mugging. We see this as providing a way to make initial contact with men newly arrived on Skid Row. We believe that the sooner this contact is made, the greater is the likelihood that men will accept other alternatives to the Skid Row style of life. Without doubt, the housing would also be used by spree drinkers, who tend to be residentially mobile and who also tend to be more amenable to the idea of treatment. The facilities could at least protect their personal belongings while they are being detoxified and provide rooms for them when they come out of the hospital.

Almost inevitably the question will be asked: where should such housing be located? It is unlikely that any location will satisfy all community elements, and we approach the matter here from the point of view of the needs of Skid Row residents. We recommend that there be several such facilities and that they be located at some distance from each other. We also recommend that each facility be within a reasonable distance of good public transportation or within fifteen minutes walk (roughly three-quarters of a mile) of the downtown commercial district and its wholesale adjuncts. Many of the transients will not be immediately employable, but will be later from time to time. Usually within the same downtown area are medical and public welfare facilities that are most likely to be useful to transients.

An independent employment agency should be established to operate in the interests of marginal workers.

We believe that the Pennsylvania State Employment Service (PSES) is not operating in a way that will achieve maximum benefits for Skid Row men. For example, PSES is primarily engaged in placement and does not engage in labor contracting. Furthermore, it has a concern for providing job placements for many different kinds of elements in the population and cannot focus on this single group of men. Then too, it is concerned with stable placements and tends to ignore the unstable job seeker. Finally, for reasons that are not at all clear to us, PSES is not able to attract job placements from the kinds of firms that generally employ Skid Row men. We believe that there is a place for a job placement firm that will aggressively compete with the existing commercial agencies. The principal difference would be that it would be a non-profit organization. It should probably have both a job placement division and a labor contracting division. In the job placement division, a fee would be collected, just as is now done, but the fee should be less than in an ordinary placement agency. In the labor contracting division, there would be the same sorts of advances and deductions that now exist, but it should be possible to pay a higher hourly wage because the new organization would be non-profit. Two organizational modalities may be suggested: a union of marginal workers, which would operate the facility somewhat along the lines of the hiring hall of the longshoremen; an autonomous cooperative, similar to one now being proposed in Winnipeg, Manitoba, as Independent Co-Operative Enterprises.

The program is aimed at not only the transient single men, but also the resident men for whom casual labor has become a way of life. There are approximately five hundred of these men, who, for the most part, are receiving some form of social assistance to offset the difference between their wages and their needs. Some work out of the private casual help agencies, while others, rejecting this alternative, prefer to wait on street corners for passing trucks. Needless to say, during the winter, this recourse usually proves not only fruitless but also somewhat uncomfortable. The fact that these men choose the latter alternative and/or some form of social assistance is clearly indicative of their hostilities toward the "exploitative" practices, or in the final analysis, to the very concept of private temporary help agencies.[3]

The proposed agency would be an autonomous one run by people who themselves have experienced the marginal employment way of making a living. All funds above costs would be used for the expansion of services—creating new jobs, establishing a hostel (or residential facility) for transient single men, developing a drop-in recreation center, and setting up a job training program. These objectives would be secondary to the primary one of according the participants the dignity which is their due. It is hoped this would become evident during the process of job assignment as well as an aspect of the cooperative ownership of the agency. It is estimated that the break-even point for the agency is 21 men working full time. Under conditions existing in Winnipeg in 1971, the plan is to charge client firms $2.25 an hour and to pay the men $1.75 an hour—fifty cents an hour more than they are now getting. While the plan has yet to be put into operation, it is an interesting step in the right direction. Some variant of it should probably be attempted experimentally in this country. There are probably financial control problems that would require careful audit supervision as well as power control problems that would need to be guarded against—for example, preventing the seizure of the organization by labor racketeers. But these anticipated difficulties are insufficient reasons for arguing that the plan is impractical.

The District Attorney, in conjunction with the Better Business Bureau and the Central Labor Federation, should maintain a watchdog supervision over the activities of commercial employment agencies.

Employment agencies vary considerably in practice, and charges of exploitation are often clearly in the gray area between legality and illegality. It will therefore take more than the investigative powers of the District Attorney's office to protect marginal workers. A commitment from the Better Business Bureau and the Central Labor Federation should make it possible to pressure both employers and agencies to reduce the scope of these borderline activities. Thus, in the job placement situation where the agency collects its fee off the top before the man gets his money, the outcome is that the man often finds himself working for nothing. This is of course not strictly true, for if the man had not quit, he would have had some money of his own in a couple of weeks. But agency operators as well as employers know the instability of the men, and make no adjustments for it. Often the men do not have a chance to quit—they say that they are fired when the agency no longer gets a cut from their wages. Again, it would be desirable if the agency could be persuaded to be less rapacious and to take its fee at a less rapid rate. There are also instances in which localities collect an occupation tax from a man for each job he takes. Thus, other citizens who maintain a normal home in the township pay the occupation tax once; Skid Row men, who can least afford it, may pay the same tax several times. Again, this practice may be legal, but it is questionable and should be subject to examination by an attorney. There are times when men believe that they are being cheated: short hours, manipulated board and lodging charges, false promises, failure to deduct Social Security payments. Again, we observe that most of the abuses that we have found are legal. The men are notoriously unable to protect themselves.

Marginal workers should be granted supplementary income from public funds to make it possible for them to maintain a decent standard of living.

What a decent standard of living may mean is of course subject to considerable interpretation; but since Skid Row men earn less than the recognized minimum, a first effort should be made to bring their pay up to at least the bottom. We recognize that there is the persistent argument that they would only drink it up anyway—which may be true for some men. However, many would probably use the money to improve their diet and their housing.

A system of surveillance should be maintained over live-in job situations, and, wherever possible, such job arrangements be discouraged.

We recognize that some institutions and family employers, as well as parts of the recreation industry, depend upon live-in job arrangements. On the face of it, there should be no objection to such arrangements. However, such employers often make inadequate provision for the employees to have a satisfactory private life. Often the living quarters themselves are crowded and badly ventilated and lighted, and the food is variable in quality. What is even more to the point, the jobs are often in isolated areas, and adequate recreational facilities are not available outside the nearby tavern. The jobs, in short, may help a man stay sober for a time, but more often they function to reinforce whatever drinking tendencies he may already have. Should live-in jobs continue to be available in the labor market, it would seem desirable for employing institutions and commercial establishments to be placed under a system of licensing and inspection to insure that the minimal standards of living for employees are maintained. Since these jobs are often outside the metropolitan area, it is clear that a state or federal agency must establish such a system.

There should be a vigorous supervision of agricultural day labor practices.

As we have already pointed out, large numbers of day laborers work on farms in New Jersey and in other outlying parts of metropolitan Philadelphia. These workers are more or less at the mercy of the bus driver-labor contractor, and indications are that they are widely exploited. We would like to see at least a more careful inspection of working conditions at these farms. This poses some difficulties: farmers would be sure to resist; we have heard also of some laborer contractors who are armed. Clearly it will take the authority of either the state or the federal government. Stopover points should be put under surveillance to prevent cheating and to control the bootlegging that seems to be common. We believe that neighborhood store-front locations should be established where agricultural day laborers can come and where driver-contractors would be required to register. The driver-contractors should be required to keep at least simple records (assistance in doing this should be offered), which should be inspected on a spot basis. It would probably also be desirable to conduct spot interviews with the field workers to determine what abuses need attention and correction. We see no immediate hope that the field workers will stop their drinking, but we believe that it should be possible to arrange for sales to them directly and at legally established prices in both Pennsylvania and New Jersey. Information on alcohol treatment programs as well as on the availability of other public health services could be a part of the service of the store-front centers. Since such a program could not possibly be effective without the active assistance of farm operators, it may be necessary to require them to keep records of the labor contractor they are dealing with and the essentials of the transaction. The development of a viable agency for marginal workers might make possible negotiations with farm operators to secure a living wage for these workers.

Ways should be developed to reduce the apparent economic exploitation of the men in work rehabilitation programs.

We recognize that when a man first comes out of a Skid Row type of living situation he is in poor health and a bit shaky. For a period of several weeks, he may indeed be costing the rehabilitation program more than he is earning. Justification may never exist for paying a man more than the minimum wage. However, we believe that after an initial period of, say, one month, a man should be placed on the payroll at a rate of pay that is not far below the minimum wage. After possibly another month, he should be at the legal minimum, and thereafter should be raised above the minimum in accordance to the level of skill he uses in the job. The program should be truly rehabilitative in the sense that he should be encouraged to work in sheltered workshops that are independent of the rehabilitation agency or to work with other employers. Insofar as housing and work may be available through the same agency, we can see the possibility of a night hospital arrangement for some men. Being paid a legal minimum wage, the man will be in a position to make his own housing choices. We believe that when the rehabilitation program is involved in the collection and resale of furniture, household articles, and used clothing, payment of a minimum wage should be accompanied by a reform of the existing incentive system.

Long-term hospitalization facilities should be made available for persons with alcohol problems.

By long term, we mean more than six months—possibly from a year to 18 months. Our analysis of different styles of treatment suggests that at the present stage of our knowledge it is advisable to have the Skid Row alcoholic withdraw from his Skid Row associations in order to increase the possibility of developing a new style of relating to people and situations. We have some misgivings about this procedure, because the objective of a treatment program should be to learn how to live within the community, and because there are so many difficulties that Skid Row people face when they reenter the community. In part, these difficulties stem from the fact that when the men leave the institution, they have relatively few non-Skid Row relationships on which they can base a new style of life. While they can deemphasize old Skid Row relationships during their institutional life, they cannot develop the new ones that they will need to support a changed life style. Our bias is that this facility should be located within the city that it serves, so that it will be relatively easy to reach by public transportation. It would probably be best if it were either a separate and specialized institution or a special unit of an existing mental hospital.

A simple clinic offering minor medical and referral service should be available on a walk-in basis, operating seven days a week, 18 hours a day, in localities with relatively high concentrations of Skid Row-type persons.

Such a facility could be located in an empty store, in a trailer parked on an empty lot, or in a comprehensive service center such as we have already discussed. While this facility would be able to handle medical problems expeditiously—in some senses, it would be analogous to a front-line casualty station, with referral to hospital emergency wards or to inpatient bed care where indicated—its real purpose would be to provide a rewarding point of contact with Skid Row residents as a part of a larger rehabilitation program. This can hardly be called early case finding, but it can be conceived as a way to identify and develop treatment care for persons with chronic health problems. We have in mind more than alcoholism of course. Tuberculosis is endemic to Skid Row, and such a center might be extremely helpful in postinstitutional care and supervision of men with arrested cases of this disease. We have in mind also the problems of anemia and hepatitis. The clinic could conduct tests which would identify many of those with hepatitis, even on the basis of existing technology. In addition to the dangers associated with blood banking by persons with hepatitis, there are also the chronic aftereffects of serum hepatitis, characteristically, some degree of debilitation. Once the serum hepatitis cases are identified, such a clinic could undertake whatever treatment is indicated on an outpatient basis or make hospital referrals if necessary.

The system of blood banking should be reorganized and placed under greater supervision.

Substantial quantities of blood are needed in modern medical and surgical practice. We are not insensitive to the position put forward by Titmuss in his comparison of blood banking in the United States and in Great Britain.[4] In the United States, most blood is available on either a commercial or an encumbered basis; in Great Britain, most blood is available from volunteers without cost. We believe that efforts should be made to expand the quantity of unencumbered blood available for nonmilitary purposes. This will require a campaign conducted over a long period of time. In addition, Titmuss points out that the American system of blood banking is inefficient; large quantities of blood are allowed to spoil, apparently because of an inefficient distribution system. We believe that, aside from blood collected in hospitals, all other blood should come under the control of a nonprofit agency that would be able to distribute it where needed on the basis of computerized and teletyped procedures. A regional approach to blood banking should be adopted, so that the total needs for blood on a daily basis are known and allocations of blood can be made. We cannot see such a reform occurring in the immediate future. The system of control now being developed should be extended: all existing blood banks should be licensed annually and should be required to demonstrate the competence of their staff, the adequacy of their procedures, and the quality of the blood that they collect. No blood should be permitted in interstate commerce which is not from a laboratory licensed by the state. Further, we believe that the profit factor should be removed from the blood banking system. We propose that this be done in two directions: the charges to consumers should be reduced; the sellers of blood should get a greater share of the cost to the consumer. We believe that a nonprofit blood bank service should be established that is separate from the clinic facilities proposed above. There should, however, be active cooperation between these facilities. For example, men who are known to have hepatitis would not be permitted to sell blood. When better technology becomes available, it should be mandatory that all blood banks take blood only from those who have had a prior screening and who have been issued a recent certificate to this effect. Skid Row area residents could secure this certificate from their neighborhood medical clinic. Since this is so important from a public health point of view, the certificate should also have a photograph of the person, to avoid the problem of clients' using multiple names. Until technology permits this, spot checks should be made of all blood banks, and samples should be tested for hepatitis. Blood banks that yield "clean" samples should be awarded an A rating, similar to ratings of restaurants in some sections of the country.

A program of intensive casework should be developed for the rehabilitation of people who live a Skid Row life style.

Chapters 10, 11, and 12 discussed efforts to rehabilitate Skid Row residents. Group therapy in prison was not successful. Nor was a halfway house which moved men directly from the Skid Row locality into the program. Rather, some measure of success was achieved with a program of intensive casework which was conducted over a period of several years. We believe that, while not successful in all cases, this program offers the best hope for working with Skid Row men at the present time. When a man has an alcohol problem, the intensive casework procedure will complement long-term hospitalization. When a man has no alcohol problem but has other problems of health and poverty, the intensive casework approach will be needed to carry him through until his new life circumstances have become sufficiently routinized to be maintained with some reasonable degree of success. It should be clear by now that we do not see rehabilitation in simplistic terms, such as getting a man to stop drinking, or living a normal family life, or getting a job. Rather, we see rehabilitation as a process of moving away from a Skid Row style of life and toward one that is qualitatively better. It is to the meaning of "qualitatively better" as well as to other equally controversial notions that we now turn.

PROPOSITIONS

Skid Rows are civic problems.

We mean this in the sense that Skid Row people are a part of the metropolitan community both in terms of their relationship to the economy and in terms of their long-term residence. Most of their employment, despite its marginal character, contributes to the total metropolitan product; their support is normally drawn from local resources as well. A large proportion of the Skid Row people have lived in the metropolitan area for a long time—many have lived there almost all their lives. They are not much different in this respect from other working-class poor people who also live in metropolitan areas. Furthermore, in most cases a person does not suddenly become a Skid Row bum. It is a process that takes place over a period of years, although there are problems that speed the process. The solution to the Skid Row problem lies, we believe, in the metropolitan area and its closely related environs. By the same token, the solution to the problem does not rest in abstractions like society or the government. It is the civic leaders and officials of local governments who need to provide leadership. They are of course responsive to their constituencies and, in turn, help influence the behavior of their constituencies.

Alcoholism is not a sin; poverty and homelessness are not crimes.

Without respect to whether a drunken man brought it on himself or not, the fact is that he is at that moment suffering from alcohol poisoning. He is sick. He is likely to be a danger to others as well as to himself. Furthermore, if he has been engaged in a prolonged drinking bout, he may be suffering from a number of additional ailments, such as severe malnutrition, liver damage, and brain damage; delerium tremens is a likely side effect as he comes off the binge. Just as we do not punish a diabetic who willfully neglects treatment by refusing medical attention, so we should not punish a heavy alcohol drinker by refusing appropriate medical treatment or by putting him in jail rather than providing adequate detoxification facilities. We are not prepared to judge a person's poverty, even if it can be demonstrated that it is "caused" by his drinking, and thereupon to refuse to create the conditions which may enable him to live a more healthy life. We see alcohol use as a major obstacle to the possibility of a healthy life—an obstacle which the alcoholic should be encouraged to deal with on a day-to-day basis and one which the larger community can help overcome by programs of early case finding and prevention. We reject such motivation tests as participation in a religious service as a prior condition for food and flop. And we reject work tests as a basis for providing appropriate assistance to people living a Skid Row life style. Insofar as there are governmentally accepted calculations of a minimum standard of living for families, these same principles should apply to single persons. If it is a community responsibility to see that each family has enough to maintain a minimum standard of living, then it is likewise a responsibility to see that each single person also has enough. More abstractly, we are inclined to believe that each person has some minimum "drawing rights" by virtue of his very being, so that the issue is a question of the size of these drawing rights and how they should be administered when people are demonstrably inept in their management.

We see no reason why all citizens must be compelled to have a home—that is, we see no reason why citizens should be subject to arrest and punishment because they are vagrants. The requirement that each person must have a home and the punishment of the homeless are rooted in the vagrancy law of Edward III in 1349.[5] For years our society has required a high degree of labor mobility as a condition of relatively rapid industrial growth. Our national period of rapid industrial expansion is over, but there are still large numbers of people who drift around the country: the seminomadic trailer park residents, the beach bums, the race track hangers-on. Rarely are these people arrested as vagrants. It is hard to understand the present-day application of vagrancy laws to Skid Row people except as a kind of oppression.

The rights of all citizens include protection from exploitation.

As we have said a number of times in this book, it is hard to prove that Skid Row people are being exploited, but evidence gives support to the charge by Skid Row men. Furthermore, the exploitation is pervasive; we have reason to believe that there is exploitation by some hotel and rooming house operators, bar operators, employment agencies, employers, police, and under-takers. We believe that Skid Row people need protection from this exploitation and that it is the responsibility of public officials to provide this protection. Indeed, we are inclined to think that protection from exploitation must be an early step in the process of rehabilitation, for without such protection the resources of the Skid Row resident cannot readily be used toward the creation of a better quality of life.

The objective of the rehabilitation of Skid Row people is to assist them to improve the quality of their lives.

From time to time in this book we have asserted that the Skid Row life style is qualitatively poor. We see the issue of the quality of life along several dimensions.

1. Health. If we conceive of a continuum in health from "in the pink" to death, Skid Row people should be placed near the lower end of the scale. Chronic illness is common; some persons are clearly incapacitated, many are sufficiently handi-capped that they cannot work without considerable medical-psychiatric care, and the probability of early death is relatively high. Skid Row, as a neighborhood, is a dangerous place to live.

2. Happiness. We conceive of a continuum in happiness from a typically elevated mood and a general satisfaction with the way one's personal affairs are going to a pervasive anxiety, poor self-image, lack of self-esteem, inappropriate anger, and a permanent chip on the shoulder. Our data suggest that rela-tively few people involved in a Skid Row life style are at the positive end of the continuum, and that a relatively large proportion are at the negative end. Skid Row people are generally unhappy people.

3. Effectiveness. We conceive of effectiveness as involving the

ability to establish one's goals, to develop a range of alternatives, and to choose from among these alternatives an effective means of reaching one's goals. We conceive of this dimension of effectiveness along a continuum from high to low. Insofar as most Skid Row residents say that they are dissatisfied with the neighborhood, job, their social relationships, and the like (even if they accept the stereotype that they are indeed Skid Row men), we believe that they demonstrate a relatively low level of effectiveness. Skid Row residents have generally been downwardly mobile with respect to prestige class in a society which stresses upward mobility. Many of them were somewhat upwardly mobile earlier in their lives. We believe that their subsequent shift in class position was an evidence of ineffectiveness—not only were they no longer upwardly mobile but they generally wound up lower than their fathers. In their immediate circumstances too, many Skid Row people, especially the spree drinkers, should be considered to have a low level of effectiveness. We cannot avoid the issue by arguing that they have chosen alcohol as a central value, for, while this may be true of the blood-level drinker, the very loss of control involved in the spree, with its subsequent debilitation, is indicative of ineffectiveness.

We believe that Skid Row men may move from an unhealthy, unhappy, and ineffective quality of life, but we believe also that it is unlikely that many of them will be able to achieve the opposite extreme of life quality. That is, we conceive of modest gains as more probable. Rehabilitation is to be seen as a process of movement away from the lowest extreme. Successful rehabilitation is relative both to the point of origin and to the reasonably possible. In saying this about movement toward a better quality of life, we are not insensitive to the charge that the society itself—the social environment in the largest sense—is a factor contributing to the poor quality of life of many persons. We are not advocating simple adjustment to a possibly destructive social environment. Relatively good health, happiness, and effectiveness are achievable in rejecting the society and in working for its change as well as in accepting the society and in working within its constraints.

The most effective goals for those working with Skid Row men are small and modest gains.

We have called this the optimal discrepancy theory, which means that the goals should be optimally discrepant from the present status. Practically, this means that we believe that the men will work harder with more positive affect for goals that are not greatly different from those which they have at present. Programs should be proposed and implemented in which small gains are made and consolidated so that the risk of failure is relatively small and a continuity of gains is more probable. The investment of social credit made by the agency interested in rehabilitation is necessary to maximize the possibility that there will be gains, especially in the early stages of rehabilitation, and to provide the necessary encouragement during the occasional periods of discouragement and relapse.

Planning with respect to Skid Row should proceed along multiple lines, involving rehabilitation, treatment, and prevention.

Elsewhere we have considered a possible application of the epidemiological-public health model to social problems.[6] We wish to touch on the subject only briefly here. The model suggests that planning programs for civic problems require differentiated strategies. That is, different kinds of programs will be needed for: treating the acute condition; treating the chronic aftereffects; and preventing the illness. Each type of strategy has its own justification and its own requirements. To use a simpler—and possibly more persuasive—example, it was not enough to provide rehabilitative assistance for the crippling effects of poliomyelitis. Although every effort was made to treat the victim during the acute stages of the disease, considerable investment went into the development of a successful vaccine to prevent contracting the disease in the first place. Furthermore, this approach recognizes that different strategies may be expected for different kinds of illnesses, despite their superficial similarity. Thus, in the present case, we recognize that Skid Row is heterogeneous. For example, there are: spree drinkers, blood-level drinkers, and nondrinkers; younger, older, and elderly men; recent arrivals, and old-timers; the handicapped, and the relatively intact; the ever married, and the never married; the nonidentifiers who dislike the Skid Row neighborhood, and the acculturated who like the neighborhood; the homeless unemployed vagrant, and the residentially stable marginal workingman; those who can make it on their own, and those who cannot. There are modest intercorrelations among some of these categories, it is true, but the reality of Skid Row does not lend itself to the stereotyping that is characteristically applied by the general citizenry and by some professionals as well. It was these modest intercorrelations that we used in some of our program proposals in the earlier part of this chapter.

With the aid of the epidemiological model, then, we can consider the Skid Row life style to be a chronic condition. That is, the shift out of the normal community life represents a critical event that is difficult to reverse—it represents a transition from an acute pre-Skid Row period into a relatively stable chronic stage that is likely to continue until the person dies unless some active rehabilitative intervention occurs. We can also consider the pre-Skid Row condition, which lasts for a period of perhaps 5 to 15 years before the adoption of a distinctively Skid Row life style, as fitting the model of the acute stage. Treatment of the acute condition, then, involves finding those who are in this acute stage and attracting them to programs that will help to alter their direction. Clearly this is an urgent task. Finally, we can consider strategies of prevention which involve finding occupationally unstable, socially marginal, or disaffiliated persons less than 30 years of age, especially those who have already begun to drink heavily and whose drinking has led to difficulties with other people or with the law. Thus, prevention involves reaching out to people in the community who have a poor quality of life at an early period of their adult lives. It is in the preventive modality that we see most clearly that the Skid Row problem is linked with other major community problems.

In this chapter we have presented a point of view about Skid Row. It supplements and complements what we have written in earlier chapters as well as what we have written elsewhere.[7] We have presented much data, and we have not attempted a mechanical summary of it in this last chapter. Rather, in the first section, we presented a series of proposals for programs that we believe are worth betting on. In making these recommendations, we have not been hesitant to go beyond the data and to draw upon our feeling about what is appropriate—our values and our hunches. Nonetheless, we have kept our roots in the data. In the second section of this chapter, we have set out some of our broader conclusions. That is, we have set forth some propositions that we believe should provide the setting for programs directed to Skid Row men.

We look at this book as a contribution to the policy debate that is essential to the American political process. Civic leaders outside of Philadelphia should recognize that we have been talking about their hometown as well as our own; every metropolitan area in the United States has people living the Skid Row life style. Much that we recommend is also applicable to alcoholics who are skidding into that life style. In order to help these people find a way out of degredation and into a position of dignity and respect in their own eyes and those of the members of the larger community, we believe that it is desirable for the larger community to change some of its practices. This will complement the changes that we seek in Skid Row men and in non-Skid Row alcoholics. Insofar as we can find the time, money, and compassion to re-arrange our priorities in order to accomplish some of these changes we believe that we will have a better society.

Appendixes

A   Design, Methodology, and Procedures

The 1960 survey was designed as a census of the "homeless and unattached male population of the Franklin Square Redevelopment area and adjacent areas and in those Philadelphia institutions which house men of similar socio-economic characteristics."

Survey Population

The population to be surveyed was defined as "all unattached men living in or associated with the above area." An unattached man was defined as "one not presently living with a wife or other family member and not an owner of the lodging house in which he resided." At its best, the target population should have included all the men who live in, or who are dependent upon, the institutions associated with this area for the most of the year. The actual target population was taken as all those who were actually sleeping in or associated with this area on the night of February 27, 1960. This population was probably very similar to the ideal population except for some short-term transients, longer-term residents who happened to be visiting outside the area at the time of the survey, and for men who were on live-in jobs at the particular time. Our particular compromise was to include the area from the Delaware River westward to Thirteenth Street, and from Market Street on the south to Spring Garden Street on the north. It was deliberately planned to survey beyond the area generally recognized by Philadelphians as Skid Row in order to be certain to cover all unattached men in low-rent housing. Although Chinatown is situated near the Skid Row area, unmarried Chinese men were excluded from the census. "Men associated with the area but not living there at the time of the survey" were defined as: those men listing addresses inside the survey area who were currently housed in a public or private institution, including the House of Correction, Landis State

In the preparation of this appendix, we wish to acknowledge the assistance of the classes of 1960 and 1961, Temple University School of Medicine; James Rooney; and Dr. Francis Hoffman, Dr. Victor LoCicero, and Dr. Herman Niebuhr, Jr.

229

Tuberculosis Hospital, Graduate Hospital of the University of Pennsylvania, and Philadelphia General Hospital; all residents of missions
outside the survey area which serve principally the unattached male
population.

Table A-1 gives the estimated population in each of these areas and
types of institutions, and also the number of these residents who were

TABLE A-1   ESTIMATED POPULATION AND NUMBER OF
                    RESIDENTS INTERVIEWED, 1960

Area	Residents Interviewed	Estimated Number of Residents
Franklin Square Environs		
Lodging houses and missions	1851	2404
On the street	64	64
Police lockup	35	35
Total within area	1950	2503
Outside Franklin Square		
Missions	215	244
Hospitals	39	45
House of Correction	45	65
Total outside area	299	354
Total number	2249	2857
Percentage of estimated population interviewed: 97%		

contacted and interviewed. The total of 2,249 represents all those who
completed at least a part of the interview. The best single estimate of
the percentage of the target population who completed part of the
interview is 79 percent. Of this group, over 98 percent completed the
interview. The 21 percent of the target population who did not complete part of the interview represent those who were never contacted
(about 10 percent) and those who were contacted but refused to be
interviewed at all (about 10 percent). We believe that some of our
losses were due to the hostility of a small number of lodging house
managers who remained uncooperative after efforts were made to tell
them about the program.

Questionnaire Design

In 1960 we developed two interlocking interview forms called the
short form and the long form. We also planned to use a recheck form
with a 1 percent sample of the respondents in order to assess reliability;
but since only from 60 to 70 percent of these checks were actually
completed, and we did not consider this to be a large enough proportion to give an accurate estimate of the reliability of responses, we did

not analyze those data further. The recheck form was a nicety of research design which did not work out under the pressure of administering the primary survey instruments in the field.

The survey design called for the administration of the short form to 80 percent of all interviewees. The long form was to be administered to 20 percent. These were preselected by designating which resident bed before the survey was to receive either a long or a short form by a random procedure. Actually the short form was given to 83 percent (N = 1870) of the sample, while the long form was given to the remaining 17 percent (N = 377). These discrepancies from the original design may be explained in part by the fact that the long form was not given to any hospital residents and in part because the preselected resident beds were not all filled on the night of the survey.

The short form interview took about 20 minutes to complete in the field. It included questions on personal and family history, work record, education, alcohol consumption, living accommodations, and attitudes about redevelopment. The long form interview took about 40 minutes to complete in the field. It included all the questions in the short form as well as additional questions on the personal and family history, living accommodations, social attitudes, personality traits, and health. The questions and form of both questionnaires were pretested extensively at the Philadelphia House of Correction before the survey.

Training and Orientation of Interviewers

The interviews on Skid Row were done by third- and fourth-year medical students of the Temple University School of Medicine. Each student was given one orientation lecture and five hours of supervised training and practice in the administration of both the short and long questionnaires. This was considered enough training on structured questionnaires in general and these two specifically to supplement the elaborate training in interviewing that these students had already received during their clinical years in the medical school. In the field, the medical students were divided into smaller groups under the supervision of resident psychiatrists and staff of the Department of Psychiatry of the Temple University Medical School. These resident psychiatrists had undergone similar training with the questionnaires. They were responsible for immediate call-backs if the medical student was turned down. Consequently, it may be assumed that all the men who refused to be interviewed initially were later confronted by well-trained and skilled interviewers.

Survey Procedures and Special Problems in the Field

Chronology. A preliminary survey was made several months before the main survey in order to estimate the population of the Franklin Square area by determining the number and location of all the sleeping accommodations within the area. A week before the weekend of the main survey, interviews were held at those missions which were outside the Franklin Square area. These interviews served not only as a final test of the questionnaires but also as additional training for the interviewers under relatively well-controlled conditions and in a generally cooperative atmosphere.

The survey proper was carried out during a period of approximately 24 hours starting at noon on Saturday, February 27, 1960, and extending to 5 P.M. on Sunday, February 28, 1960. After interviews were completed on Saturday evening at 11 P.M., they were again started at four-thirty the following morning. At this time, an attempt was made to interview all those who had spent the night walking the street or sleeping in all-night restaurants. Men were interviewed in the police lockup later in the morning.

During a two-week period following the weekend survey, follow-up calls were made at all the rooming houses and hotels with rooms to interview those who had been missed. Although follow-up interviews were attempted in some of the cubicle hotels, these were found to be pointless because of the rapid rate of turnover for any given cubicle. The follow-ups were discontinued when the rate of successful call-back interviews dropped to near zero.

Finally, interviews were held at the Philadelphia House of Correction during several weeks following the weekend of the main survey. Only those men were interviewed who had been inmates over the weekend and who had given a residential address within the survey area. Patients in the major hospitals with addresses within the survey area were interviewed during the week before the survey.

Interview Procedure. To capitalize on the familiar and the stereotypic, all interviewers were introduced as "Doctor" and were dressed in familiar white clinical uniforms. It is difficult to estimate how much this precaution helped facilitate the initial contact and allay natural suspicions, but it was felt that it helped by putting the survey in a context with which all the respondents were familiar.

The cooperation of the respondent was also encouraged by the payment of 25¢ for the short interview and 50¢ for the long one. In terms of the values of Skid Row, these payments can be regarded as a sizable down payment on a night's lodging or a bottle of wine. It was anticipated that the fee might tempt some men to make a tour to repeat the interview throughout the day. Hence, a stain recommended for this purpose by the police detectives was stamped on the back of the hand following payment. This stain turned out to be removable with an ingenious concoction of Sterno and ashes. Following this discovery, interviews in the street were stopped. In hotels and rooming houses, repetition was impossible because a man could be identified as belonging to one specific room. Consequently the problem of repeaters was not a serious one. The payment itself was our attempt to answer the anticipated question: "What am I going to get out of it?" It might assure our getting the interview, although there was no necessary implication that the replies would be honest.

Preparation of the Data for Analysis

For purposes of machine analysis of the data, a code booklet was prepared for both the short and long questionnaires. The coders were all trained and checked out for reliability at the beginning of the operation; the coding, punching, and tabulating operations were checked for reliability after the final cards were prepared. This check was made by rescoring a 1 percent random sample of the short form questionnaire and an independent 1 percent random sample of the long one. Questionnaires scored by each of the coders were included in both samples of protocols; this was the only limitation placed on the randomness of the selection. The results of this check indicated that the coding and punching operations were sufficiently reliable to warrant further analysis; on independent rescoring, there was perfect agreement with the original score in 95 percent of all items. There was an additional source of error of 1 percent on the short form attributable to errors in card punching. There were no card punching errors found on the long form. The single biggest source of error in coding was found on the occupational rating scales. This was particularly true for the occupational prestige ranks. An additional check on these items showed that over 80 percent of the original scores were within one rank difference out of seven of the rescored ranks. Hence, these items also were considered reliable enough for further analysis.

In summary, we may consider the processed data as reliable as the initial interviews. The initial interviews appear to be reliable when they were evaluated in terms of the interviewer's ratings and certain comparisons of the basic parameters of the population with those of similar surveys.

THE 314 DEMONSTRATION GRANT STUDY

The Sampling Process

From its inception, the demonstration project was an exercise in accommodation—accommodation between fantasy and reality, research and practice. Whenever possible, a happy compromise was sought— and not always found. These changes are discussed below under

"Research Design." Most of these changes and revisions are of substantive interest in their own right. The 1960 study was influential in the subsequent design of the demonstration project research and the action. For instance, the conclusion from the 1960 study—that differences in the living accommodations of the Skid Row men entailed many differences in the status and style of life of those same men—had consequences for the design of the sample of the present study.

Formally, the present project was designed to be an experiment in relocation and rehabilitation in which clients were selected on a probability sample which could then be examined in terms of an analysis of variance. Details of the relocation process are discussed elsewhere in this book. However, from the beginning, it was apparent that any strict adherence to a probability sample was impractical because the project was scheduled to run for one and a half years, and the definition of a stable population for Skid Row over such a time period was impossible. Nevertheless, we proceeded to define a sample based upon the 1959–60 census.

The demonstration project consisted of a survey combined with a pilot relocation project. Because of the relocation phase of the present program, the survey area was restricted to coincide with the area to be acquired by the Philadelphia Redevelopment Authority for site clearance: from the Delaware River westward to Ninth Street and from Cherry Street on the south to Spring Garden Street on the north. Because of the relocation focus of this second phase of research, missions and other institutions located outside the central Skid Row area were not retained in the sampling frame. The sampling frame of the demonstration project was based on the 1960 listing of dwelling units in the newly defined area. Changes in dwelling units were found by checking against a complete survey of buildings conducted by the Philadelphia Redevelopment Authority in 1962.

Respondents were drawn for the sample by: names selected at random from a complete census of occupants in all lodging houses and missions in the area; or "instant sample," utilizing numbers randomly drawn from a master list of all sleeping accommodations in the area.

Our initial sampling procedure was to draw names of area residents at random from a total listing of names which had been gathered from the landlords or managers of each lodging house in the area. It was anticipated that the occupancy list would be updated each month to provide a corrected sampling frame for the interviewing of the succeeding four weeks. However, we came to the conclusion that the lists were inaccurate, and we account for the inaccuracy in a number of ways:

The most salient problem was in the high residential mobility rate of the study population. Large numbers of men were found to have moved from their place of residence between the time of the census and the call of the interviewer from one to five weeks later.

The use of the census occupancy list coincided with the maximum seasonal mobility out of the area by the residents during the late spring months. At this time, when summer resorts serving Philadelphia and New York metropolitan areas were readying for opening, as many as one-quarter of the Skid Row population might have moved out of the area for seasonal employment.

The completion of the occupancy list and the subsequent clerical work preparatory to the selection of the sample required more than one week. This time lapse, coupled with the high mobility rate of the population, served to diminish the possibility of contact with a significantly large portion of the population, particularly with the mobile segment of the group. Under these circumstances, the respondents available for interview tended to be the more residentially stable residents of Skid Row.

We believe that the occupancy lists which were the basis of the sampling universe were incomplete. Although there was no refusal to provide a listing of residents in April 1963, the management of one hotel containing more than 200 dwelling units completely refused cooperation after that. Some other hotels offered lesser degrees of resistance. The critical factor was the presence of the owner: in three hotels, the owner was present during the mornings, and no interviewing was possible during this time; however, the afternoon and evening clerks, not under the surveillance of the owner, offered acceptable cooperation to the interviewers. The owner of another hotel was present all day each Tuesday, and refused cooperation; therefore interviewing was restricted to the other four days of the week. No problems were encountered in five of the hotels at any time. It is suspected that the management of two hotels withheld the names of their steadily paying clients lest they accept the offer of relocation. This phenomenon did not occur in three hotels and the missions because the names of residents were copied directly from the registry books. The process of providing the names of residents irritated the landlords and hotel clerks. This was noticeable when the second occupancy list was prepared. In general, the landlords felt that they had done enough to provide the first list.

A final problem was the great amount of time and manpower required to complete the listing within all lodging houses. With a limited staff, the preparation of the list required that we temporarily stop the efforts to locate and to interview sample members as well as all other research activity.

Sampling from the occupancy list of the area was officially terminated on June 23, 1963, after two such lists had been compiled.

Instant sampling of occupants of randomly selected dwelling units was done in 1963 and again in 1964. The sampling frame and method of designating respondents were the same for both periods. Potential respondents were selected on the basis of occupancy of predesignated dwelling units, stratified on the basis of the type of lodging. A dwelling unit was defined as any type of sleeping quarters in a multiple-unit dwelling: a bed in a mission dormitory, a cubicle in a hotel, a single room in a rooming house, or an apartment in a multiple-dwelling structure. Dwelling units were stratified on the basis of divisions within each type of lodging house.

1. Hotels were divided into two strata on the basis of geographical proximity and similarity of number of dwelling units.
2. Rooming houses were likewise divided into two strata, although the principles of stratification differed in 1963 and 1964. In 1963, all rooming houses were rank-ordered according to the number of their rooms. Rooming houses were divided into two strata at the median size. In the summer of 1964, the area was stratified into a northern and a southern sector, and rooming houses were ranked within each stratum according to the number of rooms they contained.
3. Initially each of the three gospel missions was made a separate stratum. However, one mission operated three types of dormitories: free beds for whites; free beds for blacks; and beds for whites renting at 40¢ per night. Each section of this mission as well as of the other two missions was made a separate sampling stratum. Sampling was not conducted among individuals in the work rehabilitation programs.

In brief summary, the total sampling frame consisted of nine strata: two each in hotels and rooming houses, and five in gospel missions. Sampling in 1963 was conducted within each stratum based upon its proportion of the total population as found in the April 1963 census of all lodging houses. Sampling proportions within strata in 1964 were based upon totals derived from a Philadelphia Department of Licenses and Inspection count of hotel occupancy estimated from the previous year's census.

The survey conducted during the summer months of 1964 had two additional features: more rigid control of the relative sampling proportions among strata; and validity rechecking of interviews by calling back at lodging houses to verify actual residence in the sampled dwelling unit.

Dwelling units were selected from a master list of all units in each stratum in the sampling frame by the use of a table of random numbers. The interviewer was instructed to ask the lodging house manager or clerk if the designated dwelling unit was occupied at the time of the call. If it was vacant, the unit was excluded from the sampling procedure. If the unit was occupied, the name of the occupant was recorded and placed in the sample. The interviewer was then expected to attempt to interview the respondent if he was available. If the potential respondent was not available, the interviewer was expected to call back until he contacted the respondent. Once contact was made, the interviewer attempted to interview the potential respondent with the prepared questionnaire, explain the services of the center, and encourage the respondent to come in for services.

Summary 1963–64 Sampling

The sample was selected to represent an unbiased cross section of the unattached men living on Skid Row during 1963–64. The men were selected for the sample, interviewed "on the doorstep," and encouraged to return to the center for further processing and assessment prior to relocation. Eight hundred men were selected for the sample; of these, 603 were actually interviewed and encouraged to return to the center. Thirty-seven additional men were contacted but refused the interview. Hence, the survey sample represents about 76 percent of the target sample of the men on Skid Row. Consequently, it may be expected that the survey sample has certain biases which tend to make it unrepresentative of all the men on Skid Row during this period. These biases are:

1. About 24 percent of the men could not be contacted and interviewed.
2. The cooperation of the landlords and their agents was uneven at best.
3. Finally, the sample deviated from a strict adherence to the design because some of the contact interviewers included "volunteers" in the sample during the summer of 1963. This problem was discovered, and systematic checks were instituted during the third sampling phase. The cause of such a deviation is an interesting problem in applied research and will be discussed at greater length in the next section.

The degree of sampling bias by these factors is impossible to determine in any systematic fashion. We have therefore placed considerable stress in our analysis of the results on a comparison of different subsamples with which we have worked. Data of this sort are presented in Appendix C. Thus, extensive comparisons were made: between volunteers and nonvolunteers; between the relatively stable and the relatively unstable; between the present survey sample and the 1960 sample. Because of such possible deviations from a representative sample, and because a strict adherence to a probability sample was impractical from the outset, we have placed little reliance upon inferential statistics.

Original Research Design

The original research design of the demonstration grant called for a systematic study of three phases of the client's contact with the center. Each of these three phases was believed to be crucial to the success of the project and crucial to the success of any similar project in other cities.

The Recruitment Process. From its inception, the present project was plagued by a lack of immediacy; acquisition had not yet taken place, and consequently all appeals to the client had to be couched in terms of voluntary relocation. Nevertheless, this apparent disadvantage carried with it the necessity of emphasizing the motives which would persuade a man to give up his accustomed mode of existence to the extent of submitting to an extensive diagnostic process and relocating to a different secton of the city.

Consequently, the original design called for an analysis of two factors which might be expected to make a difference in eliciting the initial cooperation in the relocation process. The first of these factors was that of the client's identification with the initial contact interviewer. It was assumed that a man would show greater cooperation if the contact interviewer was perceived as a member of Skid Row or at least as a person who had recently moved off the Row. To study this variable, the original research design called for two different sets of initial interviews: those undertaken by members of the diagnostic center staff alone, and those undertaken by members of the center staff accompanied by an "identification figure," who was in fact a recent inhabitant of Skid Row. The intent of the identification figure was to assure the prospective client that the procedure was on the level and that it was to the advantage of the client to listen. One-half of all the sample men were to be interviewed by the staff men alone; the other half were to be interviewed by staff men accompanied by an identification figure.

The second factor we proposed to study in eliciting the initial cooperation of the clients was the degree of personal contact involved in eliciting their cooperation. To measure the effectiveness of this factor, the research design called for two different contact procedures: one-half of the men were to be interviewed and referred to the diagnostic center; the remainder were to be interviewed and accompanied personally to the center at the convenience of the client.

In other words, the original plan, which was designed to study the process of gaining the client's voluntary cooperation, may be conceptualized as a 2×2 analysis of variance. There were two independent variables involving: the client's identification with the interviewer; and the referral to the diagnostic center. The dependent variable was the degree of cooperation elicited, which was most directly measured by whether or not the client turned up at the center.

This rather elaborate field study design collapsed early in the game. The reasons for the collapse at this point are instructive. We found that it was impossible to maintain either variable for a number of different reasons. The variable of identification was killed almost immediately by success. The Skid Row identification figures proved to be so successful in contacting the men and interpreting the program of the center that they soon became irrelevant on other grounds. This is to say that there is an excellent grapevine on Skid Row, and the initial contact assumed trivial importance once the men had assessed the characteristics and quality of the center and its staff.

The apparent success of the identification figures was, however, not bought without a price. The men on Skid Row identified with the identification figures, who, in turn, identified with the men of Skid Row, to the extent that they felt compelled to include some particularly needy and worthy members of Skid Row in the sample. Consequently, an unknown number of "volunteers" was included in the sample during the summer of 1963. Reliability checks disclosed this problem, which was solved by increased vigor of reliability checking during the third phase of the project. The data were divided into three sampling periods. An analysis in terms of these sampling periods in order to assess the importance of such biasing factors showed no marked deviations in the summary figures.

The second variable designed to study the problem of referral versus accompaniment back to the center also collapsed, but for different and more pedestrian reasons. This variable was impossible to administer. It was simply not feasible to accompany a specified client back to the center at the times which were appropriate for the initial interview. The initial interview was often completed early in the morning or late in the evening when the center was closed, and hence further pursuit of the research design was impossible. Attempts to pick up such clients on succeeding days were administratively cumbersome and often did not take place as scheduled.

In retrospect, it is obvious that such a design was doomed to failure. Nevertheless, we felt that the use of identification figures for the original contact proved to be of critical importance, even though their divided allegiance led to difficulties in the sampling procedures. (These so-called identification figures have since become popularly known as "indigenous workers.")

Diagnostic and Review Process. The original research plan called for the referral of half the clients out of the center for certain diagnostic and social work services. It was our intent by such a procedure to examine the social work process in general. It was clear that not all future diagnostic and relocation centers would have such a range of services available under one roof, and hence it appeared important to be able to evaluate the success of the referral process with this kind of client.

This variable also failed simply because most diagnostic services of importance were in fact available to the client at the center; consequently, referral out of the center became increasingly cumbersome, unrealistic, and administratively difficult as time passed. It was particularly odious for the social workers to be bound by a research restriction which completely contradicted the realities of the center.

The Relocation Process. An intensive follow-up of renewed contacts and interviews with each relocated client was planned. This was believed to be particularly important in view of the high geographical mobility of this population. Consequently, five different contacts and interviews were planned after relocation: one day, eight days, one month, three months, and one year after relocation.

Again staff limitations and reality intervened to limit the number of the follow-up interviews. We learned that it requires a considerable amount of time to accomplish any given follow-up. The three-month and one-year follow-up interviews were carefully constructed to parallel the questions included on the initial doorstep interview, so that comparisons for each client over time would be possible. (In Chapter 10, we discussed a comparable procedure which was developed and used under a later NIMH grant.)

Final Research Design

The final research design evolved into a one concentrating on a comparison of the adjustment of the clients before contact with the center and three months after relocation. Thus, from an experimental field study associated with a correlational diagnostic study, the final research design evolved into a simpler one limited to a correlational diagnostic study. The main outline of this correlational study involved an emphasis on analysis of the relationship of the Skid Row man to the center at essentially two different points of contact: initial cooperation, and the subsequent adjustment.

A final facet of the overall research design was the provision for more detailed studies of particular aspects of the Skid Row complex of problems.[1] From time to time, special studies have been undertaken to provide answers to problems of more limited scope. For example, an experiment was performed to assess cheating, stealing, and dishonesty among our clients. The results of this study will be given in detail in Appendix B.

Data Collection Procedures

We used a great many different data collection procedures.

Doorstep Questionnaire. The initial questionnaire was usually given in the field at the point of initial contact with the client, often at his residence. Hence, it acquired the name of doorstep questionnaire. This was administered to the basic sample contacted on the Row and also to one in five who volunteered for the project by walking into the center (walk-ins). The rest of the volunteers were given an abbreviated form of this same questionnaire. The doorstep questionnaire included questions designed to elicit basic demographic data as well as life style, medical history, drinking pattern, and expressions of opinions about their environment, themselves, and other issues. The information collected on the doorstep questionnaire constituted some of the basic data collected on any client. Many of the questions were the same as those included on the earlier survey made in 1960, and consequently we were able to relate our present sample or special subsamples back to an earlier and more complete sample of Skid Row. Also, many of the questions were designed to parallel the same or similar questions included on subsequent follow-up questionnaires, so that we might study a man over a period of time.

Intake Questionnaire. The intake questionnaire was administered to the sample man when he first came to the diagnostic center itself. Consequently, the sample to whom this questionnaire was administered included all those members of the basic sample who were persuaded for one reason or another to participate in the diagnostic and relocation program of the center. The intake questionnaire included some of the same questions as those on the initial questionnaire to help us estimate the reliability of our data collection procedures. These estimates will be presented in the section on reliability. In general, this questionnaire placed greater stress upon information for the social worker and anchor counselor, so that they could develop a plan with the client for eventual relocation.

Clinical and Social Assessment Procedures. Once the client had established contact with the center, a number of different data collection procedures were undertaken and coordinated by the anchor counselor. An attempt was made to administer some of these procedures to all the men who fell into the basic sample. These included a social work interview, medical examination and history, psychiatric interview, and psychological examination. It was not always possible to administer each of these to all the clients, and consequently we have slightly different samples for each procedure. The reasons for the differing sizes of samples vary from procedure to procedure, but usually include a combination of difficulties in scheduling and client dropout. For example, the psychological examination was usually administered late in the assessment procedure, and consequently was done on a smaller sample. Other assessment procedures were administered only when apppropriate or when there was competent staff available to perform the examination. Thus, special questionnaires to help in planning for Public Assistance and vocational training were completed only when appropriate. The medical examination routinely included a physical examination, X-ray, a number of laboratory tests and a medical history. If more specialized diagnostic tests were required, the client was referred to a general hospital. The psychiatric interview included a diagnostic interview and the completion of a formal description of the psychiatric symptoms provided by the Lorr Scale. The psychological examination routinely included five tests: two tests of intellectual function (Quick Test and Benton Memory for Designs), and three tests for the evaluation of personality structure and motivational goals. These latter tests were adaptations of the MMPI, TAT, and Rotter test of level of aspiration. The scales adopted from the MMPI were the L, Pd, D, Ma, and the scales of social and self-alienation. The results of the MMPI and Quick Test will be discussed in Appendix C.

Follow-Up Questionnaires. The follow-up questionnaires represented the final formal points of contact with the client. The follow-up plan and its revision have already been discussed.

Reliability of Skid Row Respondents

The problem of the reliability and validity of our data has haunted us from the early stages of the 1960 Skid Row census. Questions of validity and reliability in social science research are always relevant. They become doubly worthy of our attention when an investigator, such as Wallace in his *Skid Row as a Way of Life,* proposes a theory to explain differences in response that rests on a knowledgeable inner circle and a naive outer circle of investigators.

INSIDER VERSUS OUTSIDER

Wallace argues that there is a Skid Row subculture, which involves a mutual set of duties and obligations, a set of values focused on alcohol, a common jargon, and a pattern of socialization into this subculture. We agree that this is the case for some of the men on Philadelphia's Skid Row. Wallace goes on to argue that while outsiders, like Bogue, find Skid Row men socially isolated and unhappy, insiders find that "they extend to one another those very things which society denies, beginning with toleration, if not acceptance, and ending with mutual sharing."[1] Further, the Skid Row man responds to the rejection of the larger society in turn, and to questions by outsiders "if at all, only with responses designed for the consumption, if not appeasement, of the hostile outside world."[2] According to this point of view, the findings of outsiders are radically distorted by their preconceptions as well as by the veil of concealment used by the Skid Row men; outsiders cannot possibly know the truth about these men. In terms of research procedures, Wallace relies heavily on participant-observation material both from a field staff working in Minneapolis and from books written over the previous fifty to sixty years. He also alludes to the possibility that long experience with Skid Row men may yield the insider quality information.[3]

Wisemen seeks to handle the problem in a slightly different way. She does not directly challenge the validity or the reliability of out-

In the preparation of this appendix, we express our appreciation to Dr. Joseph Spelman, Medical Examiner of the city of Philadelphia, and his staff; Richard Sharf, Tamar Shulman, William Hood, Leonard Moore, and Deanne McClain.

sider material, but argues that Skid Row men and professionals (including researchers such as Bogue and, presumably, ourselves) have different frames of reference. These may all be correct, Wiseman argues. Even a Skid Row man, she says, may shift from a Skid Row to a middle-class frame of reference and back. If he starts from a Skid Row frame of reference, let us say, he becomes a part of a rehabilitation program and takes on some of the values of that program. When he returns to Skid Row (the program has "failed"), he may initially respond in terms of middle-class values; but after he once again gets accustomed to the situation, his frame of reference shifts to Skid Row values. There are multiple realities and shifting perceptions possible, says Wiseman (consistent with the symbolic interactionist sociology to which she subscribes). If this is so, both hostile and warm positive perceptions of Skid Row are "true."[4] However, while Wiseman recognizes this shifting perception in the ambiguous situation, her presentation ultimately comes to be a contradiction: on the one hand, there is the Skid Row man's perception in which he defines events and relationships in terms of strategies of survival through the manipulation of social welfare agencies ("stations of the lost"); on the other hand, there is the professional's perception of the men and of their programs "for" the men which, on one level, appear to help the professional meet his own needs and, on another level, express the larger community through a variety of agencies dedicated to the social control of deviant behavior.[5] Wiseman goes on, in her "Methodology" Appendix, to give her own procedures for answering the issues of validity and reliability. She starts with participant observation (using a "guide" to secure initial acceptance), goes on to formal interviews in the various situations she is investigating, and finally develops a series of cross-checks of facts from different informants. Incidentally, the "tour director" was one of the authentic acculturated types of Skid Row men, as Wallace sees it, and presumably therefore guaranteed the validity of the data collected.[6] Spradley also meets the problem in his own way. He uses techniques of ethno-communication analysis. Insofar as his respondents report the same life experiences—and this becomes evident in a range of special meanings that are largely limited to their own circle—the reports of the underlying life experiences of "urban nomads" in Seattle ring true.[7]

Neither Wiseman nor Spradley presents any reliability figures or attempts to specify his sample bias. We believe that the data we present are relatively unusual. We have not found any other report of reliability for information received from Skid Row men.

The challenge of insider-outsider theories is difficult to answer. Insider data generally have a ring of authenticity; we have relied upon them throughout this book where it seemed appropriate. However, certain criticisms of insider data should be expressed. The researcher qua participant observer may be so atypical that he misses significant data; he may misinterpret what he reports because of his own imported frame of reference; and he may be tempted to present "his people" in a warm and sympathetic light. At the other extreme, there may not in fact be an insider-outsider dichotomy at all. It may be a figment of the writer's *verstehende* approach (that is, he may project his own emotions into the life of the people he is working with and then extract it as a general finding). Alternatively, and more probably, some of the population under study may be adequately considered in terms of an emergent community of insiders, but a substantial part may not be adequately considered in those terms. Thus, from our own data we have concluded that there are, indeed, some Skid Row residents who identify with, and have, a life style that they consider distinctly their own and who also have a characteristic rejecting-the-rejector ideology. But there are other Skid Row residents who are really in Skid Row, as far as the rest of the community is concerned, but who do not have a high identification with a Skid Row community. Therefore, both Wallace and Wiseman may be correct for some men.

The immediate task of this appendix is to explore the reliability of our outsider data (collected from formal interviews), keeping in mind that our interviewers, especially in the 1963–64 period, included a number of men who had themselves lived on Skid Row and had some intuitive sense about the quality of the material that they helped to collect. This discussion will ultimately lead us to briefly suggest some procedures on the borderline between the insider and the outsider which may be helpful; most of these suggestions are obvious, but they bear repeating.

SOME INTERCITY COMPARISONS

In this and the following section, we present comparisons of grouped data among cities and within Philadelphia over two points in time. By and large these data show great stability. Demographic data similar to our own were collected in studies done in Chicago, Minneapolis, and New York.[8] We have touched upon these research activities from time to time throughout this book. Tables B-1 through B-3 present comparative data on age, marital status, and educational achievement. We selected these variables chiefly because they are more or less standard descriptive items, whereas data that might possibly be intrinsically more interesting to investigators of Skid Row, such as drinking activity or friendship-social affiliation, are likely to be acquired in a variety of ways that are not readily comparable. Three of the studies were done on a sampling basis, and are subject to the restrictions of sampling error and respondent substitution; the Philadelphia data constituted an

TABLE B-1 AGE OF SKID ROW RESPONDENTS, SELECTED CITIES BY PERCENTAGE

	Chicago 1963	Minneapolis 1958	COMPLETE REV. Philadelphia 1960		Bowery 1966
Less than 45	34	17	27	24	28
45 to 54	29	23	29	30	26
55 to 64	19	24	27	28	25
65 and older	18	36	17	18	21
N	613	2,783	2,249	1,474	203
45 and older	66%	83%	73%	76%	72%

TABLE B-2 MARITAL STATUS

	Chicago 1963	Minneapolis 1958	Philadelphia Rev. 1960	Bowery 1966
Never married	43%	52%	47%	55%
Widowed	10	14	12	7
Divorced and separated	44	30	37	36
Other	—	4	2	2
DK, RA, NA	2	—	2	—
Total percentage	99	100	100	100

TABLE B-3 EDUCATIONAL ACHIEVEMENT OF SKID ROW RESPONDENTS, SELECTED CITIES, BY PERCENTAGE

	Chicago 1963	Minneapolis 1958	Philadelphia Rev. 1960	Bowery 1966
Grade school				
0–4 yrs.	18	14	12	15
5–6 yrs.	12	11	13	16[b]
7 yrs.	10	10	32[a]	
8 yrs.	20	25		19
High school				
1–3 yrs.	21	22	22	24
4 yrs.	13	12	12	19
College				
1 yr. or more	6	6	7	8
Total	100	100	98	101
DK, RA. NA			2	

[a] 7–8 yrs.
[b] 5–7 yrs.

attempt to secure a census, and reached an estimated 79 percent of the Skid Row population of Philadelphia as it was defined at that time. We have recalculated the Minneapolis data to exclude females; few homeless females were living in the Philadelphia Skid Row area as defined in 1960, and these were excluded from the 1960 data.

A Comparison of 1960 and 1963–64 Data

In Appendix C, we will make comparisons between our 1960 and 1963–64 demonstration grant data; we discuss research procedures in Appendix A. Table B-4 gives a comparison of selected questions asked in the doorstep interview with responses to the same items in the 1960 study. These are grouped data; in the next section, we will present a comparison of responses to selected items in the doorstep and the intake interviews based on individual respondents. Table B-4 shows that there was a high degree of similarity in the responses of Skid Row men interviewed several years apart. While we do not doubt that there were individual variations in response, and it is likely that some of these cancel each other, it seems reasonable to conclude that the data support the conclusion that there is a relatively high degree of reliability in the information given by Skid Row men with respect to this kind of material—at least, they had their story straight. In general, the more public the question, and the more likely that it is the kind of question that a person may be asked by agencies, hospitals, and police, the greater the tendency to reliability. This is suggested, on the one hand, by a comparison of the "wastebasket" responses in reporting on drinking patterns and length of time that the respondent had lived in the Philadelphia Skid Row neighborhood with age at last birthday, last grade of school completed, and marital status, on the other hand.

Interviewer-Reinterview Reliability, 1963–64

In our 1963–64 study, respondents were asked identical questions on the doorstep and the intake interviews. To study the reliability of the information, we selected 50 sets of these interviews at random from all sets of sample clients. We imposed the limitation that the number of doorstep interviews included for any interviewer be proportional to the total number of interviews he had done—that is, random sample stratified by interviewer. We have computed percentage agreement between the two interviews for the six questions. The error estimates may arise from several different sources, since the percentage agreement was calculated from the coded interviews. Error may arise from unreliability of the interviewee, the interviewer's recording procedures, or the coder. The error arising from coder differences was less than 2 percent; coding checks have all shown satisfactorily high reliability.

TABLE B-4   COMPARISON OF 1960 AND 1963–64 SKID
ROW POPULATION BY PERCENTAGE

	1960	1963–1964
N	1474*	552
Age at last birthday		
Less than 45	24%	21%
45–54	29	32
55–64	28	29
65 and older	18	18
DK,RA, NA	1	**
Total percentage	100	
Last grade of school completed		
0–4 yrs.	12	14
5–6 yrs.	13	14
7–8 yrs.	32	31
1–3 yrs. H.S.	22	23
4 yrs. H.S.	12	9
Some college	7	8
DK, RA, NA	2	1
Total percentage	100	100
Marital status		
Never married	47	43
Widowed	12	17
Divorced & separated	37	36
Other	2	2
DK, RA, NA	2	2
Total percentage	100	100
Drinking Patterns		
Spree drinker	29	30
Daily	16	14
Off and on throughout week	9	9
Weekends only	8	9
Few times a month	14	15
No drinking	17	16
Other & DK, RA, NA	7	7
Total percentage	100	100
Length of residence in Philadelphia		
Skid Row neighborhood		
Less than 1 yr.	17	15
1–2 yrs.	14	10
3–4 yrs.	11	11
5–9 yrs.	20	20
10–14 yrs.	13	12
15 or more years	20	25
DK, RA, NA	5	7
Total percentage	100	100

* 1474 is the total within the revised Skid Row boundaries as stereotypically conceived and applicable in the grant. See Tables B-1, B-2, B-3 above.
** Less than one-half of one percent.

The six questions selected for inclusion in both questionnaires were intended to represent a range of difficulty from the most matter of fact (age) to the relatively difficult (age at first bender). The following were the items and the percentage agreement for the coded responses: age, 100 percent; marital status, 93 percent; highest grade of school completed, 79 percent; did the respondent drink last year?, 97 percent; did the respondent go on a spree last year?, 78 percent; age at first bender, 66 percent in the same age bracket. For those who admitted to going on a bender (or spree) sometime during their lifetime (N = 23), 52 percent agreed within the same age bracket and 91 percent within an age bracket on either side.

We conclude that for questions that are relatively public facts (age, marital status, did the respondent drink last year?) there is likely to be a relatively high reliability in Skid Row respondent answers. Those facts that are less public are likely to be less reliably answered (for example, education or whether a client went on a binge or spree last year). This may be deliberate concealment directed at our interviewers, but we are not really in a position to know from these data. Finally, it seems evident that data that rely on memory of age at which certain past events occurred (and that may not have been perceived as significant at the time) must be treated with caution; we believe that the time a person reports he went on his first spree or bender should probably be considered reasonably reliable if there is agreement within several years, especially since the event may have taken place 15 to 25 years earlier. It is for this reason that we have not reported much of this kind of material which we collected.

A STUDY OF CHEATING

Skid Rowers have a reputation for being con men. One theory to explain this is that they perceive that they must lie, cheat, and steal in order to survive in a harsh world. Based on the work of Hartshorne and May, a procedure was devised to investigate the reliability of the information we received from men who came to the center.[9] Three different groups of 12 clients each were tested for lying, cheating, and stealing under three different incentive conditions. One group was given no monetary incentive for cheating; a second group could earn up to 80¢ if they cheated; and a third group could earn up to $2.40 if they did do so. Seven tests were administered which were ostensibly part of a psychological battery. Clients were scored as having cheated when they had impossibly high scores. (In order to protect the clients, these materials were not made available to other staff members and were not incorporated as a part of the client's case record.) Relatively little dishonesty was found among the clients on any of the tests used under any of the experimental conditions. Across all conditions, it was found that 13 men cheated two or more times, whereas 23 cheated on fewer than two occasions. There was no indication that the monetary incentive made a difference in the cheating or stealing behavior that was examined in the tests. There was, for instance, an average of less than one instance of stealing or cheating per man under the conditions of high incentive.

We were frankly surprised at the relatively low prevalence of dishonesty under the condition that had been structured specifically to elicit and study dishonesty. We do not conclude that these men would not be dishonest under other circumstances, but that those who came to the DRC/P were sufficiently motivated by their own problems to be willing to minimize conning behavior in the psychological testing situation as a part of an implicit bargain for the services available at the center.

OME Data

We made comparisons on age with the Office of the Medical Examiner. These data were gathered by the OME staff as a part of their legal investigations. We have been told that this information was received from the man's family and, when that was not available, from official records, such as those of the Department of Public Assistance, various hospitals, Social Security, and occasionally the center. Thus, the OME records are not entirely independent of our own. While for a majority of Skid Row men age discrepancies tended to be relatively low between various agencies giving such information, even for such public information we should bring a modest degree of skepticism and an alertness for the possibility that the age reported was not the correct one. In most cases in the real world, it is doubtful that this discrepancy really matters. Nor do we have any reason to believe that similar data collected from a general population of workingmen would be more accurate. Further, while exact age is irrelevant to relationships on Skid Row, we doubt that insiders would get more accurate information than outsiders.

These materials bring to the fore the question of how an outsider can raise the level of accuracy, especially for what we have called private information, in order to assure relatively high validity and reliability. We have used private information throughout this book wherever we have felt that it was justified. Some of these materials have come from participant-observation reports from members of our staff who have lived in or near Skid Row for varying lengths of time. But what about nonparticipant observers—that is, when the researcher does not himself live on Skid Row but questions Skid Row men? Some of our materials came from men who had lived for years on Philadelphia's Skid Row as well as from others. We believe that the information they gave us has relatively high accuracy, although even in these cases we sometimes have felt that the ex-Skid Row men were holding back and putting us on. At least they did not tell us everything on the first round. This may have been because they were concerned with helping the men and because they did not see how the information we wanted would help; it may also have been because they did not understand the kind of information we were looking for—as their later comments suggest.

One of our skillful interviewers in the realm of private information was the caseworker whose activities we discussed in Chapter 12. Generally his work indicated that in situations where interviewing was more or less expected, we could expect high reliability for answers to questions that were not threatening to the respondent. However, the very act of interviewing can be threatening when it is done in or near a rooming house, mission, or bar, if it is known that the owner, manager, or director is hostile to the interviewer and that he can withhold services or retaliate in some way. Answers to questions are more likely to be unreliable if they involve being critical of persons who provide needed services or exercise other authority, if the person being interviewed has any fear that the information may somehow get back. Furthermore, low reliability can be expected if the respondent suspects that the interviewer intends to use his influence to remove services (such as close down an unfit rooming house, bar, or bootlegger) or report the interviewee's comments to authorities who may, in turn, retaliate in some way. This was a major reason for altering names and locations in Chapter 3, in which we discussed off-hours drinking.

With the situational limitation in mind, then, the following suggestions can be made.

1. The Skid Row man must be convinced that the purpose of the interview is worth his while and that it will be confidential. This is most likely to happen when he has developed a personal confidence in the interviewer, and believes that the interviewer (in contradistinction to the agency he represents) is sincerely interested in, and trying to help, him. Such confidence may develop more rapidly if the interviewer is introduced by someone in whom he already has confidence and is told that it is OK. Such a person may well be another Skid Row man.

2. Interviews of Skid Row men with respect to sensitive issues should be conducted in an informal manner where there is no appearance of a document for a record. Interviews should move from less sensitive or less threatening questions to those that are more so. If possible, the more sensitive or threatening questions should be depersonalized. For example: "How do cheap wine drinkers

in your neighborhood get booze on Sunday?" rather than "Where do you get booze on Sunday?"

3. The interviewer should allow digression from the main point of the interview. This not only makes for more informality but sometimes leads to related valuable information that the interviewer was not aware of, and sometimes serves as an avoidance of too sensitive a question and thereby helps keep the conversation going. Thus, information on life in the Tenderloin and about the rackets during Prohibition came from a client during questions about current bootlegging.

In conclusion, some kinds of data gathering procedures do not require participant-observation techniques to get relatively high reliability. Parenthetically, we explicitly do not reject observation procedures. We do argue that whenever possible we should move toward other (external) indicators and procedures that complement participant observation. Information may be sensitive or not, depending upon the context in which it is obtained or the expectations that prevail in the situation on the part of the Skid Row man. Sensitive information can often be obtained when the Skid Row man trusts the interviewer. Trust seems to be highest when the interview is done by a man who has had Skid Row experience or who has had alcohol problems in the past or when a warm relationship has developed between the caseworker and the Skid Row man, as discussed in Chapter 12. Final solutions to problems of validity are always going to be difficult to achieve on Skid Row.

C   Who Used The Center?

On a cold February day in 1960, a team of third- and fourth-year medical students from the Temple University School of Medicine (replete with white coats and temporarily addressing each other as "Doctor") did the basic interviews for our initial study of Philadelphia's Skid Row. We had contracted to do a statement of the characteristics of all Skid Row men and to make proposals on how these men might be relocated without creating a new Skid Row. We interviewed as many men as possible who were wandering the streets ("carrying the banner") until it became evident that we were getting repeaters. A more detailed statement of the sampling frame is found in Appendix A.

The 1960 Study: A Base Line

The composite picture from our data in 1960 revealed Skid Row was the haven for middle-aged and older homeless men who were socially detached and living there because of its low cost. The ratio of white to black men was more than four to one; blacks were younger than the whites. The respondents fell below the educational norm of the average United States male. However, when Bogue made a comparison of the educational achievement of Chicago's Skid Row population and that of low-income U.S. workingmen (male operatives, service workers, and nonfarm laborers), he found that the two distributions were very similar. Chicago's Skid Row men were about average educationally for their occupational level. Our data are similar to Bogue's in this respect.[1]

Cubicle hotels and missions provided a place to stay for about seven out of ten men; an additional 10 percent were in institutions or had no place to live. (Free mission lodging, institutionalization, and work rehabilitation programs are the alternative methods of getting shelter outside jail.) Most of the residents of the area were Philadelphians in

We wish to thank the third- and fourth-year students of the Temple University School of Medicine who participated in our 1960 study. We also express appreciation to Dr. Francis Hoffman, Dr. Victor LoCicero, Dr. Herman Niebuhr, and James Rooney (all of whom had significant parts in the 1960 research); Dr. Walter Stanger and Dr. Jack Weinstein, who worked on psychological and psychiatric materials in the 314 demonstration grant.

253

the sense that they had lived a relatively long time in the city or its environs. It was evident that, for one reason or another, the homeless men did not, or were unable to, provide for themselves at a minimal working-class level. Despite the growth of the Public Welfare system as well as other "social security" devices in our country, most of the homeless men lived in poverty. In a substantial number of cases, this poverty was associated with a drinking problem.

THE 314 DEMONSTRATION GRANT SAMPLE

In this appendix, we consider the problem of who will voluntarily use the kind of service center that was developed, with our 1960 data as a basis of comparison. First, however, we must explain that we secured 2,249 interviews in our 1960 study (79 percent of our estimate of the total population), but Tables C-1 through C-7 are based on only 1,474 men. In order to facilitate comparisons with the 552 men in the 1964 sample, all men living outside the 1964 demonstration grant area have been excluded. Also, in these tables, men who were interviewed at their residences, but who did not come to the DRC, are "doorsteps"; men who were interviewed at their residences, who were invited to the DRC, and who came in, are "returnees." Those who were not interviewed at their residences, but who came into the DRC unsolicited and asked for something, we call "walk-ins."

Tables C-1 through C-7 show that the men in our 314 demonstration grant population were similar to those interviewed in 1960. About 80 percent of the men were 45 years of age or older; 59 percent had completed eight grades of school or less; 43 percent reported that they had never married; only 25 percent reported that they had lived in the Skid Row neighborhood for two years or less, while 36 percent had lived there ten years or more. Comparison of responses to a question

TABLE C-1   AGE DISTRIBUTION OF 1960 AND 1964 SAMPLES, BY PERCENTAGE

| SAMPLES | AGE DISTRIBUTION | | | | | TOTAL | |
	Less than 45	45–54	55–64	65 or Older	DK, NA, RA	Percentage	N
1960 Sample	24	29	28	18	1	100	1474[b]
1964 Sample (total)	21	32	29	18	a	100	552
Doorstep	18	25	31	26	a	100	288
Returnee	25	39	26	10	0	100	264
1964 Walk-in	36	33	26	5	a	100	269[c]

[a] Less than 0.5 percent.

[b] Respondents in the 1960 Sample living outside the 1964 geographical area were excluded from all tables in this chapter.

[c] Not part of the 1964 Sample. Included for comparison purposes in all relevant tables in this chapter.

TABLE C-2   EDUCATIONAL LEVEL OF 1960 AND 1964 SAMPLES, BY PERCENTAGE

| SAMPLES | EDUCATIONAL LEVEL | | | | | | | TOTAL | |
	0–4 Years	5–6 Years	7–8 Years	1–3 H.S.	4 Years H.S.	Some College	DK, NA, RA	Per-centage	N
1960 Sample	12	13	32	22	12	7	2	100	1474
1964 Sample (total)	14	14	31	23	9	8	1	100	552
Doorstep	18	16	30	19	10	7	a	100	288
Returnee	11	12	33	27	9	8	a	100	264
1964 Walk-in	9	10	33	29	11	7	1	100	269

a Less than 0.5 percent.

TABLE C-3   MARITAL STATUS OF THE 1960 AND 1964 SAMPLES, BY PERCENTAGE

| SAMPLES | MARITAL STATUS | | | | | | TOTAL | |
	Never Married	Ever Married	Widowed	Divorced or Separated	Other	DK, NA, RA	Per-centage	N
1960 Sample	47	51	12	37	2	2	100	1474
1964 Sample	43	55	17	36	2	2	100	552
Doorstep	48	50				2	100	288
Returnee	39	59				2	100	264
Walk-in	36	63				1	100	269

TABLE C-4   LENGTH OF RESIDENCE IN PHILADELPHIA SKID ROW NEIGHBORHOOD OF 1960 AND 1964 SAMPLES, BY PERCENTAGE

| SAMPLE | LENGTH OF RESIDENCE IN NEIGHBORHOOD | | | | | | | TOTAL | |
	Less than One Year	1–2 Years	3–4 Years	5–9 Years	10–14 Years	15 or More Years	DK, NA, RA	Per-centage	N
1960 Sample	17	14	11	20	13	20	5	100	1474
1964 Sample (total)	15	10	11	21	12	24	7	100	552
Doorstep	10	9	7	22	12	32	8	100	288
Returnee	21	10	15	21	12	14	7	100	264
1964 Walk-in	35	8	4	17	14	15	7	100	97a

a 172 respondents were not asked this question.

TABLE C-5   TYPE OF BUILDING OF RESIDENCE OF 1960 AND 1964 SAMPLES, BY PERCENTAGE

SAMPLES			TYPE OF BUILDING			TOTAL	
	Gospel Mission	Hotel	Rooming or Apartment House	Other	DK, NA, RA	Percentage	N
1960 Sample	24	61	12	1	2	100	1474
1964 Sample (total)	26	40	27	2	5	100	552
Doorstep	18	43	33	1	5	100	288
Returnee	34	38	21	3	4	100	264
1964 Walk-in	39	16	12	16	17	100	269

TABLE C-6   ROOM RENTAL PERIOD OF THE 1960 AND 1964 SAMPLES, BY PERCENTAGE

SAMPLES		TIME PERIOD FOR WHICH RENT WAS PAID						TOTAL	
	Free	Daily	Weekly	Twice Monthly	Monthly	Other	DK, NA, RA	Percentage	N
1960 Sample	10	31	28	9	11	7	4	100	1474
1964 Sample (total)	15	26	23	17	15	3	1	100	552
Doorstep	8	24	32	14	20	1	1	100	288
Returnee	23	25	14	21	10	6	1	100	264
1964 Walk-in	37	19	14	6	7	14	3	100	269

TABLE C-7   RACE DISTRIBUTION OF 1960 AND 1964 SAMPLES, BY PERCENTAGE

SAMPLES		RACE DISTRIBUTION			TOTAL	
	White	Black	Other	DK, NA, RA	Percentage	N
1960 Sample	87	10	1	2	100	1474
1964 Sample (total)	72	22	a	6	100	552
Doorstep	76	18	0	6	100	288
Returnee	67	26	1	6	100	264
1964 Walk-in	60	18	0	22[b]	100	269

[a] Less than 0.5 percent.
[b] This high rate of nondefinitive responses is due to interviewers' reluctance to ascribe racial identifications to the walk-ins.

about the first time that a man lived on any Skid Row supports the proposition that for most of them Philadelphia's was the first and only Skid Row in which they had lived. Systematically, we further found that the younger the man, the more recently he had moved there, and the older the man, the longer he had lived there. The data challenge the stereotype of the outsider drifting into Philadelphia to exploit local charitable resources. Rather, they suggest the stereotype used by the migratory worker of several generations ago when he referred to "homeguards" in contrast to "bindlestiffs."

In general, we are satisfied that our 1964 procedures reached much the same kind of man that we reached in 1960, and so we believe it is reasonable for us to use both sets of data together in our discussions about the characteristics of Skid Row men. There are, however, two important differences that we need to consider. These are revealed in Tables C-5 and C-7. Table C-5 shows that while 61 percent of the 1960 sample lived in cubicle hotels, only 40 percent of the 1964 sample did so. This difference is evident also in the percentage living in rooming houses or apartments. These data partly reflect field research problems. In 1960, we had such excellent cooperation from hotel operators that from time to time police officers popped in and made clear their active support of the project, which they would not have done without the consent of the owner-operators of the hotels. The owners cooperated at that time because it was a part of the initial redevelopment procedures, which required a statement of the number of persons involved, their characteristics, and a plan for rehousing them. The hotel owners saw this procedure as in their own interest, because at the time they were full or nearly so, and the survey thereby established a basis for a high level of payment when the Redevelopment Authority bought the property. In any case, a survey of the number of persons to be displaced was a legally required procedure before a federal grant could be made; if the owners had failed to cooperate, they would have incurred the wrath of the mayor, who supported the project. At the same time, we had less than enthusiastic cooperation from rooming house operators, owners of several run-down apartments, and one gospel mission. The rooming house operators were themselves renters, and they saw only a disruption of their operation—revelations of health and fire hazards that might then lead to city action; loss of anonymity for their roomers, which might encourage them to move out; the decrepit condition of the rooms in some cases; and the slovely housekeeping in their own personal quarters. Probably the same was true for the apartment owners. The gospel mission director was cold to any interviewing in his place, which was located out of the Skid Row neighborhood; he knew clearly what the men needed, and he did not see a city agency bringing Jesus to the men.

Things were different during the 1963–64 demonstration grant study. We had resistance from several cubicle hotel operators—eventually our staff was excluded from one of them. On the other hand, the cheap rooming house and apartment house operators were as cooperative as we could reasonably expect. The shoe was now on the other foot. The rooming house and apartment house owners (rather than the managers) believed the Redevelopment Authority was in a position to acquire some of the properties, and they wanted to get their money (possibly for reinvestment in other real estate). The cubicle hotel operators, on the other hand, were deeply concerned that the center might successfully rehabilitate and relocate the men away from Skid Row. Plainly, each time a contact counselor talked to a man and persuaded him to come to the center, the hotel operators faced the possibility of a declining occupancy rate. Not only would this hit them in the pocket directly, but they believed it would hit them indirectly, because they would find their position worsened when it came time to negotiate with the Redevelopment Authority.

Table C-7 shows that 22 percent of the 1964 sample was black, in comparison with 10 percent of the adjusted 1960 sample. Throughout the entire period of both studies, we had relatively good cooperation with the gospel missions that were located in the Skid Row locality, although relationships later deteriorated. (They deteriorated because we began to make recommendations about relocation and changes in program that displeased the directors of the two principal missions.) We believe that we can partly explain changes in the percentage of blacks in the adjusted 1960 data and the 1964 data in terms of the following: there was an increase in the use of the missions by black men during the period between the two studies. Blacks do not live in the cubicle hotels. In part, this is an example of the pervasive racial segregation of our society—it prevails in Philadelphia even at the lowest class levels. In part, it may also be a manifestation of the greater poverty of the blacks, since it is only in the missions that free beds are found. Although not all mission beds are free, even those that cost money are less expensive than those in the hotels. Finally, we suspect that white Skid Row men have been more effective in getting placed on Public Assistance rolls—that is, they generally know how to exploit the community resources better than do the black Skid Row men. In examining the differences between mission occupancy and hotel occupancy, and between free and paid beds in terms of our problems in getting into cubicle hotels, we believe that while the proportion of blacks has risen on the Philadelphia Skid Row, it is somewhat less than the data in Table C-7 suggest.

SOME PSYCHOLOGICAL AND PSYCHIATIC MEASURES

An Intelligence Measure

Throughout our work with Skid Row men we have been concerned with changing the relationship of the Skid Row man to the rest of the community. At one time or another we have given considerable attention to such concepts as rehabilitation, employability, social relations and social isolation. For this reason, a series of psychological and psychiatric tests and interviews were planned.

When men in the sample came into the center (returnees), they were interviewed by our caseworkers and given a medical examination as soon as possible; they were also asked to complete a number of psychological tests and a half-hour interview with the center's psychiatrist. These contacts with the men took a number of days; since the psychological-psychiatric interviews were less urgent than the medical, they were placed later in the schedule. As a consequence, we do not have such information on men who quit us before these interviews were undertaken. We are aware of the analogy to the mission nose dive (that the testing program was our price for giving them service which is functionally similar to participation in a prayer meeting as the price for getting food and a bed for the night), but we saw no other way to develop adequate plans for assisting the men and communicating these to persons of power and influence in government and in civic affairs. The principal issue, as we see it, is whether such efforts can produce programs which enhance the dignity as well as physical comfort of the men.

The IQ estimate was obtained from the Quick Test, a four-picture, word identification test that has the liabilities of all vocabulary measures—scores tend to be readily influenced by differences in educational and cultural background. Nonetheless, the IQ scores obtained from this test probably yield a reliable estimate of a man's ability to compete intellectually in the larger community, for the number of words a man knows is a measure not only of his learning ability but also of his fund of verbal information.[2] We believe that cultural differences, especially when ethnic differences are combined with isolation from the mainstream of our society, will show up to the disadvantage of the person taking the test and give a spuriously low measure of his potential. Consequently, racial and ethnic isolation (inversely, cultural differences—the culture of poverty) must be kept in mind, because they would seem to understate the individual's potential. It is for this reason that we will not dwell on the IQ scores of the blacks, which were in fact somewhat lower than those of the whites. Rather, we will discuss the scores for all the men tested, since programs developed for Skid

Row men, while they can pinpoint certain kinds of programmatic populations, should have sufficient generality to transcend the limitations of race. Indeed, not only should they have this property, but we believe that it is the social policy of our society that they must.

The mean IQ score for all those who were tested (N = 178) was 88.5, a score surpassed by more than 75 percent of the general population. Using a number of variables, we found no significant difference between clients who took the battery of psychological tests and those who did not. There is reason for some caution in these results, because a number of the men were possibly still in a confused condition—one of the temporary aftereffects of heavy alcohol consumption and poor nutrition.

Nonetheless, there is a consistency in the data. A direct relationship exists between years of school completed and mean IQ score: those completing four or fewer grades of school had a mean IQ of 64.7; those completing five to seven grades, 76.1; in contrast, those completing 12 or more grades of school had a mean IQ of 105.1. In general, there is the same relationship between grades of school completed and IQ that we have come to expect in the general population. In spite of the limitations of the test, our data suggest that the returnees were poorly equipped intellectually for the economic and social competition of the larger community. And while we realize that it is risky to reach too far beyond the data, these findings suggest a partial explanation for the downward class mobility that will be discussed in Appendix D. The data also suggest a more cautious approach to rehabilitation than the one we used when we began our work in 1959.

The MMPI: Pd and D Scales

In addition to the Quick Test, several scales of the Minnesota Multiphasic Personality Inventory (MMPI) that seemed to be particularly appropriate for use with this population, notably the Pd and D scales, were selected for administration and analysis. The Pd, or Psychopathic Deviancy, scale was originally developed to measure "the personality characteristics of the amoral and asocial subgroup of persons with psychopathic personality disorders. . . . The major features of this personality pattern include a repeated and flagrant disregard for social customs and mores, an inability to profit from punishing experiences as shown in repeated difficulties of the same kind, and an emotional shallowness in relation to others, particularly in sexual and affectional display."[3]

The mean score obtained by the diagnostic sample of the Pd scale was 64.0, a score surpassing those attained by nearly 90 percent of the subjects in the original standardization group, these being persons described as normal. Our finding on the Pd scale is essentially the same as that of Brantner, who found a mean score of 70.1 for 296 homeless men tested in a Minneapolis Salvation Army Men's Social Service Center in 1958.[4] This finding suggests that a high proportion of the men who returned to the center for help exhibited a degree of social pathology which would be a severe hindrance to their being accepted as a member of the larger community.

The D, or Depression, scale, was included in this battery as a comparison with the Pd scale and also to explore the general affective tone of the Skid Row men. According to its developers, the Depression scale was created to identify a "mood state . . . characterized generally by pessimism of outlook on life and the future, feelings of helplessness or worthlessness, slowing of thought and action, and frequently by preoccupation with death and suicide."[5] The mean score for the diagnostic sample on this scale was 61, a score surpassing those attained by 82 percent of the normal population in the standardization group, which is about the same score Brantner found.[6] Although D scores generally increase with age (and this factor may contribute to the high scores of the present population), it is evident from the above that those men who returned to the center found little happiness in their life on Skid Row. Most were, instead, dissatisfied with their present lot, their future, and themselves.

We found no significant relationships between Pd and D scores and other variables such as age, race, length of residence on Skid Row, or relocation from Skid Row. The D scale in fact failed to discriminate between any groups except when scores of alcoholics were compared with those of nonalcoholics (Table C-8). This gives support to other MMPI studies which suggested that alcoholics tend to score high on both the D and Pd scales.[7]

TABLE C-8   ALCOHOLISM DIAGNOSIS AND PD AND D SCORES

| | ALCOHOLISM DIAGNOSIS | |
	Alcoholic	Nonalcoholic
Pd score	65.5	58.8
D score	63.7	55.7
N	120	58

TABLE C-9   EDUCATION AND PD SCORE

| | NUMBER OF GRADES COMPLETED | | | | |
	0–4	5–7	8	9–11	12 or More
Mean Pd Score	55.1	62.5	63.6	68.1	64.8
N[a]	21	38	43	46	29

[a] NA omitted.

Finally, Pd scores were related to years of schooling, as reported in Table C-9. The implication of these findings would appear to be this. Men who came to the center for help appeared to possess intellectual, educational, or social handicaps that prevented their adaptation to Skid Row and probably to the larger society as well. Thus, those men who enjoyed the intelligence required for self-maintenance did not possess the necessary social competence, and those with social values most similar to those of the larger society were handicapped by poor intellect.

The Lorr Scale: Psychiatric Symptoms

The psychological testing materials suggest long-term deficits in the ability to participate satisfactorily in our society. (We do not apply terms such as "successfully" because we want to avoid the connotation of upward class mobility, large amounts of material goods, and the like. Rather, we want to imply the kinds of satisfactions that a person in the working class may get out of life. These satisfactions may even include getting drunk occasionally, but assuredly do not involve alcohol as a dominant value. Nor does it involve the kind of poverty, ill-health, and danger that characterize Skid Row localities. To what extent is there evidence of mental disorder or psychopathology among Skid Row men? One way to answer this question is by means of the Multidimensional Scale for Rating Psychiatric Patients, or Lorr Scale, which permits several comparisons with a standardized group of hospitalized psychiatric patients.[8] The first comparison is based upon a global estimate of psychopathology—Morbidity Score. The mean Morbidity Score (17.9) was surpassed by 90 percent of the psychiatric population. Although this finding would suggest our finding a relative absence of psychopathology in the Skid Row population, further analysis of the subscores which comprise this index appears to place some doubt on this conclusion.

The Lorr Scale permits an analysis of this group on seven subscales or factors. The mean factor scores obtained by 101 men in the diagnostic sample are shown in Table C-10. (The proportions of hospitalized patients whose scores were lower than those obtained by the Skid Row sample are also given.) The only mean score falling substantially below the mean of the patient group is K—Conceptual Disorganization. This finding suggests that although Skid Row men do not appear to differ significantly from a psychiatric population with respect to most of the symptoms described here, they do have less of a tendency toward psychotic-like thought disturbances. The Skid Row sample scores higher than the patient group on factors A and E, suggesting that Skid Row men are probably more distressed by feelings of anxiety and depression. In view of the difficult circumstances of the

Who Used the Center? 263

TABLE C-10   COMPARISON OF DIAGNOSTIC SAMPLE WITH
               HOSPITALIZED PSYCHIATRIC PATIENTS

Factor, Lorr Scale	Mean Factor Score	Percentage of Patients Who Score Lower	Factor, Lorr Scale
A	18.3	76.3	Retarded depression versus *manic excitement**
C	3.4	51.5	Paranoid projection
E	16.4	69.2	Melancholy agitation
F	6.4	44.1	Perceptual distortion
G	10.0	56.2	Motor disturbances
J	10.5	72.0	Self-depreciation versus *grandiose expansiveness**
K	7.8	29.4	Conceptual Disorganization

* Term in italics indicates the direction of those bipolar factors.

men at the time when they came into the center, such feelings would not seem to be unusual. (The Skid Row group also scored higher than the patient group on factor J, but this result may have been an artifact of scoring; the psychiatrist tells us that he had a tendency to overrate persons on this factor, feeling that the absence of self-depreciation in a Skid Row man was inappropriate and represented a denial of reality problems.) In brief, although the mean Morbidity Score of the Skid Row men was considerably lower than that of a hospitalized psychiatric population, this difference is largely due to a relative absence of thought disturbances in the Skid Row group; moreover, they probably exhibited more symptoms of anxiety and depression than the patient group.

Psychiatric Diagnosis

Alcoholism is not ordinarily used as a primary category when making psychiatric diagnoses; disorders associated with alcohol use are seen as a secondary problem under the more general heading of personality disorder. We recognized from the beginning that the alcohol problems on Skid Row were so common that we would need to use alcoholism as a major diagnostic label; our psychiatrist decided to use the more inclusive diagnosis of personality disorder to describe related problems that were not necessarily associated with alcohol use. Of the 124 men who received the psychiatric interview, 44 percent were diagnosed as alcoholic. (This figure differs from the one used elsewhere in this book because the latter included men who were not interviewed by our psychiatrist.) Of the balance, 14 percent were diagnosed as having personality disorders; 9 percent, brain disorder; 7 percent, psychoneurosis; 4 percent, psychosis; 2 percent, as being mentally deficient;

the balance either were without psychiatric disorder or no diagnosis was made. We want to keep in mind that although alcoholism was the major psychiatric problem of this group, it was not an easy task to make such a diagnosis. Some men were completely unaware that their drinking was of a pathological nature and therefore minimized its importance when interviewed by the psychiatrist. Other men, usually the more intelligent, had some recognition of the part that alcohol played in their lives, but because of the moral implications surrounding excessive drinking, they tended to distort their description of alcohol use. Alcoholism, the single most important problem of the group examined, was frequently found to be a complicating factor in other psychiatric disorders as well. Because alcoholism was so important among the men who came to the center, we decided to start our more detailed discussion of the Skid Row condition with our findings and conclusions in relation to it.

For the psychiatric data as a whole, mental deficiency and psychosis were not found as frequently as one might have anticipated. We see two alternative explanations for this. Perhaps mental defectives and psychotics are more easily identified within the broader community, and so get treatment or institutionalization before moving to Skid Row. To the extent that this notion is correct, it would support a view that Skid Row exists largely to serve working and lower-class men who are incompetent as well as to provide a place for others from higher socioeconomic levels, whose incompetence may well stem from their use of alcohol. If this is so, then one might expect these men to begin showing up at community health centers throughout the country, which, in turn, would mean an acceleration of tendencies that already exist for Skid Row to dry up. The relationship of alcoholism and class is discussed in detail in Chapter 3.

An alternative explanation is that the mentally incompetent are merely underrepresented in our sample—that is, they exist on Skid Row in larger numbers but failed to come to the center for help. Priest's work suggests this possibility.[9] Priest reported to us in a personal communication in 1966, his conclusions that "the therapeutic selection process tends to raise the proportion of alcoholics and personality disorders compared to schizophrenics."

If these same findings are applicable to the men on Philadelphia's Skid Row, then it would appear that the diagnostic sample was largely made up of acutely distressed Skid Row alcoholics, but that those men who did not come in might have had mental disorders of a different kind. Such men might be relatively content with the undemanding nature of Skid Row, finding a satisfactory adjustment within this environment that might not have been possible within the larger community. Thus, the men who came to the center, despite their many distressing symptoms, may possess as much or more potential for rehabilitation and relocation than those who failed to use our services.

WHO WILL COME TO A VOLUNTARY RELOCATION PROGRAM?

The center was established to offer casework referral services; however, as we pointed out in Chapter 2, it was also intended to assist in the relocation of Skid Row men away from the area. With the exception of the Noble Street area, relocation was voluntary. Site clearance had not taken place for most of the area. Consequently, the note of urgency that site clearance creates was largely absent. The doorsteps and returnees evidenced this difference. Expressed predictively, there is a greater likelihood that those who said they came to the center as a result of their own initiative will continue through to relocation, in comparison with those who said they came because they were asked by the contact counselors.

We realize the danger of converting minor tendencies into major trends, but we think it will sharpen our ability to discuss the data in Table C-11 and suggest applications to the reader. If our data are expressed predictively, the following factors will influence use of a facility such as the center:

Age

Older men of retirement age are least likely to come into a program such as that offered by the center. These men are likely to be the most stable and the ones who feel that they can make it alone. Younger men (under 44) are most likely to come to such a facility. Thus, for the doorsteps, 18 percent were less than 45 years old, in comparison with 25 percent of the returnees and 36 percent of the walk-ins; in reverse, 26 percent of the doorsteps were 65 years or older, in comparison with 10 percent of the returnees and 5 percent of the walk-ins. Once they have come, however, the younger men are probably not much more likely to continue through the program than others who have not yet reached retirement age.

Race

Black men will seek the services of a DRC-type facility a little more readily than will white Skid Row residents. Furthermore, having come, black men will be more likely to continue through the program into relocation. It will be remembered that black residents of Skid Row tend to be younger than white residents, to be less well educated, and to have a different pattern of drinking.

TABLE C-11 GENERAL PROGRAM COOPERATION OF 314 SAMPLE, BY PERCENTAGE

	NOT RELOCATED Did Not Come to DRC	NOT RELOCATED Came to DRC	RELOCATED	TOTAL Percentage	N
Why came					
Was asked	—	55	45	100	111
Initiative	—	42	58	100	99
Age					
Less than 45	37	32	31	100	108
45–54	41	25	34	100	156
55–64	48	30	22	100	149
65 and older	72	16	12	100	97
Race					
White	52	27	21	100	376
Black	40	23	37	100	113
Education					
0–4 years	57	25	18	100	77
5–8 years	51	25	24	100	230
1–3 years H.S.	36	33	31	100	114
4 years H.S. or more	47	21	32	100	87
Marital status					
Never married	54	24	22	100	230
Widower	47	27	26	100	89
Divorced or separated	40	30	30	100	174
First move to any Skid Row					
Less than 1 year	36	32	32	100	53
1–4 years ago	42	28	30	100	107
5–9 years ago	46	23	31	100	106
10 or more years ago	55	25	20	100	211
Type of building					
Hotel	51	28	21	100	211
Rooming or apartment house	58	19	23	100	145
Mission	35	31	34	100	131
Number of physical handicaps					
None	54	26	20	100	304
One or more	38	28	34	100	189
Alcohol behavior					
Nonspree	53	26	21	100	344
Spree	38	30	32	100	151
Perceived Row tenure					
Permanent	55	23	32	100	270
Temporary	39	32	29	100	225
Friends in Skid Row					
None	46	26	28	100	276
One or more	52	26	22	100	198

Education

Skid Row residents with four grades of education or less (functional illiterates) are less likely to use the services of a DRC-type agency than other Skid Row men. Men with some high school education are most likely to come and most likely to continue into relocation. There are systematic differences between the doorsteps, returnees, and walk-ins at the lowest educational levels. However, these differences disappear when the data are analyzed with age as a control. This conforms to larger trends in American society—one may expect older men to report less education, and this has little to do with living on Skid Row.

Marital Status

Men who have never married are least likely to come to a DRC-type facility, and divorced or separated men are most likely to do so. Of the doorsteps, 50 percent said they had never married, in comparison with 59 percent of the returnees and 63 percent of the walk-ins. These systematic differences are small, but they persist when the data are controlled for age. Thus 63 percent of the doorsteps under 45 said they had never married, in comparison with 51 percent of the returnees and 40 percent of the walk-ins; 51 percent of the doorsteps 65 years or older had never married, in comparison with 44 percent of the returnees and 17 percent of the walk-ins. (These marital data should be seen in larger perspective: the 1960 U.S. Census for Philadelphia found that only 16 percent of the males between the ages of 30 and 44 and only 10 percent of those 65 and older had never married.) Further, divorced or separated men are more likely to continue program involvement and on into relocation than are men who have never married or who are widowers.

Length of Residence in Skid Row

The longer a man has lived in Skid Row, the less likely he is to seek out a DRC-type facility. Thus, 10 percent of the doorsteps had lived in Skid Row for less than one year, in comparison with 21 percent of the returnees and 35 percent of the walk-ins; the differences between the returnees and the walk-ins did not, however, persist with longer periods of residence. Having come into the facility, those who have most recently arrived in the Skid Row neighborhood are more likely to be relocated; those who have lived in the neighborhood the longest are likely not to be relocated.

Type of Building in Which the Men Lived

Men from missions are more likely to come into a DRC-type facility and to continue through into relocation than are men living in hotels and rooming houses. In part this is a function of intercorrelated characteristics already discussed, but there are other factors as well. Living in a mission is the most unstable and least desirable, and only the most desperate will live there. Thus about 8 percent of the doorsteps occupied free (mission) beds the night before their initial interview, in comparison with 23 percent of the returnees and 37 percent of the walk-ins. Twenty percent of the doorsteps were paying rent on a monthly basis, in comparison with 10 percent of the returnees and 7 percent of the walk-ins. We might add that the "other" in Table C-6 were mostly walking the streets—they did not sleep in any building the night before.

Physical Handicaps

Men who report one or more physical handicaps that keep them from working are more likely to come to a DRC-type facility and to continue into relocation than men who report that they have no physical handicap.

Drinking Behavior

Spree drinkers are more likely to come to a DRC-type facility and to continue through into relocation than are other types of drinkers or nondrinkers.

In general, the condition of the walk-ins was more desperate—their alcohol problem was more pressing, and the younger men are not likely yet to have successfully worked out a minimal means of survival in the neighborhood. We did not anticipate the demands placed upon the diagnostic and referral services of the center by the walk-ins. The administrative arrangements and the demonstration grant were based on sampling procedures discussed in Appendix A. However, there were times when we were crowded with walk-ins virtually to the exclusion of the regular clients. The situation became a threat to the center because of interference with contract and grant obligations. Our solution was to gather minimal information for comparative purposes and to adopt a 20 percent interview sampling procedure. Nonetheless, as much as possible, the DRC staff continued to give at least referral service to all walk-ins. (We believe that any facility with an open-door policy will have a similar experience.) Persons who had come into Skid Row within the past month or persons who had major health problems were given substantially the same services as those in the Demonstration Project sample. While a few urgent cases probably slipped into the sample as the result of the activities of some of our ex-Skid Row contact counselors, we doubt that these were men who had recently arrived in the Row, because the recent arrivals were least likely to have lined up the necessary friendship ties. We interpret the data in Table C-11 as lending support to the argument that special services for recent arrivals into Skid Row are justified because these men are least likely to have any ties with other Skid Row persons or agencies and the most likely to have ties outside the Skid Row neighborhood that they would like to retain or redevelop. The matter is not entirely clear-cut, as evidenced by the fact that persons who say that they perceive themselves as temporarily in Skid Row are more likely to seek out a DRC-type facility, and that those who perceive themselves as permanent residents are more likely to continue through into relocation. At present we are at a loss to explain this, but it is worth mentioning that the men who were relocated from Skid Row had significantly higher IQ scores than those who were not.

In brief summary, then, under voluntary conditions, the kind of program that the DRC had during the 314 demonstration grant period is more likely to be attractive to unstable younger men—those with an alcohol problem—and to be identified by Skid Row residents in that manner. The relatively stable retired men, although they may be close to poverty, are inclined to maintain as much autonomy as they can in the light of their circumstances. Further, they actively seek to dissociate themselves from the other residents of the area, even though they may perceive that they have become permanent residents in fact, and they do not identify with Skid Row members. It seems probable that the use of a DRC-type facility by older and more stable men will be higher under conditions of site clearance, and that they will tend to define it as primarily a rehousing agency, even though many may in fact have significant health problems.

D Occupational Prestige Class and Downward Class Mobility

The most commonly used objective method of placement is in terms of participation in the division of labor as indicated by the type of occupation. Its common use is attributable to the high correlations obtainable between this single measure and other approaches. The present study utilized class placement in terms of the type of occupation. The scheme was worked out for the Lenski-Landecker studies of class crystallization, but was divided into seven categories to recognize differences at the bottom.[1] It was used in our 1960 study and therefore retained in the present analysis even though we had preliminary drafts of Bogue's approach.[2]

The following is the basic format for prestige class placement. The descriptive labels are our own.

Upper Class. Physician, top executive in national business, top government official.

Middle Class. College professor, minister with college training, architect, chemist, dentist, lawyer, judge, psychologist, engineer, school principal, banker, member of board of large corporation, factory owner employing more than a hundred persons, airline pilot, musician in a symphony orchestra.

Lower Middle Class. Public school teacher, social worker, registered nurse, captain in United States Army, building contractor, official in international union, employer of from three to ninety-nine persons, owner-operator of printing shop, undertaker, real estate agent, radio announcer, newspaper columnist, news reporter, private secretary, detective, railroad engineer, electrician, machinist, tool-die maker, department foreman, county agent, farm owner-operator.

Marginal Middle Working Class. Piano teacher, manager of a small store, owner of dignified, respectable business employing one or two persons, local union official, owner-operator of lunch stand, bookkeeper, truck salesman for wholesaler, insurance agent, bank teller, playground director, policeman, interstate bus driver, railroad conductor, carpenter, automobile mechanic, bricklayer, crew foreman, farm tenant, farmer (unspecified), and plumber.

Working Class. Store-front preacher, pawnbroker, sales clerk in store, typist, file clerk, corporal in United States Army, barber, cook, taxi driver, baker or bakery truck driver, chauffeur, singer in night club, machine operator in factory, local bus driver, gas station attendant.

Lower Class. Waiter, bartender, soda clerk, clothes presser, railroad station hand, dock worker, night watchman, janitor, farmhand, coal miner, share-crop farmer.

Lower Lower Class and Lumpenproletariat. Shoe shiner, garbage collector, muzzler.

Table D-1 summarizes from the 1960 study and both the doorstep and intake interviews. The 1960 data include all respondents, but we also made analyses restricted to those living in the 314 demonstration grant area; the results are nearly the same. The table gives information on reports of occupational prestige class aspiration—"when you were a teenager growing up"—and also gives three major points of comparison: prestige class of the parental family, prestige class of the longest or the best job, and prestige class of the most recent job. In 1960, our stress was placed on the longest job in a person's lifetime because we conceived of this period as the point of greatest lifetime stability of the respondent. In other words, the longest lifetime job was that point at which the respondent probably participated most fully in the division of labor of the larger society and therefore, from the perspective of the larger society, participated most significantly. We decided to give greater attention to the respondent's perception of his best job in the Demonstration Project sample (although we continued to ask about the longest job in the intake interview). We wanted, thereby, to get an indicator of the Skid Row man's perception of his most significant period of participation. Table D-1 suggests that there is substantial agreement that the societally most significant period of participation is at about the same prestige rank. To some extent, this may be accounted for by the fact that the same job was named for the best job and for the longest job. In 1960, we asked the respondents about their work in the week of the survey. In our subsequent analysis, we decided that it would be more desirable to ask about the last job. We believe that most of the differences between the two columns are probably accounted for by the difference in the ways in which the question was asked. For these data, we also made analyses for only the whites living within the 314 demonstration grant area. There was no significant difference between the two sets of data.

TABLE D-1   COMPARISON OF PRESTIGE CLASS OF JOBS, BY PERCENTAGE

PRESTIGE CLASS	PARENTAL FAMILY 1960	1964a	TEEN ASPIRATION 1964b	FIRST FULL JOB 1964b	LONGEST JOB 1960	BEST JOB 1964a	JOB AFTER LONGEST 1964b	SURVEY WEEK 1960	LAST JOB 1964a
Upper to lower middle	16	20	18	1	6	5	1	2	1
Marginal middle, upper working	39	32	18	1	25	20	10	7	6
Working	18	18	20	35	36	36	21	19	15
Lower	21	17	14	40	27	29	33	37	37
Lumpenproletariat	1	4	1	12	5	5	22	32	39
None	–	–	12	–	–	–	5	–	–
DK, NA, RA	5	9	10	5	1	5	8	3	2
Total percentage	100	100	100	100	100	100	100	100	100
N	2249	550	269	238	2249	547	238	1062	550

a 314 Demonstration Grant Doorstep Sample.
b 314 Demonstration Grant Returnee Sample.

The data in Table D-1 show a substantial similarity between the 1960 population and the Demonstration Project sample population with respect to the prestige class of the parental family. Between 16 and 20 percent reported that they came from distinctly middle-class families; cumulatively, over 50 percent of the parental families were either in the middle classes or were marginal to it. The respondents apparently aspired to prestige class at about the same level as their parents, and actually entered the labor force at a somewhat lower level than that of their parents. But this is not unusual; the father would be closer to any peak of status achievement, and one would expect the son to start at a somewhat lower point—a kind of one step backward and two steps forward procedure from the point of view of inter-generational mobility. The data based on longest job or best job suggest that the respondents never reached the prestige rank of their parental family. Indeed, from almost the beginning, Table D-1 suggests that the men who live in the Skid Row area have long and steadily been downwardly mobile with respect to prestige rank. This is consistent with Bahr's findings.[3]

Bogue's SES Scores. Table D-2 presents somewhat similar data. Here we present a comparison of our data and the material reported by Bogue for Chicago. We have used Bogue's SES scores; the reader is referred to Bogue's book for their development and calculation.[4] Table D-2 presents prestige class data based on best job, longest job, job after longest job, and last job for the Demonstration Project sample and for Chicago. This table shows that there are at the most only slight differences between the two populations. Both Tables D-1 and D-2 suggest

TABLE D-2   SOCIOECONOMIC STATUS SCORES,[a] BY PERCENTAGE

SES Score	Longest Job	Best Job	Job After Longest	Last Job Phil., 1964	Last Job Chicago[a]
110 and above	3	5	4	2	1.4
100–109	11	10	7	6	5.1
90–99	13	15	8	5	3.3
80–89	24	26	16	11	9.6
70–79	18	19	15	14	17.2
60–69	21	19	33	47	52.8
Below 60	10	6	17	15	10.6
Total percentage	100	100	100	100	100.0
N	264	520[b]	264[c]	522[b]	613

[a] Cf. Bogue, *Skid Row*, p. 322 ff.
[b] Based on entire 1964 Sample; DK, NA, RA omitted.
[c] Based on intake interview; DK, NA, RA omitted.

that while the longest job and the best job are variable for each man, there has been a relatively sharp break toward downward mobility at this point. This is borne out by the fact that the job after the longest job tends to be lower in prestige rank. We believe that there is a need for further investigation. What happened to terminate that longest or best job? What happened during the best or longest job period in the life experiences outside the job? Further, in order to avoid fallacious conclusions, it will be desirable to make comparisons with non-Skid Row working-class respondents who may also have similar job patterns. Bahr's data suggest that this high point took place much later in the non-Skid Row comparison population that he calls Park Slope.

Table D-3 presents our effort to repeat some of the procedures set forth by Bogue within the scope of our own data for intragenerational class mobility—that is, for change in prestige class, when we think of

TABLE D-3   INTERGENERATIONAL AND INTRAGENERA-
TIONAL MOBILITY, BY PERCENTAGE

MOBILITY	INTERGENERATIONAL	INTRAGENERATIONAL	
		1964 Sample	Chicago[a]
Up only	6	11	10.6
Down and up	3	22	13.2
Nonmobile	11	10	9.9
Up and down	15	32	45.7
Down only	65	25	20.6
Total percentage	100	100	100
N[b]	406	244	613

[a] Bogue, Skid Row, p. 328.
[b] DK, NA, RA omitted; data based in part on intake interview material.

the parental generation as the point of beginning and the person's own entry into the adult world as the point of beginning. Table D-3 shows that 65 percent of the men have been downwardly mobile for what is essentially their entire lifetime; another 15 percent of the respondents had been upwardly mobile and then downwardly mobile. (Nonresponse and consequent coding problems cut down the number of cases.) We believe that these data lend support to similar conclusions found by Bogue. Data on intragenerational mobility are also reported. Some of the information was gathered in the intake interview that was used in the coding process, and the number of cases was further cut down by coding and machine matching. There are differences between the data in Table D-3 and Bogue's conclusion that a substantial fraction of Chicago's Skid Row men were upwardly mobile and then downwardly mobile; apparently, the Philadelphia men were generally more mobile than the men in Chicago.

If Tables D-1, D-2, and D-3 may be said to be based on objective methods of class placement, the data in Table D-4 may be said to consider the subjective class placement of the respondents. The respondents were asked whether they belonged to the middle, working, or lower classes; they were asked for their subjective class placement before they came to the Skid Row area and at the time of the interview; the questions were separated by a number of others in the Door-

TABLE D-4   SELF CLASS IDENTIFICATION AT TIME OF INTERVIEW AND RETROSPECTIVELY BEFORE SKID ROW, BY PERCENTAGE

Class	Before	Now
Middle	39	26
Working	48	36
Lower	13	38
Total percentage	100	100
N[a]	530	518

[a] DK, RA, NA omitted.

step interview form. Almost one-half of the respondents perceived themselves as working-class persons before they moved to Skid Row, in comparison with about one-third who viewed themselves this way after having moved to Skid Row. While only 13 percent perceived themselves as lower class before coming to Skid Row, 38 percent did so at the time of the interview. The data are not readily translatable into terms of Table D-1 and Table D-2. It is nonetheless evident that many of the men currently living in Philadelphia's Skid Row area do perceive themselves as having been downwardly mobile. The class mobility phenomenon is therefore not a figment in the mind of the researcher, but has some meaning in the perception of the lives of the men themselves. Further, the substantial proportions who perceive that they were in the middle and working classes before coming to Skid Row lend some support to the argument that these men continue to express these class points of view and ways of looking at the world and of deciding about themselves and their relation to society.

Notes

Notes

Chapter 1

1. This position will be elaborated in Chapter 13, and may also be found in Leonard U. Blumberg, Thomas E. Shipley, Jr., and Joseph O. Moor, Jr., "The Skid Row Man and the Skid Row Status Community." We express our appreciation to the *Quarterly Journal of Studies on Alcohol*, where we have used the same words.

2. Donald J. Bogue, *Skid Row in American Cities*.

3. The concepts used in this discussion originated with Max Weber and were elaborated by Don Martindale, *American Social Structure*, p. 456, and especially by Keith Lovald, "From Hobohemia to Skid Row," Chaps. 2, 6; we have substituted Hawley's approach to sustenance functions for the Weber-Martindale-Lovald approach to wealth or economic power. Cf. Amos Hawley, *Human Ecology*, Chaps. 3 and 12.

4. Leonard Blumberg, Thomas E. Shipley, Jr., Irving W. Shandler, and Herman Niebuhr, Jr., "The Development, Major Goals, and Strategies of a Skid Row Program: Philadelphia."

5. David C. McClelland, J. W. Atkinson, R. A. Clark, and E. L. Howell, *The Achievement Motive*.

6. Blumberg *et al.*, "Development, Major Goals, and Strategies," p. 255.

7. Philadelphia Prison Society, *The Homeless Man*.

8. Leonard Blumberg, Francis H. Hoffman, Victor LoCicero, Herman Niebuhr, Jr., James F. Rooney, and Thomas E. Shipley, Jr., "The Men on Skid Row," p. 1.

9. Blumberg *et al.*, "The Men on Skid Row."

Chapter 3

1. David B. Pittman and C. Wayne Gordon, *Revolving Door*; John Patterson Brantner, "Homeless Men," Chap. 3.

2. H. Warren Dunham, *Homeless Men and Their Habitat*; Keith Lovald, "From Hobohemia to Skid Row," Chaps. 5–7; Samuel E. Wallace, *Skid Row as a Way of Life*, Chaps. 3–8; Jacqueline P. Wiseman, *Stations of the Lost*, Part II; James P. Spradley, *You Owe Yourself a Drunk*, Chap. 3.

3. Donald J. Bogue, *Skid Row in American Cities,* Parts I and II, Appendix A.

4. E. M. Jellinek, *The Disease Concept of Alcoholism,* pp. 35–41. See also the discussion on loss of control by Ruth Fox and Peter Lyon, *Alcoholism: Its Scope, Cause, and Treatment,* pp. 137–40.

5. Howard M. Bahr, *Homelessness and Disaffiliation,* Chap. 7.

6. Spradley, *You Owe Yourself a Drunk,* Chap. 9.

7. Bogue, *Skid Row in American Cities,* Chap. 19.

8. Wallace, *Skid Row as a Way of Life,* Chap. 4; Wiseman, *Stations of the Lost,* Chaps. 7 and 9.

9. Wallace, *Skid Row as a Way of Life,* Chap. 13.

10. Pennsylvania Liquor Control Board. "Listing of Retail Liquor Licenses, District Number 1."

11. Spradley, *You Owe Yourself a Drunk,* pp. 175, 252.

12. Wiseman, *Stations of the Lost,* Chap. 8.

13. Pitirim Sorokin, *Social Mobility.*

14. Carson McGuire, "Social Stratification and Mobility Patterns."

15. J. J. M. Van Tulder, "Occupational Mobility in the Netherlands from 1917 to 1954."

16. Leo Schnore, "Social Mobility in Demographic Perspective."

17. Robert K. Merton and Alice S. Kitt, "Reference Group Theory and Social Mobility."

18. Wallace, *Skid Row as a Way of Life,* Chaps. 12 and 13; Spradley, *You Owe Yourself a Drunk,* Chap. 5.

19. Joseph Greenblum and Leonard I. Pearlin, "Vertical Mobility and Prejudice: A Socio-Psychological Analysis."

20. Greenblum and Pearlin, "Vertical Mobility and Prejudice."

21. Peter Binzen, *Whitetown, U.S.A.*

22. Seymour M. Lipset and Joan Gordon, "Mobility and Trade Union Membership."

23. Julius Roth and Robert F. Peck, "Social Class and Mobility Factors Related to Marital Adjustment."

24. Jurgen Ruesch, *Chronic Disease and Psychological Invalidism,* Chap. 7, esp. pp. 118–19.

25. August B. Hollingshead and Fredrick C. Redlich, *Social Class and Mental Illness.*

26. Hollingshead and Redlich, *Social Class and Mental Illness,* p. 369.

27. Peter M. Blau, "Social Mobility and Interpersonal Relations."

28. Blau, "Social Mobility and Interpersonal Relations, p. 294.

29. Bogue, *Skid Row in American Cities,* Chap. 14; Bahr, *Homelessness and Disaffiliation,* Chap. 12.

30. David C. McClelland, *The Achieving Society;* J. W. Atkinson and N. T. Feather, eds., *A Theory of Achievement Motivation.*

CHAPTER 4

1. Donald Clemmer, *The Prison Community,* pp. 298 ff.
2. James P. Spradley, *You Owe Yourself a Drunk,* pp. 130–31.
3. Spradley, *You Owe Yourself a Drunk,* Chap. 9.
4. Spradley, *You Owe Yourself a Drunk,* Chap. 5.
5. Howard Bain, "A Sociological Analysis of the Chicago Skid Row Lifeway," Chap. 8; Paul Chevigny, *Police Power,* Chaps. 7, 15; Samuel E. Wallace, *Skid Row as a Way of Life,* Chaps. 7 and 8; Keith Lovald, "From Hobohemia to Skid Row," pp. 310–36; Jacqueline P. Wiseman, *Stations of the Lost,* Part II.
6. Bain, "A Sociological Analysis of the Chicago Skid Row Lifeway," p. 84.
7. Caleb Foote, "Vagrancy-Type Law and Its Administration," p. 636.
8. Spradley, *You Owe Yourself a Drunk,* pp. 260–62.
9. Egon Bittner, "The Police on Skid Row: A Study of Peace Keeping."
10. Wiseman, *Stations of the Lost,* Chap. 3.
11. Bain, "A Sociological Analysis of the Chicago Skid Row Lifeway," p. 87.
12. Lovald, "From Hobohemia to Skid Row," p. 333. Cf. Foote, "Vagrancy-Type Law and Its Administration," p. 637; Bittner, "The Police on Skid Row," p. 708.
13. Lovald, "From Hobohemia to Skid Row," pp. 333–34.
14. The present analysis resembles the analysis presented by Irving W. Shandler, Thomas E. Shipley, Jr., Donald J. Ottenberg, M.D., Chesterfield Cotton, and Leonard Blumberg in "Alternatives to Arrest: A Ten Day Study of Detoxification Needs of Men Brought to the Sixth Police District," a multilithed publication of the DRC/P, 1967. The present discussion gives a much more comprehensive analysis of the same data. In addition, it excludes from the analysis certain duplications of cases that were inadvertently included in the earlier statement.
15. Chi square was used as the basis of estimates of statistical significance. In these tests, the "don't know" responses were excluded when such exclusion did not do violence to the estimate; hence, the contingency tables involve one degree of freedom unless otherwise noted.
16. D. J. Myerson and J. Mayer, "Origins, Treatment, and Destiny of Skid Row Alcoholic Men."
17. Leonard U. Blumberg and Thomas E. Shipley, Jr., "Follow-Up of the Philadelphia Skid Row Project."
18. *New York Times,* July 8, 1967; November 24, 1968.
19. William H. Speers, "Down and Out in Philadelphia."

20. Spradley, *You Owe Yourself a Drunk*, p. 176.
21. Foote, "Vagrancy-Type Law and Its Administration."

CHAPTER 5

1. Charles Abrams, *Forbidden Neighbors*, p. 247.
2. Herbert Gans, *Urban Villagers*.
3. Board of Licenses and Inspections Review, "Findings and Opinions," January 10, 1963 and October 10, 1966.
4. James Reichley, *The Art of Government*, pp. 97–98.
5. Harold Wentworth and Stuart Berg Flexner, *Dictionary of American Slang*, p. 358.
6. The scheme was discussed in *The Monthly Register*, Vol. 1 (April 15, 1880), published by the Philadelphia Society for Organizing Charity, and was urged in the Second Annual Report of the Central Board of Directors of the Philadelphia Society for Organizing Charity, October 1, 1880. It is not clear whether the plan to arrange for commitment to the House of Correction was actually implemented, but later reports made clear that the work test had eliminated a large number of tramps from applicants to the society for assistance. The Seventh Annual Report of the Board of Directors (October 1885) discusses the matter. The First Wayfarer's Lodge and Woodlot was opened at 1719 Lombard Street in March 1884; the second one, at 80 Laurel Street in June 1885. During 1884–85 848 cords of wood were sawed. On May 28, 1902, one lodge and woodlot was moved across the street to 1720 Lombard Street; the new site and building cost $55,000. By 1904 the other had been moved to 1438 North 6th Street. The annual meeting of November 30, 1915, authorized the sale of the latter facility; the former was sold after World War I. The Philadelphia Society for Organizing Charity is now known as the Family Service of Philadelphia.
7. Jacqueline P. Wiseman, *Stations of the Lost*, Chap. 7.
8. For a more complete discussion, see Thomas Fedewa, SSA, "The Relationship between Skid Row Institutions and Skid Row Residents in the City of Philadelphia: A Comparative Analysis of Religious Institutions," Ph.D. dissertation in process, Department of Religion, Temple University, 1972.

CHAPTER 6

1. *Purdon's Pennsylvania Statutes Annotated* Vol. 18, Section 2032, p. 61. Cf. Caleb Foote, "Vagrancy-Type Law and Its Administration"; Judah I. Labovitz, "The Legal Status of Skid Row People," unpublished paper.
2. We selected "last month" because we believe that it is a better

indicator of the "true" employment situation; a man might well have been unemployed in the week before we interviewed him but have had steady employment for all or most of the year.

3. Jacqueline P. Wiseman, *Stations of the Lost*, Chap. 8.

4. D. W. Morse, "Peripheral Worker in the Affluent Society."

5. Eli Ginzberg, *Manpower Agenda for America*, pp. 74 ff.

6. Seymour L. Wolfbein, *Employment, Unemployment, and Public Policy*.

7. C. C. Hodge and J. R. Wetzel, "Short Workweeks and Under-employment," p. 30.

8. Morse, "Peripheral Worker in the Affluent Society."

9. Morse, "Peripheral Worker in the Affluent Society"; cf. Eli Ginz-berg *et al., Manpower Strategy for the Metropolis*, pp. 158 ff; Austin G. Loveless, "Background and Economic Status of the Unemployed of St. Francois County, Missouri, and Their Attitudes toward Retrain-ing."

10. Morse, "Peripheral Worker in the Affluent Society"; for a less sympathetic view see Don D. Lescohier, *The Labor Market*, pp. 18, 258–72.

11. Fred Frailey, "Two Seeking to Form Union of Day Laborers in Uptown."

12. From this point on, we have drawn heavily upon a confidential staff report of the East Coast Migrant Project, "New Jersey Day-Haul Report—Summer 1969," American Friends Service Committee, Phila-delphia, Pennsylvania. See also Les Payne, "The Migrant Camp: Wine Fights and Payday." Payne describes a slightly different exploitative situation on the Long Island potato farms among black migrant laborers. The American Friends Service Committee report indicates that the use of migrant labor is declining in favor of the day haul.

13. Wiseman, *Stations of the Lost*, p. 237.

14. Mark Hutter, "Summertime Servants: The Schlockhaus' Waiter." Cf. *New York Times*, July 19, 1970.

15. Wiseman, *Stations of the Lost*, Chap. 8.

16. Keith Lovald, "From Hobohemia to Skid Row"; James F. Rooney, "Societal Forces and the Unattached Male: An Historical Review."

17. Wiseman, *Stations of the Lost*, Chaps. 7–9.

CHAPTER 7

1. Well after the reports were written from which this analysis was derived, the following article came to our attention. Because the Olin research was in greater detail and with different emphasis than our own, the two sets are not readily comparable. The article is of con-

siderable importance to physicians concerned with the medical care of Skid Row-like persons. Jack S. Olin, " 'Skid Row' Syndrome: A Medical Profile of the Chronic Drunkenness Offender."

2. Richard M. Titmuss, *The Gift Relationship*, p. 89.

3. J. Garrott Allen, "The Advantages of the Single Transfusion"; News Release, Stanford University Medical Center, February 12, 1970; cf. N. R. Boeve, L. C. Winterscheid, and K. A. Merendina, "Fibrinagen-Transmitted Hepatitis in the Surgical Patient"; J. H. Walsh, R. H. Purcell, A. G. Morrow, R. M. Chanock, and P. J. Schmidt, "Post-Transfusion Hepatitis after Open Heart Operations."

4. Saul Krugman, "Etiology of Viral Hepatitis."

5. *New York Times*, "Blood Banks Get Order to Improve"; *Philadelphia Bulletin*, "FDA Moves to Regulate All Blood Centers."

6. John Senior, "Reflections Upon the Incidence of Post-Transfusion Hepatitis in Various Parts of the World"; *Science*, "Hepatitis: A New Understanding Emerges."

7. C. A. Saravis, C. Trey, and C. F. Grady, "Rapid Screening Test for Detecting Hepatitis-Associated Antigen."

8. *Science*, "FDA to Regulate All Blood Banks."

9. "A Pound of Blood," *Philadelphia Magazine* September, 1968, pp. 81–88.

Chapter 8

1. Donald J. Bogue, *Skid Row in American Cities*, p. 278.

2. R. M. Harmer, *The High Cost of Dying*, and Jessica Mitford, *The American Way of Death*. Both discuss funeral costs in the United States. Apparently embalming can be done for less than a dollar; the minimum wholesale price of a casket in California was about $40 in the early 1960s. At present, the Philadelphia Memorial Society reports that it can arrange simple cremation funeral rites for as low as $125—arrangements that are apparently profitable since undertakers accept the contract with no difficulty. Philadelphia's contract costs for indigents are not very different from those reported for California. The City Finance Department pays a flat fee of $35 to undertakers for city burials of unclaimed bodies. Whenever possible, the city is reimbursed directly by Social Security.

3. Bogue, *Skid Row in American Cities*, p. 224.

4. F. Herbert Colwell, *Annual Statistical Report, Community Health Services*, Table 15.

5. C. C. Attkisson, "Suicide in San Francisco's Skid Row."

6. Milton Terris, "Epidemiology of Cirrhosis of the Liver: National Mortality Data," p. 2087.

CHAPTER 9

1. Don Martindale, *American Social Structure,* pp. lx, 132–33. Cf. Leonard U. Blumberg, Thomas E. Shipley, Jr., and Joseph O. Moor, Jr., "The Skid Row Man and the Skid Row Status Community."

2. Leonard U. Blumberg, Thomas E. Shipley, Jr., and Joseph O. Moor, Jr., "The Skid Row Man and the Skid Row Status Community," pp. 928–29.

3. James P. Spradley, *You Owe Yourself a Drunk,* Chap. 9.

4. Richard K. Centers, *The Psychology of Social Class.*

5. Samuel E. Wallace, *Skid Row as a Way of Life,* Chap. 13.

6. Jacqueline P. Wiseman, *Stations of the Lost,* pp. 223–24.

7. Wallace, *Skid Row as a Way of Life,* pp. 181–82. Cf. Leonard U. Blumberg *et. al.,* "The Skid Row Man and the Skid Row Status Community," pp. 929–34.

8. Wallace, *Skid Row as a Way of Life,* p. 182.

9. Donald J. Bogue, *Skid Row in American Cities,* pp. 169–70; Howard M. Bahr, *Homelessness and Disaffiliation,* pp. 25, 210–12, 291.

10. Spradley, *You Owe Yourself a Drunk,* Chap. 9, esp. p. 255.

11. Wallace, *Skid Row as a Way of Life,* pp. 159–60.

12. Wallace, *Skid Row as a Way of Life,* p. 9.

13. Wallace, *Skid Row as a Way of Life,* p. 25.

CHAPTER 10

1. John Patterson Brantner, "Homeless Men"; C. C. Hewitt, "A Personality Study of Alcoholic Addiction"; A. D. Button, "A Study of Alcoholics with the Minnesota Multiphasic Personality Inventory"; H. E. Hill, C. A. Haertzen, and H. Davis, "An MMPI Factor Analytic Study of Alcoholics, Narcotic Addicts, and Criminals"; Craig MacAndrew and Robert H. Geertsma, "An Analysis of Responses of Alcoholics to Scale 4 of the MMPI."

2. R. S. Wallerstein, "Hospital Treatment of Alcoholism: A Comparative, Experimental Study."

3. M. E. Chafetz, H. T. Blane, H. S. Abram, J. G. Golner, E. Lacy, W. F. McCourt, E. Clark, and W. Myers, "Establishing Treatment Relations with Alcoholics"; Harold W. Demone, Jr., "Experiments in Referral to Alcoholism Clinics."

4. V. J. LoCicero, "A Multidisciplined Approach to the Skid Row Habitué."

5. Brantner, "Homeless Men," p. 154; Ruesch, *Chronic Disease and Psychological Invalidism,* pp. 118–19.

6. Brantner, "Homeless Men," p. 159.

7. James P. Spradley, *You Owe Yourself a Drunk,* Chaps. 5–7.

8. James M. Weber, "Final Evaluation Report."

CHAPTER 11

1. Robert E. Harris and James C. Lingoes, "Subscales for the MMPI."
2. H. G. Gough, *California Psychological Inventory Manual.*
3. Samuel E. Wallace, *Skid Row as a Way of Life,* Chaps. 12, 13.
4. Jacqueline P. Wiseman, *Stations of the Lost,* pp. 236–37.
5. H. M. Tiebout, "Alcoholics Anonymous," p. 55.
6. Harrison M. Trice, *Alcoholism in America,* pp. 55–61.
7. Wiseman, *Stations of the Lost,* Chap. 8.

CHAPTER 12

1. James T. McMahon, "The Working Class Psychiatric Patient: A Clinical View."
2. To test for reliability, 15 cases each were drawn at random from the 20 cases of clients judged as having better social function and from the 24 judged as unimproved. For each of these cases, facts pertinent to social functioning were written from the intake interview about the status of the client at that time, along with relevant background information. Added to this were all pertinent data following intake of the final follow-up interview. These 30 case summaries were then presented through the DRC/P psychology department to a staff member for his independent judgment. Two cases were judged differently, although in different directions, so that the overall statistics remained the same. The 28 of 30 cases judged the same represent a 93 percent measure of agreement.
3. D. J. Myerson, "An Approach to the Skid Row Problem in Boston"; D. J. Myerson, "The 'Skid Row' Problem: Further Observations on a Group of Alcoholic Patients, with Emphasis on Interpersonal Relations and the Therapeutic Approach."

CHAPTER 13

1. Keith Lovald and Holger R. Stub, "The Revolving Door: Reactions of Chronic Drunkenness Offenders to Court Sanctions."
2. H. Richard Lamb and Victor Goertzel, "Discharged Mental Patients—Are They Really in the Community?"
3. Independent Co-Operative Enterprises, "I.C.E. Inc.: Information for Members," and "Co-Operative Employment Agency Proposal."
4. Richard M. Titmuss, *The Gift Relationship.*
5. William Chambliss, "A Sociological Analysis of the Law of Vagrancy."
6. Leonard Blumberg, "A Possible Application of the Epidemiological-Public Health Model to Civic Action-Research."

7. Leonard Blumberg, Thomas E. Shipley, Jr., Irving W. Shandler, and Herman Niebuhr, Jr., "The Development, Major Goals, and Strategies of a Skid Row Program: Philadelphia"; Leonard U. Blumberg, Thomas E. Shipley, Jr., and Joseph O. Moor, Jr., "The Skid Row Man and the Skid Row Status Community."

APPENDIX A

1. We have discussed some of these problems and considerations elsewhere. Leonard Blumberg, Thomas E. Shipley, Jr., Irving W. Shandler and Herman Niebuhr, Jr., "Development, Major Goals, and Strategies of a Skid Row Program: Philadelphia"; Leonard Blumberg, Irving W. Shandler, and Thomas E. Shipley, Jr. "The Philadelphia Skid Row Project"; Leonard Blumberg, Thomas E. Shipley, Jr., and Irving W. Shandler, "Seven Years on Skid Row: Diagnostic and Rehabilitation Center/Philadelphia"; some of the problems of follow-up are discussed in "Follow-Up of the Philadelphia Skid Row Project."

APPENDIX B

1. Samuel E. Wallace, *Skid Row as a Way of Life,* p. 156.
2. Wallace, *Skid Row as a Way of Life,* p. 159.
3. Wallace, *Skid Row as a Way of Life,* p. 160.
4. Jacqueline P. Wiseman, *Stations of the Lost,* p. 43.
5. Wiseman, *Stations of the Lost,* p. 271.
6. Wallace, *Skid Row as a Way of Life,* pp. 193–200.
7. James P. Spradley, *You Owe Yourself a Drunk,* pp. 68ff, 268–69.
8. Donald J. Bogue, *Skid Row in American Cities;* Theodore Caplow, Keith A. Lovald, and Samuel E. Wallace, *A General Report on the Problem of Relocating the Population of the Lower Loop Redevelopment Area;* Howard M. Bahr, *Homelessness and Disaffiliation.*
9. H. Hartshorne and M. A. May, *Studies in Deceit.* Our data are from an unpublished study carried out by Richard Sharf and designed in collaboration with him.

APPENDIX C

1. Donald J. Bogue, *Skid Row in American Cities,* pp. 109–10.
2. While generalizations based on the Quick Test are limited because of its ceiling of 135 and the small adult group used in its standardization, IQ scores on this test were found to be significantly correlated ($r = .81$) with similar measures obtained on the Wechsler Adult Intelligence Scale (WAIS) in a sample of 38 Skid Row men. Cf. D. Wechsler, *The Measurement of Adult Intelligence.*
3. W. G. Dahlstrom and G. S. Welsh, *An MMPI Handbook,* p. 60.

4. John Patterson Brantner, "Homeless Men, A Psychological and Medical Survey," pp. 148, 153–54.

5. Dahlstrom and Welsh, *An MMPI Handbook,* p. 55.

6. Brantner, "Homeless Men," p. 148.

7. C. C. Hewitt, "A Personality Study of Alcohol Addiction"; J. V. Quaranta, "Alcoholism: A Study of Emotional Maturity and Homosexuality as Related Factors in Compulsive Drinking," p. 354; D. P. Hoyt and G. M. Sedlacek, "Differentiating Alcoholics from Normals and Abnormals with the MMPI"; A. D. Button, "A Study of Alcoholics with the MMPI." But see Craig MacAndrew and Robert H. Geertsma, "An Analysis of Responses of Alcoholics to Scale 4 of the MMPI," for a critical review of the implications of these studies.

8. M. Lorr, "Multidimensional Scale for Rating Psychiatric Patients."

9. R. G. Priest, "A USA-UK Comparison."

APPENDIX D

1. Gerhard Lenski, "Status Crystallization: A Non-Vertical Dimension of Social Status."

2. Donald J. Bogue, *Skid Row in American Cities,* pp. 516–21.

3. Howard M. Bahr, *Homelessness and Disaffiliation,* Chap. 12.

4. Bogue, *Skid Row in American Cities,* Chap. 14.

Bibliography

Bibliography

Abrams, Charles. *Forbidden Neighbors.* New York: Harper, 1955.

Allen, J. Garrott. "The Advantages of the Single Transfusion." *Annals of Surgery* 164 (1966):475–81.

Atkinson, J. W., and N. T. Feather, eds. *A Theory of Achievement Motivation.* New York: J. Wiley, 1966.

Attkisson, C. C. "Suicide in San Francisco's Skid Row." *Archives of General Psychiatry* 23 (August, 1970):149–57.

Bahr, Howard M. *Homelessness and Disaffiliation.* New York: Columbia University Bureau of Applied Research, 1968.

Bain, Howard. "A Sociological Analysis of the Chicago Skid Row Lifeway." Unpublished M.A. dissertation, University of Chicago, 1950.

Binzen, Peter. *Whitetown, U.S.A.* New York: Random House, 1970.

Bittner, Egon. "The Police on Skid Row: A Study of Peace Keeping." *American Sociological Review* 32 (1967):699–715.

Blau, Peter M. "Social Mobility and Interpersonal Relations." *American Sociological Review* 21 (1956):290–95.

Blumberg, Leonard. "A Possible Application of the Epidemiological-Public Health Model to Civic Action-Research." *Social Problems* 12 (1964):178–85.

Blumberg, Leonard; Thomas E. Shipley, Jr.; Irving W. Shandler; and Herman Niebuhr, Jr. "The Development, Major Goals, and Strategies of a Skid Row Program: Philadelphia." *Quarterly Journal of Studies on Alcohol* 27 (1966):242–58.

Blumberg, Leonard; Francis H. Hoffman; Victor LoCicero; Herman Niebuhr, Jr.; James F. Rooney; and Thomas E. Shipley, Jr. "The Men on Skid Row: A Study of Philadelphia's Homeless Man Population." Lithographed. Philadelphia: Department of Psychiatry, Temple University School of Medicine, for the Greater Philadelphia Movement and the Redevelopment Authority of the City of Philadelphia, 1961.

Blumberg, Leonard; Irving Shandler; and Thomas E. Shipley, Jr. "The Philadelphia Skid Row Project: An Action-Research Program." In *Sociology in Action,* Arthur B. Shostak, ed. Homewood, Ill: The Dorsey Press, 1966.

Blumberg, Leonard, and Thomas E. Shipley, Jr. "Follow-Up of the

Philadelphia Skid Row Project." In *Putting Sociology to Work,* Arthur B. Shostak, ed. New York: McKay, in press.

Blumberg, Leonard; Thomas E. Shipley, Jr.; Irving W. Shandler. "Seven Years on Skid Row: Diagnostic and Rehabilitation Center/Philadelphia." In *Creating Social Change,* G. Zaltman, P. Kotler, and Ira Kaufman, eds., pp. 429–37. New York: Holt, Rinehart and Winston, 1972.

Blumberg, Leonard; Thomas E. Shipley, Jr.; and Joseph O. Moor, Jr. "The Skid Row Man and the Skid Row Status Community." *Quarterly Journal of Studies on Alcohol* 32 (1971):909–41.

Boeve, L. C.; L. C. Winterscheid; and K. A. Merendina, "Fibrinogen-Transmitted Hepatitis in the Surgical Patient." *Annals of Surgery* 170 (1969):833–38.

Bogue, Donald J. *Skid Row in American Cities.* Chicago: Community and Family Center of the University of Chicago, 1963.

Brantner, John Patterson. "Homeless Man: A Psychological and Medical Survey." Ph.D. dissertation, University of Minnesota, 1958.

Button, A. D. "A Study of Alcoholics with the Minnesota Multiphasic Personality Inventory." *Quarterly Journal of Studies on Alcohol* 17 (1956):267–81.

Caplow, Theodore; Keith A. Lovald; and Samuel E. Wallace. *A General Report on the Problem of Relocating the Population of the Lower Loop Redevelopment Area.* Multilith. Minneapolis: Minneapolis Housing and Redevelopment Authority, 1958.

Centers, Richard K. *The Psychology of Social Class.* Princeton: Princeton University Press, 1949.

Chafetz, M. E.; H. T. Blane; H. S. Abram; J. G. Golner; E. Lacy; W. F. McCourt; E. Clark; and W. Myers. "Establishing Treatment Relations with Alcoholics." *Journal of Nervous and Mental Diseases* 134 (1962):395–409.

Chambliss, William J. "A Sociological Analysis of the Law of Vagrancy." *Social Problems* 12 (Summer, 1964), 67–77.

Chevigny, Paul. *Police Power: Police Abuses in New York City.* New York: Pantheon, 1969.

Clemmer, Donald. *The Prison Community.* New York: Holt, Rinehart and Winston, 1958.

Colwell, F. Herbert. *Annual Statistical Report, Community Health Services.* Philadelphia Department of Public Health, Division of Statistics and Research, 1963 and 1964.

Dahlstrom, W. G., and G. S. Welsh. *An MMPI Handbook.* Minneapolis: University of Minnesota Press, 1960.

deLint, Jan, and Wolfgang Schmidt. "Mortality from Liver Cirrhosis and Other Causes in Alcoholism." *Quarterly Journal of Studies on Alcohol* 31 (1970):705–9.

Demone, Harold W., Jr. "Experiments in Referral to Alcoholism Clinics." *Quarterly Journal of Studies on Alcohol* 24 (1963): 495–502.

Dunham, H. Warren. *Homeless Men and Their Habitat: A Research Planning Report.* Detroit: Wayne State University, Department of Sociology, 1954.

Foote, Caleb. "Vagrancy-Type Law and Its Administration." *University of Pennsylvania Law Review* 104 (1956):603–50.

Fox, Ruth, and Peter Lyon. *Alcoholism: Its Scope, Cause and Treatment.* New York: Random House, 1955.

Frailey, Fred. "Two Seeking to Form Union of Day Laborers in Uptown." *Chicago Sun-Times,* February 1, 2, 16, and March 6, 1970.

Gans, Herbert. *Urban Villagers.* New York: Free Press of Glencoe, Division of Macmillan Co., 1962.

Ginzberg, Eli. *Manpower Agenda for America.* New York: McGraw-Hill, 1968.

Ginzberg, Eli, and the Conservation of Human Resources staff. *Manpower Strategy for the Metropolis.* New York: Columbia University Press, 1968.

Gough, H. G. *California Psychological Inventory Manual.* Palo Alto: Consulting Psychologists Press, 1957.

Greenblum, Joseph, and Leonard I. Pearlin. "Vertical Mobility and Prejudice: A Socio-Psychological Analysis." In *Class, Status, and Power,* eds. Reinhard Bendix and Seymour M. Lipset, pp. 480–91. Glencoe, Ill.: Free Press, 1953.

Harmer, R. M. *The High Cost of Dying.* New York: Collier, 1963.

Harris, Robert, and James C. Lingoes. "Sub-Scales for the MMPI: An Aid to Profile Interpretation." Mimeographed. San Francisco: Department of Psychiatry, University of California, 1955.

Hartshorne, H., and M. A. May. *Studies in Deceit.* New York: Macmillan, 1928.

Hawley, Amos. *Human Ecology.* New York: Ronald Press, 1950.

Hewitt, C. C. "A Personality Study of Alcoholic Addiction." *Quarterly Journal of Studies on Alcohol* 4 (1943):368–86.

Hill, H. E.; C. A. Haertzen; and H. Davis. "An MMPI Factor Analytic Study of Alcoholics, Narcotic Addicts, and Criminals." *Quarterly Journal of Studies on Alcohol* 23 (1962):411–31.

Hodge, C. C., and J. R. Wetzel. "Short Workweeks and Underemployment." *Monthly Labor Review* 90 (1967):30.

Hollingshead, August B., and Fredrick C. Redlich. *Social Class and Mental Illness: A Community Study.* New York: Wiley, 1958.

Hoyt, D. P., and G. M. Sedlacek. "Differentiating Alcoholics from Normals and Abnormals with the MMPI." *Journal of Clinical Psychology* 14 (1958):69–74.

Hutter, Mark. "Summertime Servants: The Schlockhaus' Waiter." In *The Participant Observer*, Glen Jacobs, ed. New York: Braziller, 1970.

Independent Co-operative Enterprises. "I.C.E., Inc., Information for Members." Mimeographed. Winnipeg: *ca.* 1971.

Independent Co-operative Enterprises. "Co-operative Employment Agency Proposal." Mimeographed. Winnipeg: *ca.* 1971.

Jellinek, E. M. *The Disease Concept of Alcoholism*. New Haven: College and University Press, 1960.

Krugman, Saul. "Etiology of Viral Hepatitis." *Hospital Practice* 5 (1970):45–49.

Lamb, H. Richard, and Victor Goertzel, "Discharged Mental Patients— Are They Really in the Community?" *Archive of General Psychiatry* 27 (1971):29–34.

Lenski, Gerhard. "Status Crystallization: A Non-Vertical Dimension of Social Status." *American Sociological Review* 19 (1954): 405–13.

Lescohier, Don D. *The Labor Market*. New York: Macmillan, 1919.

Lipset, Seymour M., and Joan Gordon. "Mobility and Trade Union Membership." In *Class, Status, and Power*, eds. Reinhard Bendix and Seymour M. Lipset, pp. 491–500. Glencoe, Ill.: Free Press, 1953.

Lo Cicero, Victor J. "A Multidisciplined Approach to the Skid Row Habitué." Paper delivered at annual meeting of the National Council on Alcoholism, Washington, D.C., 1960.

Lorr, M. "Multidimensional Scale for Rating Psychiatric Patients." *Veterans Administration Technical Bulletin*, TB10-507, 1953.

Lovald, Keith. "From Hobohemia to Skid Row: The Changing Community of Skid Row." Ph.D. dissertation, University of Minnesota, 1963.

Lovald, Keith, and Holger R. Stub. "The Revolving Door: Reactions of Chronic Drunkenness Offenders to Court Sanctions." *The Journal of Criminal Law, Criminology, and Police Science* 59 (4, 1968):525–30.

Loveless, Austin G. "Background and Economic Status of the Unemployed of St. Francois County, Missouri, and Their Attitudes Toward Retraining." Ph.D. Dissertation, University of Missouri, 1962.

MacAndrew, Craig, and Robert H. Geertsma. "An Analysis of Responses of Alcoholics to Scale 4 of the MMPI." *Quarterly Journal of Studies on Alcohol* 24 (1963):23–38.

McClelland, David C. *The Achieving Society*. Princeton: Van Nostrand, 1961.

McClelland, David C.; J. W. Atkinson; R. A. Clark; and E. L. Howell.

The Achievement Motive. New York: Appleton-Century-Crofts, 1953.

McGuire, Carson. "Social Stratification and Mobility Patterns." *American Sociological Review* 15 (1950):195–204.

McMahon, James T. "The Working Class Psychiatric Patient: A Clinical View." In *Mental Health of the Poor,* Frank Riessman, Jerome Cohen, and Arthur Pearl, eds., pp. 283–301. New York: The Free Press, 1964.

Martindale, Don. *American Social Structure.* New York: Appleton-Century-Crofts, 1960.

Merton, Robert K., and Alice S. Kitt. "Reference Group Theory and Social Mobility." In *Class, Status and Power,* eds. Reinhard Bendix and Seymour M. Lipset, pp. 403–10. Glencoe, Ill.: The Free Press, 1953.

Mitford, Jessica. *The American Way of Death.* New York: Simon and Schuster, 1963.

Morse, D. W. "Peripheral Worker in the Affluent Society." *Monthly Labor Review* 91 (1968):17–20.

Myerson, D. J. "An Approach to the Skid Row Problem in Boston." *New England Journal of Medicine* 249 (1953):646–49.

Myerson, D. J. "The 'Skid Row' Problem: Further Observations on a Group of Alcoholic Patients, with Emphasis on Interpersonal Relations and the Therapeutic Approach." *New England Journal of Medicine* 254 (1956):1168–73.

Myerson, D. J., and J. Mayer. "Origins, Treatment, and Destiny of Skid Row Alcoholic Men." *New England Journal of Medicine* 275 (1966):419–25.

New York Times, July 8, 1967; November 24, 1968; October 12, 1972.

Olin, Jack S. " 'Skid Row' Syndrome: A Medical Profile of the Chronic Drunkenness Offender." *Canadian Medical Association Journal* 94 (1966):205–14.

Payne, Les. "The Migrant Camp: Wine Fights and Payday." *Philadelphia Evening Bulletin,* September 10, 1970.

Pennsylvania Liquor Control Commission. "Listing of Retail Liquor Licenses, District Number 1." November 1, 1969 to October 31, 1970.

Philadelphia Bulletin, August 27, 1972.

Philadelphia, Department of Licenses and Inspection, Board of Licenses and Inspections Review. "Findings and Opinions." January 10, 1963 to October 10, 1966.

Philadelphia Magazine. "A Pound of Blood." September, 1968, pp. 81–88.

Philadelphia Monthly Register of the Society for Organizing Charity, Vol. 1 (April 15, 1880).

Philadelphia Prison Society. *The Homeless Man: A Philadelphia Study.* Philadelphia: Prison Society, 1956.

Philadelphia Society for Organizing Charity. *Annual Reports* for 1880, 1885, 1915, and others (available at the Family Service of Philadelphia or the Historical Society of Pennsylvania).

Pittman, David B., and C. Wayne Gordon. *Revolving Door: A Study of the Chronic Police Case Inebriate.* Glencoe, Ill: The Free Press, 1958 (for Publications Division of the Yale Center of Alcohol Studies, New Haven, Connecticut).

Priest, R. G. "A USA-UK Comparison." *Proceedings of the Royal Society of Medicine* 63 (May, 1970):441–45.

Purdon's Pennsylvania Statutes Annotated. Vol. 18, Section 2032. St. Paul, Minn.: West, 1963.

Quaranta, J. V. "Alcoholism: A Study of Emotional Maturity and Homosexuality as Related Factors in Compulsive Drinking." *Quarterly Journal of Studies on Alcohol* 10 (Sept., 1949): 354 (abstract of M.A. thesis, Fordham University, 1947).

Reichley, James. *The Art of Government: Reform and Organization Politics in Philadelphia.* New York: Fund for the Republic, 1959.

Rooney, James F. "Societal Forces and the Unattached Male: An Historical Review." In *Disaffiliated Man,* Howard M. Bahr, ed., pp. 13–38. Toronto: University of Toronto Press, 1970.

Roth, Julius, and Robert F. Peck. "Social Class and Mobility Factors Related to Marital Adjustment." *American Sociological Review* 16 (1951):478–87.

Ruesch, Jurgen. *Chronic Disease and Psychological Invalidism.* Berkeley: University of California Press, 1951.

Saravis, C.A.; C. Trey; and C. F. Grady. "Rapid Screening Test for Detecting Hepatitis-Associated Antigen." *Science* 169 (1970): 298–99.

Schnore, Leo. "Social Mobility in Demographic Perspective." *American Sociological Review* 26 (1961):407–23.

Science. "FDA to Regulate All Blood Banks." 177 (September 8, 1972):869.

Science. "Hepatitis: A New Understanding Emerges." 176 (June 16, 1972):1225.

Senior, John. "Reflections upon the Incidence of Post-Transfusion Hepatitis in Various Parts of the World." *American Journal of Gastroenterology* 49 (1968):298–303.

Sorokin, Pitirim. *Social Mobility.* New York: Harper, 1927.

Speers, William H. "Down and Out in Philadelphia." *Sunday Today: Philadelphia Inquirer Magazine,* March 8, 1970.

Spradley, James P. *You Owe Yourself a Drunk: An Ethnography of Urban Nomads.* Boston: Little, Brown, 1970.

Terris, Milton. "Epidemiology of Cirrhosis of the Liver: National Mortality Data." *American Journal of Public Health* 57 (1967): 2076–88.

Tiebout, H. M. "Alcoholics Anonymous: An Experiment in Nature." *Quarterly Journal of Studies on Alcohol* 22 (1961):52–68.

Titmuss, Richard M. *The Gift Relationship: From Human Blood to Social Policy.* London: Allen & Unwin, 1970.

Trice, Harrison M. *Alcoholism in America.* New York: McGraw-Hill, 1966.

Van Tulder, J. J. M. "Occupational Mobility in the Netherlands from 1917 to 1954." *Transactions of the Third World Congress of Sociology,* Vol. III: *Changes in Class Structure,* pp. 209–18. London: International Sociological Association, 1956.

Wallace, Samuel E. *Skid Row as a Way of Life.* Totowa, N.J.: Bedminster, 1965.

Wallerstein, R. S. "Hospital Treatment of Alcoholism: A Comparative, Experimental Study." *Menninger Clinic Monograph Series No. 11.* New York: Basic Books, 1957.

Walsh, J. H.; R. H. Purcell; A. G. Morrow; R. M. Chanock; and P. J. Schmidt. "Post-Transfusion Hepatitis after Open Heart Operations." *Journal of the American Medical Association* 211 (1970): 261–65.

Weber, James M. "Final Evaluative Report." Mimeographed. St. Louis Detoxification and Diagnostic Evaluation Center, *ca.* June 1967.

Wechsler, D. *The Measurement of Adult Intelligence.* Baltimore: Williams and Wilkins, 1944.

Wentworth, Harold, and Stuart Berg Flexner. *Dictionary of American Slang.* New York: Crowell, 1960.

Wiseman, Jacqueline P. *Stations of the Lost: The Treatment of Skid Row Alcoholics.* Englewood Cliffs, N.J.: Prentice-Hall, 1970.

Wolfbein, Seymour L. *Employment, Unemployment, and Public Policy.* New York: Random House, 1965.

Index

Index

Abrams, Charles, 76
Accidents, death by, 127
Agricultural day labor: blacks in, 99–101; exploitation of, 99–101
Albuminuria, 115
Alcohol, ethyl (grain), 122
Alcohol, methyl (wood), 122
Alcohol, nonbeverage, 48, 69, 121–23, 128
Alcoholics, biographies of, 18–36
Alcoholics Anonymous (AA), 10, 67, 138, 155, 161, 168–69, 174–75, 176–81, 185, 186, 194–95, 197, 200–202
Alcoholism: acute, 13; and albuminuria, 115; and anemia, 117; and cardiovascular disease, 114; and central nervous system disorders, 114; and cirrhosis, 114; death from, 127–28; definitions of, 39–42; and downward class mobility, 51–59; and elevated cholesterol, 115; and elevated thymol turbidity, 115; and employment, 93–95; group therapy for, 144–54; and hemorrhoids, 114; hospitalization for, 196–97, 201–2, 217; Halfway House, treatment program for, 167–87; and hypertension, 114; and liver disorders, 114; medical history of, 108; and musculoskeletal disorders, 114, 116;

numbers affected by, 111–12, 116; and poverty, 120; and prostatism, 114–15; and pulmonary diseases, 113; and trauma, 114; and tuberculosis, 112–13, 116; and varicose veins, 113; Weinrott decision on, 64. *See also* Drinking patterns
American Friends Service Committee, 99–101
American Red Cross blood donor program, 117–19
American Soldier, The, studies, 52
Anchor counselors, 12–16, 19, 154, 168–69, 171–72, 174, 182, 188–89
Anemia, 111–12, 117; and sale of blood, 117
Anomie, 52. *See also* Social Alienation scale; Social isolation
Antabuse, 184
Arthritis, 109
Asthma, bronchial, 113
Atkinson, J. W., 58

Bahr, Howard M., 41, 55, 139
Bain, Howard, 63, 64
Bar-hotels, 49, 51, 83–84; bars in, 83–84; economic exploitation in, 84–85; liquor licenses of, 83; political exploitation in, 85–87; prices in, 84; racial seg-